Praise for *Spark*

This book helps you find that spark and burn bright! When we can be creative with courage and conviction, it's a beautiful thing.

—Bear Grylls, adventurer, writer, and broadcaster

Al reminds us that creativity isn't for a few; it's the birthright of every believer. *Spark* will stir your imagination, strengthen your faith, and send you into the world convinced that your creativity really can change things.

—Jennie Allen, bestselling author and speaker

Spark is a catalytic, prophetic gift for anyone anywhere seeking to reimagine contemporary culture (in whatever medium) through the power of the Spirit in the name of Jesus Christ.

—Pete Greig, author and founder of 24-7 Prayer International

An inspiring, hope-filled invitation to unlock the God-given creativity within us all.

—Nicky Gumbel, pioneer of the Alpha Course

Al delightfully delivers the clarity and encouragement leaders need to keep moving forward with hope, creativity, and enthusiasm.

—Carey Nieuwhof, bestselling author, podcaster, and speaker

Al Gordon is a connoisseur at the intersection of creativity and spirituality. He carries a deep passion for catalyzing a movement where the church becomes the epicenter of human creativity.

—Erwin McManus, author, futurist, and lead pastor of Mosaic, Los Angeles

This book is more than a spark; it's a wildfire of creativity waiting to happen! Al Gordon writes with an authentic and prophetic voice. It's real, it's raw, and it's redemptive. It's a rallying cry for creatives to rise up and be part of the "new thing" God is doing.

—Mark Batterson, pastor, *New York Times* bestselling author

We urgently need another movement of artists and creatives. God is using Al to fan the flames of this today.

—Jon Tyson, author and pastor, Church of the City New York

This book is beautifully written, theologically rich, and deeply inspiring. But most of all, *Spark* tells the story of ordinary people, ignited by the love of an extraordinary God, bringing beauty and flourishing to the world around them.

—Jo Saxton, speaker, author, founder of the Ezer Collective

Al takes us on a journey, igniting in us the heart of God, the source of all creation and creativity, navigating the pressures and challenges creatives face, and calling us deeper and higher into the renewal of all things. Al writes with clarity, warmth, and real personal experience.

—Dr. Amy Orr-Ewing, international author, speaker, and theologian

Al Gordon is on a mission to see the church reclaim her ancient identity as a cathedral of creativity. That's a mission I can get behind. The pages of the book tell the story that mission and the local community where it is being formed, fostered, and shared.

—Tyler Staton, author of *The Familiar Stranger* and *Praying Like Monks, Living Like Fools*

When it comes to faith-fuelled, Spirit-filled creativity and leadership, Al Gordon is a voice like no other. His passion for God, life, the church and culture is totally infectious and jumps off every page of this book. Reading *Spark* will disrupt you, inspire you, fire up your imagination and help you dream bigger kingdom dreams.

—Pete Hughes, leader of KXC

Al Gordon has given us a great gift. With humor, depth of insight, and theological savvy, he offers us a vision of creativity that we all can benefit from. This is a book we all need—one that reminds us of our creative potential to bring goodness into the world.

—Rich Villodas, lead pastor of New Life Fellowship, author of *The Narrow Path*

In an age where cultural energy so often seeks only to deconstruct and critique, Al Gordon carries a passion for the Spirit-empowered work of building and dreaming. His message is a timely call for a world longing for a new renaissance—one fueled by holy creativity.

—Mark Sayers, lead pastor of Red Church, author of *A Non-Anxious Presence* and *Platforms to Pillars*

Spark is a needed book for the season the church is in, written by a playful prophetic voice, Al Gordon, who has found himself in the middle of renaissance and renewal.

—Zach Meerkreebs, author of *Lower*, pastor at Asbury University, encourager via Barnabas Collective

I realised during my first conversation with Al that the renovation of St John-at-Hackney was a very special project: a rare encounter with a building and with people of drive and vision. St John-at-Hackney is an exceptional place, not least because the richly varied ways in which its spaces are populated have allowed it to become nothing less than a spiritual, social, and cultural dynamo, whose charge is felt most strongly within its own community, but whose wider impact and influence transcends geography.

—John Pawson, architect

In a world increasingly filled with artificial intelligence and constant noise, this book is a bold invitation to rediscover imagination and step into the fullness of who we are created to be.

—Ruth Yimika Afolabi, founder and CEO, Magnify

With joyful wit and a warm embrace, Al breathes life into a very important truth: A creative fire burns in all of us.

—Ije Nwokorie, CEO of Dr. Martens

What a privilege to read *Spark* on the road. It's full of the wonder of creativity—the process, the mystery, and the potency that comes when we acknowledge the true source of it all.

—Nick Mulvey, Mercury Prize–nominated musician and songwriter

If you're someone trying to connect to the creative side you may not even feel exists, someone who wants to revive the creative side you once had, or someone who's simply interested and pondering these ideas, this book is for you.

—Mark Maciver, SliderCuts

If you want to be reminded who you truly are and be realigned to your creative purpose, dig deep into these words.

—Agyness Deyn, model and actor

SPARK

SPARK

Ignite Your God-Given Creativity

Al Gordon

ZONDERVAN REFLECTIVE
Spark
Copyright © 2026 by Al Gordon

Published by Zondervan, 3950 Sparks Drive SE, Suite 101, Grand Rapids, MI 49546, USA.

Zondervan is a registered trademark of The Zondervan Corporation, L.L.C., a wholly owned subsidiary of HarperCollins Christian Publishing, Inc.

HarperCollins Publishers, Macken House, 39/40 Mayor Street Upper, Dublin 1, D01 C9W8, Ireland (https://www.harpercollins.com)

Requests for information should be addressed to hccp@harpercollins.co.uk.

Zondervan titles may be purchased in bulk for educational, business, fundraising, or sales promotional use. For information, please email hccp@harpercollins.co.uk.

ISBN 9780310184249 paperback | ISBN 9780310176947 ebook

Unless otherwise noted, Scripture quotations are taken from the Holy Bible, New International Version®, NIV®. Copyright © 1973, 1978, 1984, 2011 by Biblica, Inc.® Used by permission of Zondervan.

Unless otherwise noted, Scripture quotations are taken from the Holy Bible, New International Version®, NIV®. Copyright © 1973, 1978, 1984, 2011 by Biblica, Inc.® Used by permission of Zondervan. All rights reserved worldwide. www.Zondervan.com. The "NIV" and "New International Version" are trademarks registered in the United States Patent and Trademark Office by Biblica, Inc.®. Scripture quotations marked AMP are taken from the Amplified® Bible (AMP). Copyright © 2015 by The Lockman Foundation. Used by permission. www.lockman.org. Scripture quotations marked ESV are taken from the ESV® Bible (The Holy Bible, English Standard Version®). Copyright © 2001 by Crossway, a publishing ministry of Good News Publishers. Used by permission. All rights reserved. Scripture quotations marked MSG are taken from The Message. Copyright © 1993, 2002, 2018 by Eugene H. Peterson. Used by permission of NavPress. All rights reserved. Represented by Tyndale House Publishers, Inc. Scripture quotations marked GNT are taken from the Good News Translation® in Today's English Version— Second Edition. Copyright © 1992 American Bible Society. Used by permission. All rights reserved.

Any internet addresses (websites, blogs, etc.) and telephone numbers in this book are offered as a resource. They are not intended in any way to be or imply an endorsement by Zondervan, nor does Zondervan vouch for the content of these sites and numbers for the life of this book.

All rights reserved. No part of this publication may be reproduced, stored in a retrieval system, or transmitted in any form or by any means— electronic, mechanical, photocopy, recording, or any other— except for brief quotations in printed reviews, without the prior permission of the publisher.

The author is represented by Tom Dean, Literary Agent with A Drop of Ink LLC, www.adropofink.pub.

Without limiting the exclusive rights of any author, contributor or the publisher of this publi-cation, any unauthorised use of this publication to train generative artificial intelligence (AI) technologies is expressly prohibited. HarperCollins also exercise their rights under Article 4(3) of the Digital Single Market Directive 2019/790 and expressly reserve this publication from the text and data mining exception.

ISBN 978-0-310-17695-4 (audio)

Cover design: OMSE.CO
Interior design: Sara Colley
Printed in the United Kingdom

For Olivia, Kester, Talia, and Grayson

CONTENTS

Prologue: The Creativity of All Believers 1

Movement One: Imagination
1. Your Secret Superpower 21
2. Ignite Your Imagination 41

Movement Two: Inspiration
3. The Spark That Lights the Fire 67
4. Lightbulb Moments 85
5. The Priesthood of the Creative 107

Movement Three: Innovation
6. Courageous Creativity 133
7. Make Friends with Failure 152
8. Start the Work 172

Movement Four: Impact
9. High Hopes 193
10. Overwhelmed with Wonder 216

Epilogue: Cathedrals of Creativity 233

Embers 247
Thank You 249
Notes 253
Renaissance: Join the Movement 269

Start a Spark Circle?

To help you ignite your God-given creativity, gather a few friends and start a Spark Circle. Get everyone to read the chapter in advance, meet up in person or online, and circle back through *Spark* with these three prompts:

1. **Notice** what stands out.
2. **Name** what it means to you.
3. **Next Step:** put it into practice.

Use these with your friends, your team, your community. Together you'll fan your spark into a flame.

Scan here to invite your friends to read with you:

PROLOGUE

The Creativity of All Believers

> *See, I am doing a new thing!*
> *Now it springs up; do you not perceive it?*
> —Isaiah 43:19

The first sign that something was going horribly wrong was the sharp, searing pain—right between my eyes. I shrieked, swatted wildly, but then came another sting, this time just behind my ear. The third sting really made me panic. It turns out, when it comes to beekeeping, that enthusiasm does not make up for ~~little~~ zero training.

It wasn't long after we planted SAINT—our church community in East London—that we decided to try keeping bees as a sort of spiritual discipline. After all, monks, mystics, and missionaries had kept bees for centuries, and they had to contend with some big challenges like the Vikings and the plague. So how hard could keeping a couple of beehives in the churchyard be?

Our intentions were noble. Bees don't just make honey—they bring life. They pollinate. They help the entire ecosystem, not just themselves. Everything literally becomes more fruitful. It was the perfect metaphor for the creative, outward-looking community we longed to build. So when the bees arrived, I was buzzing with excitement—pun intended. Eric, our friendly beekeeper, unloaded two hives from the back of his Land Rover and set them up in a quiet corner of the

PROLOGUE

graveyard enclosed by old, five-foot-high metal railings. The hives held hundreds of thousands of tiny bees. Standing next to Eric, ready to witness the launch of our beekeeping adventure, my naive enthusiasm was about to collide with the visceral reality of the natural world in a spectacular way.

For the briefest of moments, I felt like the proud father of an entire bee nation. I stood in the shadow of Adam naming the animals. Or of Francis of Assisi—at one with God's creation. Would the bees be pleased to see me? Would there be an emotional—dare I say, even *spiritual* connection? I pictured them landing gently on my hands and doing a little nectar dance while beating their tiny wings in recognition. I've probably watched too many Disney movies.

In hindsight, the fact that Eric was sealed head to toe in an outfit resembling a hazmat suit should have set off alarm bells. I was wearing a thin T-shirt, shorts, and sunglasses (for protection). In his usual dry fashion, Eric glanced at me as he lifted the lid on the hive, and said, "You might want to take a few steps back." The eternal optimist, I swatted his advice away and leaned in to embrace my new bee family with joyous enthusiasm. Immediately—to my surprise and horror—I was met by a wall of very, very angry bees. The first three stings landed before I had time to react. Within seconds, a small swarm had begun to form around me.

Lesson One: When very, very angry bees feel their hive is under attack, they don't mess around. They launch a full-scale assault, and each sting releases a pheromone marking you as the enemy. That signal spreads fast, and before you know it the entire hive is mobilised. They will not stop stinging until you're either gone—or, well ... dead.

At this point, Eric—calmly, quietly, and from behind the safety of his bee suit—turned to me and added laconically, "You may want to think about running now." Death by beesting wasn't the end I had pictured for myself, so, with the swarm growing by the second, I took his advice and sprinted. Top speed. Straight toward the graveyard railings.

Now, full disclosure: I'm neither particularly tall nor known for my athletic prowess. But somehow, in that moment—fuelled by a potent mix of adrenaline, desperation, and the unique terror that comes from being chased by a swarm of very, very angry bees—a sort of supernatural anointing came over me. With the strength of Samson, I vaulted clear over the five-foot metal graveyard railings. I kept running—and screaming—with my arms flailing violently around me like a demoniac until I reached the sanctuary of St John-at-Hackney Church. Once inside the church, I collapsed to the ground. There, for the next hour, I sat clutching an ice pack to my swollen face, popping antihistamines, and waiting for the swelling to go down.

It's not a mistake I've repeated.

The Sting of Failure

Many times in my life I've stepped out—tried something new, taken a creative risk, followed a dream—only to get stung. I've felt the pain of rejection: that disappointment when things don't work out, the fear of looking stupid, that nagging feeling that everyone else is more talented, more skilled, and more equipped. Often, when I've dared to stretch myself creatively, I've felt the searing pain of embarrassment, and that same primal instinct rises within me. *Run!*

When creativity goes wrong—when your idea flops, the feedback stings, or your courage falters—it is easy to opt for self-preservation and sprint in the other direction. To play it safe. To give up and go home. This is where we begin the story: We're hiding in the dark, seeking sanctuary from attack, holding the ice pack to our face. We regret our decisions. And we wonder if we'll ever taste the sweetness of what we dreamed the world would be like.

Have you ever felt like that? Maybe you've stepped out creatively only to be met with rejection and disappointment. Did someone sting you with criticism? Were you chased away with harsh remarks? Many of us experience this early in life when our creativity gets laughed out of the playground, our ideas mocked, or when the precious dreams emanating from our innocent imagination are shot down by someone's harsh opinion or unkind word. We turn and run, arms flailing, into the shadows, denying our gift and vowing we'll never go back, fearing we might get stung again.

The unplayed instrument.
The unfinished novel.
The empty sketchbook.
That idea that never sees the light of day.

Our creative wounds can become self-fulfilling prophecies. We compare ourselves to those who seem preternaturally gifted and convince ourselves: *I could never do that*. And so we don't. There are also those deeper wounds—the ones that come from pouring out the passion and longing of our dreams only to watch them flop miserably. The embarrassment. The rejection. The shame of that failure.

The Big Lie

Eventually we start to believe our internal narrative: Creativity just isn't for us. We determine never to step into the sunshine again. And so, hiding in the dark, we play it safe and cling to the familiar. Or worse, we convince ourselves that it was a mistake all along, that we're just not that creative, that creativity is for other people. It's for the talented ones, those exceptional people, the gifted. And so, in an act of self-sabotage, we tell ourselves the Big Lie: "I'm not creative."

What we usually mean is that we haven't excelled enough in the classic artistic fields—music, art, literature, design. We don't feel naturally gifted or able to harness originality. Or we confuse artistic ability with creativity. We end up seeing creativity as something reserved for professionals, those who are paid for their work or have the luxury of time to create—as if creativity belonged to an exclusive club of artists, musicians, and designers. *Creative*, with a capital *C*.

Let me burst that bubble for you right now: You are creative.

All of human life is creative—every act of self-expression, every flicker of imagination, the way you work, the way you love, the stories you tell, the relationships you build. From the smallest habit to your biggest dreams, your very being bristles with creativity.

Already I can hear the objections rising. You don't understand; I'm just not creative. Other people are naturally good at this. They're gifted. Talented. That's just not me.

But here is where we must begin, because this is for everyone. Everything we do with our lives involves creativity—you can't escape it. Everyone everywhere, a million times a day—with every decision, every action, every daydream, every idea—pulsates with creative energy. I like how author Brené Brown puts it: "'I'm not very creative' doesn't work. There's no such thing as creative people and non-creative people; there are only people who use their creativity and people who don't. Unused creativity doesn't just disappear. It lives within us until it's expressed, neglected to death or suffocated by resentment and fear."[1]

The real issue isn't whether we're creative; it's whether we have the courage to ignite our latent creativity. Creative acts take a little faith because they involve some risk. This book is an invitation to unlock your creative potential by reconnecting with the most dynamic part of you: your soul. So, let's talk about you.

You Are a Miracle

Pause for a moment and consider the sheer miracle of your existence. The fact that you are here—breathing, thinking, and alive—is statistically staggering. The odds of your existence? One in four hundred quadrillion. That's a four followed by fifteen zeros: 4,000,000,000,000,000. To put this into perspective—you're more likely to win the lottery every day for thirteen thousand years straight than to exist right now.

Your life is a genealogical miracle. You are the result of a long, unbroken line of succession—an epic backstory that puts any Hollywood plot to shame. If one ancestor had failed—missed the chance to fall in love, didn't survive a harsh winter, failed to cross oceans and deserts, been eaten by wild hairy things, succumbed to horrid plagues or deadly pestilence—you wouldn't have made it. Biologically, your life is astonishing, with every fingerprint unique, the product of the delicate dance of your DNA, each hidden helix spinning with infinite potential.

Today you'll think thousands of original creative thoughts as your soul is stirred by beauty, emotion, and hope.[2] You'll make tens of thousands of decisions while your heart beats a hundred thousand times.[3] Nearly half your waking hours will be spent in your imagination—where everything is possible. Your brain alone contains more neural connections than there are stars in the known universe. Right now, as you read these words, electromagnetic energy is firing across billions of your neural pathways—every secret synapse singing with life. Your body is an inner galaxy of breath and bone, light and life. Everything about you is miraculous, original, and remarkable.

But none of this gets at the most extraordinary thing about you, that you have a supernatural origin. You're not a cosmic accident or the lucky winner in the natural lottery. Your life—body, soul, and spirit—has been crafted with deliberate care by a spiritual force: a Creator. The Bible puts it like this: "For we are God's handiwork, created in Christ Jesus to do good works, which God prepared in advance for us to do" (Ephesians 2:10). The word used here for handiwork was originally written in the Greek of the New Testament. The word is ποίημα (*poiēma*), and it literally means a work of art. You are God's masterpiece—a unique creation crafted with intention and loving care by your Creator. As poet Maya Angelou has said, "Everybody born comes from the Creator, trailing wisps of glory."[4]

The Creative Soul

Your creativity is spiritual—it flows from your soul. And because everyone—not just a select few—has a soul, this creativity is an indivisible and indispensable part of who you are whether you think you're a "creative" or not. You are made in the image of this Creator with the same spiritual DNA. Your creativity is built into your very identity, your soul's

THE CREATIVITY OF ALL BELIEVERS

design. It's the way you are. Just as you breathe, you also create. You are, therefore you create. It is the core longing of every soul, as Plato described it, to create "in the medium of the beautiful."[5]

To be human is to create.

You are here, alive and breathing, because God created you. Your life, against all odds, is possible because you were imagined and crafted with care by a Maker, the one who called you into being. You are, as the psalmist put it, "fearfully and wonderfully made" (Psalm 139:14). Creativity is your birthright, the rich spiritual inheritance of your soul. And understanding this truly has the power to change everything. It's a reality being worked out in as many billion ways as there are people alive, in every corner of human life.

So let's agree to do away with the trash talk of "I'm not creative." Instead, let me invite you to step up to this splendid and singularly important starting point: Your soul, your imagination, your ideas—everything about you—is a work of art, woven with purpose and intention. Your very existence is a creative act: Every word you speak, every relationship you nurture, every moment you shape is an act of creation. Wherever we look, we see creativity at work. Our world is stitched together by millions of small creative actions, each one adding depth, meaning, and beauty. This everyday creativity is more than an enhancement of regular life; rather, it is the very engine that makes life possible.

Creativity is the birthplace of the new.

Without creativity, there is no life. There is nothing fresh, nothing original, nothing transformative. Everything that has ever come into being—every invention, every breakthrough, every shift in history—was birthed through creativity. Creativity is the realisation of possibilities—bringing life into being. The real question isn't whether you are creative but whether you'll choose to cultivate the creativity hardwired into your soul.

That's what this book is about: igniting the extraordinary relationship between your creativity and your soul. Understanding the connection between your innermost being and your output will revolutionise how you create. Think of it like this: Creativity is a spiritual muscle you're

PROLOGUE

born with, and like any muscle, it can be neglected and wasted or worked and strengthened. This is going to be a moment in your life when you suddenly find yourself making giant leaps forward, using muscles you didn't know existed, spurred on to overcome the things that fence you in.

For now, as we start, let's simply agree to leave the Big Lie behind us.

If you have a pulse, breath in your lungs, and fire in your soul, know that creativity is already at work within you. You are creative. You are wired for imagining, building, and bringing new things into existence. The New Testament describes faith as "being sure of what we hope for and certain of what we do not see" (Hebrews 11:1).[6] All creative acts are an act of faith—a sacred endeavour filled with miraculous potential.

To create is to partake in the divine.

Creativity transforms the unseen into reality.

Creativity makes the invisible visible.

Creativity shapes the future.

Creativity is a holy endeavour.

Welcome to the creativity of all believers.

God Is a Creative

God—the Creator, with a capital *C*—is in the creative business. Throughout Scripture, we meet a God of endless innovation. In the beginning of the story, God is introduced as *the* Creator of all things. In the middle of the story, we see God continuing his act of creation by making new things: "See, I am doing a new thing! Now it springs up; do you not perceive it?" (Isaiah 43:19) And at the end of the Bible, Jesus affirms, "I am making everything new!" (Revelation 21:5).

God is the prime mover.

The original instigator.

The ultimate sign-off.

The only true source of newness.

He is, and therefore he creates.

From beginning to end, God is making all things new. And because you are made in his image, carrying his likeness, you hold a residue of this divine creativity woven into your soul. Now, if this is all news to you—welcome to the adventure. Fasten your seat belt, because it's going to be a crazy ride. The reality is that you are not just bursting with potential because God created you in his image; something electric and alive is buzzing deep in your soul, something holy and divine placed there by God himself.

The Spark

You have a spark in you.

In the Jewish mystical tradition there is a word that was understood as something of a divine spark—*nitzotzot* (ניצוצות). It was seen as a flicker of God's power that ignites creative potential. This *nitzotzot* was that point of ignition, and the Bible tells us that the Holy Spirit has placed this spark in you. It's the genesis of your best ideas, your real dreams, and your deepest hopes—all of these come from that divine spark, that splice of the Creator's DNA inherent in you. That same spark of the Spirit once ignited the big bang through words spoken from our Creator's lips. It's the same spark that danced in Adam's heart as God breathed him to life. It's the spark that engulfed the burning bush, lit the flame on the altar, consumed the sacrifice, and fuelled the pillar of fire in the wilderness wanderings.

This same holy spark also wants to ignite your imagination and set your soul ablaze. And the good news is that you don't need to have it all together. The kindling for this flame? The dry ground of your weakness, your trembling, your fear, and your empty hands. When you reach the limits of human creativity, when you come empty and have nothing but a blank canvas, it's here that you will experience that spark catching fire in you.

Think of this book as a love letter to your creative soul. It's a call for a holy re-enchantment of your creative hopes, a manifesto for a new renaissance.

PROLOGUE

The Renaissance Story

Now would be a good moment for me to share a little about Renaissance—the creative movement that inspired this book. It began at SAINT, the church I help to lead in East London, as we were emerging from the Covid pandemic and stepping out from the isolation and disruption of those lonely years. The idea was simple. What if we gathered some friends and aimed to do three things:

Encounter the Creator
Equip the creative
Empower the church

We launched as lockdown lifted, and I was convinced no one would come. But when we opened our doors, we were stunned—there was a queue around the block. Hundreds had flown in from all over the world, from Tasmania to Peru, hungry to explore how to ignite the creative potential of their souls.

We laughed, prayed, danced, cried, and sang karaoke and worship songs. We held our breath as string quartets played brand-new symphonies. We stepped out of our comfort zones. We got our hands dirty. We learned wild baking and honey making—chewing on mind-blowing ideas. We picked up skills and we unpicked preconceptions. And within a few crazy years, Renaissance gatherings had started on four continents. Thousands of creative leaders were coming together for events across the globe.

It has been a wild ride. We've been flooded with encouragement from artists and entrepreneurs, like my friend Scott Harrison, founder of the extraordinary initiative Charity: Water, who called it "a game changer." We knew we'd ignited something. It felt like oxygen to a generation who were just clinging on and needed to tend to their souls.

Since that first Renaissance, two things have struck me. First, no one can agree on how to pronounce *Renaissance*. Everywhere I go, it's different. For the Brits, it's *Ren-ay-sance*. For our American cousins, *Ren-aaaay-sance*.

THE CREATIVITY OF ALL BELIEVERS

Our Spanish language conference is called *Re-ness-ence* (it sounds so good in Spanish). And for our Australian friends, it's *Reeen-ayeee-saaaaaance*. You Aussies really know how to stretch a syllable, and we love you even more for it. All over the world, people are making this idea their own. And I think it's great that everyone brings their own flavour.

Second, everyone *can* agree on how much we need a new renaissance. Across the world, people are gathering on their own to make space for their creative souls. Pete Greig, author and founder of 24–7 Prayer, says, "In a disenchanted world littered with dead religious imagery, no task matters more than the re-animation of a truly Christian imagination. How else are we to provoke the great questions to which Christ is the answer, and the answers to which he remains the greatest question? Renaissance promises to catalyse, connect and resource a new generation of creative pioneers with a message of disruptive hope."[7]

Much of what you're about to read is shaped by the thousands of leaders now involved in Renaissance. It's a summary of countless late-night conversations with creatives, change makers, community leaders, entrepreneurs, writers, and artists of every kind. My hope is that these pages will spur you to dream again, take risks, heal, and begin to imagine a different kind of world. And if you have the privilege of helping others—if you're a leader, encourager, coach, parent—may this book equip you to fan the spark in every person you meet. This is more than just another nice idea; it's an emergency—a crisis we must address.

The Urgency of Creativity

The world needs you to dream and imagine again. There is a fervent urgency to all of this. Why? Because we're living in a crisis of creative confidence. Our culture is addicted to replication, where novelty is mass produced and then quickly forgotten, "junk food" for the creative soul. We have traded in our imaginations for an algorithm and have outsourced our originality. Rather than daring to dream, we reach for the familiar (Command [⌘] + C) copy and (Command [⌘] + V) paste.

That's why nurturing, encouraging, championing, and caring for the creative soul has never been more urgent. Of course religion and creativity haven't always gone hand in hand. People who try to express their God-given creativity are often misunderstood, alienated, rejected, or exploited by a culture that cashes in on novelty and commodifies cool. The church has all too often been just as guilty. We've sometimes viewed the gifts of creative people as a commodity to be exploited rather than a spark to be uncovered, nurtured, and gently and carefully but very intentionally fanned into flame. The good news is that's changing, and you're part of that change. A new renaissance is starting to bubble up.

We are at a crossroads. A choice lies before us: Will we tend to our creative souls? Or will we settle for more of the same, being just another cog in the machine? Creativity has never been more urgently needed than it is right now. It's the quality everyone is searching for. The tech giant IBM recently surveyed over a thousand top CEOs, asking which leadership quality they believed most vital in navigating today's fast-changing, complex world. The overwhelming answer? Creativity. Sixty percent of those surveyed named it the number one trait they value above all others.[8]

The stakes have never been higher, and in the years ahead our uniquely human creativity will matter more than ever. The world is changing at unprecedented speed, and unless we learn to harness our creative potential, we risk being left adrift in a future we didn't shape. We face a world where the norm is to neuter the God-given creative trait in the human spirit and replace it with machine learning or mechanized processes. If we do not reverse this trend, the consequences will be devastating. Wendell Berry sums it up prophetically: "It is easy for me to imagine that the next great division of the world will be between people who wish to live as creatures and people who wish to live as machines."[9]

Being Human in the Age of the Algorithm

Now we're getting to the juicy stuff, because this is a book about making a choice about the kind of life you want to live. It's a stark choice

THE CREATIVITY OF ALL BELIEVERS

about how you will exist in this new world and what it means to be human in the age of the algorithm. We are currently living through one of the most extraordinary technological revolutions in human history. Artificial intelligence is advancing so rapidly that some have suggested this could signal the beginning of the end of humanity as we know it. In his best-selling book *Homo Deus: A Brief History of Tomorrow*, Yuval Noah Harari poses a haunting question: "What will happen to society, politics, and daily life when non-conscious but highly intelligent algorithms know us better than we know ourselves?" His conclusion is chilling: "We are probably one of the last generations of *Homo sapiens*."[10]

So what does it mean to be human in a world shaped by algorithms and artificial intelligence? AI can think faster, process data more efficiently, and even mimic creativity by reorganising information. But there's a key difference: AI lacks the divine spark. Algorithms don't truly dream; they only regurgitate and hallucinate. Generative AI is built entirely on existing data; it does not create anything truly new. It can reconfigure, remix, and refine, but it cannot originate. It cannot bring something from nothing—*ex nihilo*; that ability belongs to the Creator alone. No one else in the whole universe has ever or could ever create something from nothing.

Only God truly creates. The rest of us are rearranging the atoms and electrons that flow from him. But the prophetic spark—the ability to originate, envision, and bring newness into existence—also comes from God and is given to us human beings. And when we learn how to ignite this holy fire, it becomes our soul's great superpower. Straight out of Eden, the creative spark is humanity's secret sauce, our divine imprint and the unique signature of our souls. Without a Creator, there can be no lasting creativity—no meaning, no beauty, no purpose. There are just fleeting moments when we spin in the infinite darkness of the cosmic vacuum. The future of humanity, our future, depends on reconnecting with this holy creativity.

Creativity isn't an optional extra, it's the natural overflow of the divine DNA within you. The question is not if, but what: What do you

13

PROLOGUE

want to create? And perhaps more importantly: How seriously will you take this sacred calling?

In the pages ahead, we're going to uncover the creative spark inside you. We'll invite the Creator to breathe on that spark until your soul catches fire with the same creative force that called the universe into being. We'll explore how you were *created to create* and made to make. And while the stakes have never been higher, the opportunities have also never been greater. We'll journey to the source of that creativity, find the spark in your soul, and then fan it into flame until your world is ablaze with beauty and wonder.

This journey will require us to take off our shoes because we'll be standing on holy ground. We'll tread gently between majesty and mystery, between wonder and the working out of creativity in everyday life. We'll step into the holy space of how ideas take shape, why your soul creates the way it does, and how God wants to cultivate your deepest and most powerful ideas. We'll learn to walk in the way of your creative calling—to carry truth, beauty, and goodness to a world bereft of wonder.

And yes, sparking creativity *really* is urgent. Why? Because our disenchanted world is desperate for people ablaze with divine creativity who will light up the night. You must fight for that spark because the world will try to extinguish it. And there is no greater tragedy than ignoring it, just as there's nothing more exhilarating than watching your God-given creativity set ablaze. The world is changing at a speed we can barely comprehend through tech, politics, war, and environmental crises. Crazy times need courageous souls, and what we need now isn't more information or better strategies; we need people like you who find that quiet ember deep inside and fan it until it blazes.

Tending to this spark will take vulnerability, reflection, space, and deep work. But the reward is beyond worth it. So journey with me through these pages. I believe God will meet us here, reaching into the dark corners of your imagination, the broken places of your confidence, and the untapped depths of your talent to ignite something extraordinary.

THE CREATIVITY OF ALL BELIEVERS

Along the way, I'll share some stories from our church's own creative journey at SAINT, how we accidentally started an award-winning brewery and ended up collaborating with some of the world's leading creatives. We'll discover how some of the most influential artists on the planet are longing for every local church to become a cathedral of creativity. We'll meet fascinating people, learn from spectacular mistakes, and hopefully have a lot of fun.

This journey is for the believers and the doubters, the lovers and the haters, those who feel they have it all together and those whose dreams feel like they've been burned to ash. We're going to ask God, the Creator Spirit, to help us. And if you're a "I'm just not that into a higher power" type person, hang in there. I promise it will be a fun ride, and, well, life is full of surprises. And for the pragmatist in you, we're going to get practical. This isn't just theory; it's activation. We'll let iron sharpen iron—until sparks fly.

Plan Bee

In case you're wondering what happened with our bees, this story ends well. Once they calmed down and the stings on my face healed up, we got along just fine. Fast-forward from those painful early hours hiding in the church with an ice pack on my face. We took a crash course in beekeeping, got the hives established, and figured out how to harvest honey. We learned how to care for our bees and then watched as they brought flourishing to the wider neighbourhood.

Today we have a thriving apiary at St John-at-Hackney: eight hives, home to hundreds of thousands of bees. Over the years, nurturing them has become part of the rhythm of our community. They remind us of the outward motion of God's creativity—always moving beyond the safety of the hive to bring life. Our bees have become a living metaphor for what happens when you care for your creativity. Such is the impact of the humble honeybee on pollination and food production that without them humanity would face a pretty bleak future.[11] In the same way, your creativity and the creativity of local churches and communities have a pollinating effect on culture.

Recently I received an email from a neighbour. I slightly dreaded opening the message, as he would usually write to complain about the church activity, the traffic, and the noise—often with just cause. But then my eyes fell on the subject line: "Thank you." Intrigued, I clicked and read on. He explained that he was a keen gardener. His house backed onto the churchyard, and that year—without explanation—his fruit tree had been twice as fruitful. His rosebush was bursting with blooms. He couldn't figure out what had changed. It wasn't the weather or climate, as conditions had been consistent with previous years. Then one day he solved the mystery. He noticed there were more bees in his garden than ever before. Hundreds of our little bees, busy flying from flower to flower and bringing life wherever they landed. He began tracing the direction of their flight and noticed them heading back to the church. Astonished, he wrote, "Your bees are making my garden more fruitful.... I just wanted to say thank you." Our little bees now travel miles across the city, pollinating and bringing life. They don't exist just to make us honey; they exist to create fruitfulness for our whole community. This is what divine creativity in motion looks like.

You and I are here to pollinate the culture, to bring flourishing to the spiritual ecosystem all around us. We are here to re-enchant the skeptic and to make the cynic smile again.

I'm praying that over the pages of this book, God will ignite something extraordinary in your soul, and that one day, if we should ever get to meet, you'll tell me stories of how the spark in you caught fire and spread to those around you. In your work. Your home. Your friendships. Your soul. Stories of how God brought a renaissance to your creativity—to your calling, your community, your church, your life.

Because creativity isn't just for a few gifted individuals. This is about the creativity of all believers. It's your inheritance. Your identity. Your birthright.

THE CREATIVITY OF ALL BELIEVERS

Are you ready? It's time to put away the ice pack and unmask the Big Lie. It's time to dream, to risk, to be brave and step back out into the sunlight.

So turn the page—what comes next just might surprise you.

Because it's time to unlock your secret superpower.

SPARK CIRCLE

Circle back through this chapter of Spark.

Notice
What challenged or inspired you in this chapter?
What story, phrase, or idea stuck with you?

Name
Where have you believed the lie that you're not creative? What part of you needs to be reawakened to the truth that you're made to create?

Next Step
What's one way you can express your creativity this week—however small? Pick something. Commit to it. And share it with your circle.

MOVEMENT ONE
Imagination

CHAPTER 1

Your Secret Superpower

> *God created the world by imagination.*
> —Nikolai Berdyaev

If there's one thing guaranteed to wake you up faster than coffee, it's the sight of an enormous stranger defecating through the railings in front of your house.

We had recently moved as a family to Hackney, East London, to lead the church community that would eventually become SAINT. One morning as we enjoyed breakfast together in our new home, our young children opened the kitchen curtains and were greeted by this unusual scene.

Let me assure you, nothing—and I mean nothing—commands the attention of small children like the sight of a two-hundred-fifty-pound person contributing to the circle of life. Our children were transfixed. Mesmerised. Awestruck. It was a formidable welcome—and a fitting introduction to a crazy, buzzing neighbourhood. Hackney, we were quickly learning, would be many things—surprising, overwhelming, heartbreaking—but never boring.

That morning I stepped outside, taking care to avoid the new addition to the garden's compost, and made the short walk to the church. As I walked, I noticed patterns that would become all too familiar over the years to come: the drug addict shaking on a cold corner, waiting to score; the anxious fashion model striding to a casting, her nail-bitten fingers clutching a portfolio; three homeless men slumped on a bench, sharing a bottle of cheap cider for breakfast.

The neighbourhood pulsed with contradiction. Bougie bars and high-end coffee shops sat cheek by jowl with the betting shop, where defeated-looking souls loitered. A few doors down, the smell of fresh bread wafted from a craft bakery next to a store with a freshly boarded-up shop window—broken into just the night before. Thousands of tiny, jewel-like pieces of shattered glass littered the pavement, crunching underfoot. They were known locally as "Hackney diamonds" and would be referenced by the Rolling Stones in their 2023 album *Hackney Diamonds*.

Thin Red Line

Suddenly a thin red line on the ground caught my eye. The colour was unmistakable—rich, haemoglobin red: a trail of dried blood. The colour of pain, of anger, of life seeping away. My eyes followed this crimson thread as it snaked down the street. Each step I took traced the story of a life fighting for survival. I found myself wondering who was at the end of this thin red line, and were they still alive?

Dozens of people—many of them teenagers—had lost their lives that year on the streets of London, swallowed up by gang violence.[1] In my first few weeks in Hackney, I had conducted the funeral of one of these kids—a bright seventeen-year-old caught up with the wrong people. He was a smart kid with a good future ahead of him. Tragically, he got involved in a drug deal gone bad and was stabbed to death just metres from the church. His life, full of potential, was cut short by a meaningless cycle of violence and retaliation. It was heartbreaking.

That funeral still haunts me all these years later. Hundreds of teenagers packed into the church, holding on to one another, not knowing what to do with their pain. We stood shivering together at the bitter graveside. I will never forget the unimaginable sorrow etched onto his parents' faces. This was a child with a family and a future. I've walked with families through the numb weight of grief and stood in the valley of the shadow of death, fighting back my own tears at bleak, hopeless gravesides. Surely there must be another way.

Creativity so often smoulders in the ashes of pain, sorrow, and loss. Something deep within each of us yearns for a better world. Hope calls us to imagine a different future. I wonder, what are the ashes for you? Maybe it's a long-buried grief, an absence you still feel, a longing that won't let go. Perhaps it's the desire to bring light into the dark, to offer hope where it's needed most. Pay attention to those embers. Rage against the dying of the light, as Dylan Thomas put it.[2]

East London is a place of extremes. On one hand, it's densely packed with culture shapers; on the other, it's rife with poverty and addiction. Like so many similar neighbourhoods around the world, social deprivation once meant cheap rents and empty warehouses. In Hackney successive waves of artists flocked in—garment weavers, silk traders, tailors, non-conformists, Bohemians, writers, actors, musicians. Today the neighbourhood has more creatives per square mile than almost anywhere else on the planet. And yet, many children here still grow up below the poverty line. Beneath the creative veneer lie many challenges: addiction, loneliness, desperation, hopelessness.

We had been sent to this place with a mission: to help revive the ancient Anglican parish of Hackney and its cathedral-like church, old St John-at-Hackney. Built in 1792, the church replaced an earlier structure from 1275—the remains of which still stand in the graveyard, a single tower rising from the mist like something out of a Tolkien novel. In those early days, the church was barely hanging on: a decaying giant, its grandeur fading, the hulk of the building held together by scaffolding and goodwill. Like so many inner-city churches, it was once the beating heart of the community; now it was a crumbling relic.

That morning I followed the thin red line across the main road and into the church gardens, where it disappeared into the greenery of the graveyard and into the unknown. Crossing the road, I said a prayer under my breath. This road used to be known as the infamous "Murder Mile," once home to the highest murder rate in the UK. The

IMAGINATION

churchyard, meanwhile, had its own claim to fame. According to local police, 80 percent of Hackney's hard drugs trade happened here on the grounds of the church. I stepped inside the old church. Above the entrance, a single bullet hole had punctured the glass. A grim full stop to this litany of despair.

The building had seen better days. Besides gunshots, it had survived riots, the bombs of two World Wars, a devastating fire that gutted the church, and, finally, the slow, creeping death of being ignored by most people. The decline had been staggering. Less than 1 percent of the population of the city attended their local parish churches. Once upon a time, that number was, well, everyone. (To be fair, if you didn't show up back then, you got fined.) By the 1980s, attendance had collapsed and the authorities nearly called time on this crumbling relic. There was even an ill-fated attempt to sell off the building, to turn it into a shopping centre or flats, but the developers had the good sense to walk away. And so it remained, nursed by a small group of faithful, prayerful people but gently decaying in slow motion. Each time it rained, water would pour through the ceiling. On wet Sundays, buckets would be interspersed with the chairs. The whole place was crying out for resurrection.

This was testing my faith. And yet, I still believe in resurrections. I believe creativity can change things, even bring things back from the brink. And I suspect you do too: That's why you're here, reading this. Nevertheless, there are moments when we have no idea how. Hope is all very well in theory, until we're faced with hard reality and the way forward seems impossible. If you ever feel like that, know that you're not alone.

The Empty Whiteboard

So just a few weeks into this adventure in Hackney, I found myself standing in front of an empty whiteboard, chewing on a pen lid. I'd set aside time to dream of what resurrection could look like here in this place. I'd locked myself in a room to think, pray, and imagine. What would it take to turn this around? I usually love an empty whiteboard. There's something inviting about its smooth surface—no lines, no marks—just a blank canvas waiting to come alive. That empty slate. The endless possibilities. The vast potential of what could be. But that day it was not going well. For hours I'd been staring at the wall, my thoughts turning over and over. Pen in hand, I waited... and waited... and waited. Nothing. Minutes drifted by, then hours. Still nothing. I felt overwhelmed.

One thing was obvious: We would need to tear up the playbook. What got us here wouldn't get us there. What worked yesterday wouldn't work tomorrow. We were in a different world. A different culture. A generation that spoke a different language. We had to think outside the box with fresh ideas. New approaches. Anything that would reverse the cycle of decline and death. But right then, that all felt irrelevant. I was stuck and starting to regret the decision to move here. I didn't know where to begin. The need was too great. Three hours later I was still staring at a blank whiteboard. No ideas. No vision. No clue. I didn't have a strategy. I had no solution. And I started to feel a rising sense of anxiety.

> *There are only two ways to live your life.*
> *One is as though nothing is a miracle.*
> *The other is as though everything is a miracle.*
> —Albert Einstein

I needed a miracle. And this story starts where all miracle stories start—with the need. The nothingness. The brokenness. The chaos. The silent void. The vacuum. We experience a particular sense of panic when we are longing for a solution we can't yet see. And the longer we wait, the more impossible the situation seems.

All the things.
Back up against the wall.
Hoping for change.
Longing for breakthrough.
Dreaming of a better day.
All the clichés.

IMAGINATION

But for all the hyped talk, we just get stuck. So we fall back on old habits and dead patterns—familiar comforts, digital distractions—buying time while we postpone our failure. Finding a way through all of this feels utterly inconceivable. Totally implausible. Simply impossible. In this moment, my mind began to drift. I caught myself daydreaming.

Imagine if I had some secret superpower that could change things. What if we all did?

What if we had a supernatural ability that kicked in at moments like this—something that could change the game and shift the outcome?

What if there was something wired into us from the very beginning—a built-in skill, an unseen force—that could turn our deadlocks into doorways, our obstacles into opportunities?

A power that could create something out of nothing.

A way to make the impossible *possible*?

The irony is—by slipping into this daydream—I was already tapping into that very superpower.

Your Forgotten Superpower

You have a superpower. You were born with it. No one had to teach you how to use it. In fact, when we were younger it likely got you into trouble.

If you've ever been reprimanded by a teacher for staring out the window, you're in good company. And I hate to break it to you, but your teacher got it wrong. Those minutes lost daydreaming? Not wasted. Even if your grades suffered, you were tapping into the most powerful faculty of the human mind. That teacher shouldn't have given you detention—he or she should have given you an A because you were hitting on the most important source of creativity in your life: your imagination. As a kid, you didn't need a course on how to use your imagination. For you, it was as intuitive as breathing. From the very start, you instinctively displayed this marvellous set of abilities: You imagined, played, toyed, scribbled, and invented. You built camps, sketched, told stories, and wove imaginary worlds that filled your mind with visions in bright Technicolor.

You had to be taught how to eat, walk, speak, wash, and dress. But no one has ever had to teach you how to dream. Is it any wonder that Jesus said the kingdom of heaven belongs to little children?[3] They are the dreamers, the ones for whom the borders of reality are porous and playful. For them, imagination dances at the junction of faith and possibility.

Next time you're anywhere near a group of small children, watch how they approach life. They can't help but use their imaginations to express themselves. They dip in and out of them all the time, and no one has to teach them to do this. They use their imaginations in a way that is observably different from adults.

One recent neuroscience study showed that when children were asked to improvise creatively, entire networks of their brains lit up, especially the regions linked to joy, reward, and spontaneity.[4] But something changes as we grow up: We trade daydreams for deadlines, delight for duty, and play for program. In response, our brains start to streamline, rejecting information not deemed essential. We stop relying on our creative imagination. A developmental study by NASA found that 98 percent of five-year-olds score in the category of creative geniuses, yet by adulthood only 2 percent retain the ability to think creatively in this way.[5]

Your imagination is still there: It just needs reconnecting, waking up and sparking to life. So maybe that seven-year-old version of you, the one who got detention for staring out the window too much was actually onto something all along.

Let's take it even further. We weren't just onto something—we were doing the important work of developing our minds. Our ability as children to weave imagination into reality is considered by developmental psychologists a core driver of our emotional, mental, and intellectual growth. As the influential psychologist Lev Vygotsky wrote, "A child's greatest achievements are possible in play, achievements that tomorrow will become her basic level of real action."[6] The creative trajectory of the human race—the ability to initiate and improvise—is forged in the furnace of a child's imagination.

Your imagination is your forgotten superpower.

Have you noticed that as we get older, we dream less? We spend less time in our imaginations and "waste" fewer hours daydreaming. We're busy and distracted. Our imaginations don't evaporate; we just subconsciously choose to ignore them. Somewhere along the way, the grown-up us stopped dreaming and we shut off the most powerful and potent engine of our creativity.

Creativity isn't lost—it's unlearned. As we grow from childhood into adolescence and adulthood, the bandwidth once dedicated to imagination becomes crowded out and diminished by a million other thoughts: systematised education, the pressures of achievement, and the endless distractions of daily life. The writer Madeleine L'Engle captures this shift perfectly: "All children are born artists, and it is not that some retain this creative gift and others do not. Rather, it is the fact that too often it is educated out of us."[7] Imagination isn't just play—it's possibility, problem-solving, and the birth of vision.

The good news—as we shall see in the next chapter—is that our capacity for imagination is still there, waiting to be enthused and reenergised. We just need to learn to connect the dots again. When the imagination is reclaimed, it can be rewired to unlock a powerfully different future—not just for you, but for the world around you.

Imagination rules the world.
—Napoleon

The Future Is First Imagined

Nothing new in history has ever been achieved without first unlocking the power of imagination. Philosopher Jean-Jacques Rousseau is reported to have said, "The world of reality has its limits; the world of imagination is boundless." Imagination is the superpower that solves the great problems of every generation. Imagination sends rockets into space. It brings down empires. The pillow forts of your childhood become the cities of the future. Those first notes on the piano may one day be woven into concertos. The scribbles of a toddler may one day mature into a piece hung in an art gallery. Imagination changes things. History belongs to the dreamers. For better or for worse, each generation deploys its imagination to build up and make good—or when turned toward darkness and destruction, commit terrible atrocities. For good or evil, history is shaped by those who harness their imaginations and follow their dreams.

Just think for a moment about the ideas that have moved the human spirit throughout history. Consider the acts and endeavors of kings and emperors. The words of philosophers and the works of artists. The ingenuity of scientists and inventors. Martin Luther King Jr. didn't fight racial injustice with strategy alone, despite being one of the most prolific community organisers. He had a *dream*. He moved hearts by imagining a different future. Those who change history lead out of the superpower of their imaginations. Nothing great has ever been achieved without it. But to mobilise this superpower, we first need to grasp how precious—or rather, holy—the imagination has the potential to be.

All the way through the story of the people of God, we see the centrality of creative imagination. A third of the Scriptures handed down to us are made up of poetry.[8] God spoke through the dramatic visions of the prophets and the raw passion and poetry of the psalmists' cries. Consider how great heroes of the Bible used their imaginations:

> Miriam, on the shore of deliverance, vocalised that first hymn of praise.
> Joseph—of Technicolor coat fame—was a dreamer.
> Jacob visualised a ladder bridging heaven and earth.
> Solomon dreamed of wisdom.
> Esther saw a different future for the people of God.
> Daniel dreamed of empires falling.

Centuries later, another Joseph—a carpenter—would see in his dreams a little baby: a child like no other, on whose shoulders the government of the cosmos would rest. And here, as we shall see, is the thrilling mystery of mysteries: The author of life enters into his story.

IMAGINATION

Understand the great power of your imagination. It is the sketchbook of the future world you will shape. Those who write history first draft it in pencil in their dreams as a blueprint for what is possible, before inking it into reality. In our waking and sleeping, conscious and subconscious, dreaming and scheming, hopes and fears, the imagination is the sandbox where our souls play with possibility.

Origin Story

To unlock this superpower, let's rewind to the beginning: the genesis of all things. While some might be tempted to believe that the universe is just a meaningless vacuum—and imagination is nothing more than a survival trick of neurons firing as evolution does its thing—this explanation doesn't quite wash with the wild places of the human soul. Reducing everything to a material explanation kills the mystery, and when mystery evaporates, something in us shrivels. The world feels colder, smaller, harsher, and flatter. Artists, scientists, and storytellers—they've always known better. The imagination isn't just a brain function. It carries weight and holds power. It pulls us toward something beyond ourselves. The imagination has a spiritual quality to it, serving as a doorway into the divine.

C. S. Lewis, who taught English literature at Magdalen College, Oxford, was a man of extraordinary intellect—but it was the doorway of his imagination that ultimately led him to an encounter with Jesus. His friend J. R. R. Tolkien, author of *The Lord of the Rings*, played a key role in his conversion, challenging Lewis to see imagination as a gateway to meaning and a place where God interacts with us. Lewis reflected: "For me, reason is the natural organ of truth; but imagination is the organ of meaning."[9] As a consequence, Lewis began to create the imaginary world of *The Chronicles of Narnia*—tales that have captivated hearts for generations.

Our imaginations have a spiritual quality. The most spiritual act we will ever engage in is the act of creating. But you already know this—because what moves you isn't cold logic. It's an encounter with wonder, love, beauty, and hope. The creative soul has always strained to see through the lens of imagination, reaching for that sacred place where our wildest dreams run free. It is the doorway to a holy hope. And at the foundation is this essential truth: God is the original dreamer.

> *In the beginning God created.*
> —Genesis 1:1

At the very start, everything that is begins as an idea in the mind of the Creator. In the first verses of the Bible, we learn something mind-blowing about the nature of this Creator: The only uncreated thing in the universe is God himself.

He's never not been.

He just is, necessarily.

There is no before or after with God.

He is the great "I Am," from everlasting to everlasting.[10]

This means that everything else that exists flows from him. The big bang existed as an idea in God's imagination before it exploded into life. God's ideas and words spun space and time into motion. Everything that exists traces its origin back to the divine imagination. As Trevor Hart describes it in *Making Good*, "Not only is God radically and incomparably other than the world; it is precisely his act of creating the cosmos that, more obviously than anything else, marks him out as such."[11]

Apple Pie

There's a scene in James Joyce's 1922 masterpiece *Ulysses* where the wonderful character Molly Bloom makes the argument that if you want to make an apple pie, you must first create the universe. Her point is that creativity itself—just like creation—points to the existence of God. Without one, you can't have the other. Work back through the logic here: no Creator, no creativity. No creativity, no apple pie. Which leads Molly Bloom to conclude, "As for them saying there's no God, I wouldn't give a snap of my two fingers for all their learning. Why don't they go and create something?"[12]

IMAGINATION

We need a divine Creator for creativity to exist. Because without an eternal creator in the operating system of our creativity, all we're doing is rearranging atoms. Beauty and love and hope are left as just opinions, and you and I are mere cold shells. Everything is meaningless. It's therefore the creativity of God—uniquely—that gives human creativity its meaning and beauty.

Only God truly creates something from nothing. For all our best intentions and genius inventions, it's God—the single uncreated reality in the universe, who is the original source. In that sense, every idea, every work of art, and every scientific breakthrough flows from him alone. As philosopher George Steiner put it, "Tautologically, only God creates. Man 'makes' or 'produces.'"[13]

Spark! Bang! Wow!

God uniquely is in the business of true creation. The rest of us are simply creatures formed from something by Someone. Let's dig a little deeper into this for a moment. In the Genesis account of creation, two Hebrew words are used to describe the creative act:

Bara (בָּרָא): Meaning to create something out of nothing. Spark! Bang! Wow!
Asah (עָשָׂה): Meaning to fashion, to form, to make and to shape what God has created.

Bara is a unique kind of divine creative act that only God does; it is never used to describe human creativity. When the psalmist cried out, "Create in me a pure heart, O God" (Psalm 51:10), it was a *bara* heart that he was longing for, a divine newness that could only come from the Creator. *Asah*, however, is used for both God and human creativity; it means to fashion, to form, to make, and to shape from the raw material God has made. It's the shaping of the clay in the hands of the potter.

In the beginning, God *bara*-ed the heavens and the earth into being.

Then he formed—*asah*-ed—the sun, moon, earth, seas, and animals from the dust of the cosmos. When he got to the creation of humanity, something extraordinary happened:

> *So God bara-ed mankind in his own image,*
> *in the image of God he bara-ed them;*
> *male and female he bara-ed them.*
> —Genesis 1:27[14]

Spark! Bang! Wow! In one short sentence, the three-in-one God creates us with three-time divine novelty—*bara, bara, bara*—in his image. So when we talk about being made in the image of God, it's really not an exaggeration. Our identity, originality, and creativity spark from this three-pronged point of ignition. We explode into life in order to *asah* the world: to join in with this Creator in the forming and shaping of the raw materials of the cosmos in order to bring about order, beauty, and life. Creativity is the mission and mandate: the way we make good.

This realisation is the spiritual equivalent of when your favourite superhero learns of the origin story of their superpower: when Superman discovers kryptonite or when Spider-Man realises his spider-sense comes from his exposure to whatever those mutant, genetically-modified, freaky spiders are. It's the *wow* moment in our backstory that starts to make sense of the rest of the arc of our creative lives. All of your creativity traces its genesis back to the big bang of God's originality. The existence of creativity, beauty, and the ability to make, shape, and imagine are telltale tracers pointing back to the *wow* of the glory of God. There is causality in our creativity: Behind every artist's brushstroke, every poet's turn of phrase, every scientist's formula, the universe has a single splendid source of ultimate newness, beauty, and love.

This is good news for the creative soul, whatever your religious persuasion. It's this argument that the apostle Paul made when explaining the message of Jesus to the Epicurean and Stoic philosophers in Athens. He began with first principles: "The God who made the world and everything in it..." (Acts 17:24). Then, speaking the language of his ancient

Greek audience, he quoted the Stoic poet Aratus: "For in him we live and move and have our being... We are his offspring" (Acts 17:28). Paul's argument is clear: All human wisdom, all original thought, even our poetry and creativity—flows from God to us because we are made in his image. Here is the golden thread that directly links your soul to the Spark! Bang! Wow! of God's creativity. Welcome to your origin story.

Your Creative Soul

Your soul is the beating heart of your creativity. As a result, your spiritual life—the place of interface and interaction with God—is the key to unlocking your richest and most profound creative work. Understanding the source of all creativity liberates us from trying to create in our own strength. This is revolutionary: In a culture concerned with creativity, where we idolise creators, we need to recover this deeper reality—only God truly creates.

If God is the source of all creativity, then everything we have is received as a gift. Every idea, every stroke of artistic originality, every moment of beauty and truth ultimately flows from God. In this sense, every human act of creativity is a participation in God's divine work—whether we acknowledge it or not. It is impossible to create without tracing our own creativity back to the point of origin in God the Creator. And from this reality—as we surrender to something bigger than ourselves—we find we begin to unlock the true power of imagination. When we find the source of it all, we discover that all things really are possible.

The Fountainhead

I have a friend who grew up on a farm in rural Gloucestershire, England. His family has worked the land for generations, and flowing through the rolling patchwork of green fields that stitch their farm together is a small, bubbling stream. Follow it up to the source and you'll discover a hidden pool nestled in a glade of old trees. And there you'll find something extraordinary—a glistening cataract of water welling up from the depths of the earth. This quiet, unassuming pool is the source of the Thames—England's longest and most powerful river. The first time I saw it I felt a sense of wonder. Here it was—the genesis of a river that has shaped Britain for centuries. The River Thames flows through the heart of the nation, past palaces and Parliament, a great artery tracing the course of British influence far beyond London to the edges of the earth. And now I stood at its beginning: a fresh spring welling up from the darkness of the earth.

In the same way, when we connect with our Creator we touch the very source of imagination itself. This is the great fountainhead of the imagination: a holy place where—standing at the headwaters of wonder in the presence of God himself—we begin to unlock the power of our creativity in a way we never could on our own. And what do we find at the source? The great surprise, as we'll discover, is that our Creator isn't distant or indifferent; instead, he welcomes us in. He invites us to draw close, to navigate the fields of our dreams, and to meet him there.

We find that the Creator is not a cold theory or a distant tyrant. He is pure love, and his act of creating is an overflow of that love, a work of pure joy. He is the original artist, and he delights in his handiwork. As we shall see, we are not just spectators in observing his works of art—he invites us to create alongside him.

God's Pleasure

Have you ever made something you're truly proud of? Consider the moment when a painter steps back after the final brushstroke, seeing the work complete. The quiet satisfaction of an author typing the last full stop, the story finally told. The thrill as the mathematician cracks the code, the solution falling into place. We know it instinctively—there is joy in the creative process. It's rewarding, even exhilarating. We inherit this trait from our heavenly Father. In the beginning, God created—and then "God saw that it was good." You can feel his joy in those words.

IMAGINATION

Seven times in the opening chapter of Genesis, the Creator steps back, takes in his handiwork, and celebrates. He says, "It is good," and of humans, "It is very good." In the same way, when we create, we experience that deep pleasure because we're made from the same creative DNA.

The film *Chariots of Fire*, winner of four Academy Awards, including Best Picture, tells the story of Eric Liddell, a devout Christian and a gifted runner who would go on to represent Great Britain at the 1924 Olympics in Paris, winning two medals—including gold in the 400 meters. In one of the film's most memorable scenes, Liddell, portrayed by Ian Charleson, expresses the pure delight of living out his calling: "I believe God made me for a purpose, but he also made me fast. And when I run, I feel his pleasure."[15] When you unlock the power of your imagination, God delights in you because you're doing the very thing that brings him joy. When you create, you are doing what you were designed to do. You are coming fully alive, and in that you can feel God's pleasure. So, the imagination is holy ground, a place of deep encounter.

The realm of your imagination is like the garden of the soul, your inner Eden, that place where God often likes to take a walk in the cool of your subconscious. And here, in that inner world, he's searching for you. Just as the Celts spoke of "thin places," spaces where heaven feels closer, so your imagination is a place where the Creator longs to meet you, a gateway to encountering the mystery of God. The imagination is a sacred place, the holy of holies of human experience—a realm of mystery, awe, and wonder. Here your faith resides; here all things are possible. If faith is being sure of what we hope for and certain of things we cannot see, then the imagination is the delicate canvas on which those hopes are painted into reality. In this precious space, your soul communes with your Creator. Here, as the astronomer Johannes Kepler suggested, we are "thinking God's thoughts after him."[16]

Thinking God's thoughts after him sounds wonderful, but if you're anything like me, the reality is a little bit more mundane. On any given day, most of us struggle to find our house keys or where we've left our phones, let alone think wildly creative thoughts emanating from a divinely inspired imagination. We hit walls and have writer's block, brain freeze, stage fright, and everything in between. The problems we're trying to solve feel impossible, the ideas won't come, and the breakthroughs feel out of reach.

I have good news for you. The power of the imagination can be cultivated. As we shall see in the next chapter, the imagination can be nurtured, encouraged, and stirred back to life. It can become an inner world humming with creative potential, a fertile space for holy dreaming again. As with the young superhero in training, your God-given superpower can be nurtured and developed. You can learn how to slow down to tap into its power, and God can unlock a world of possibilities within your soul.

In the world of the imagination, faith becomes a reality. All things are possible. This adventure starts with an invitation to walk into the secret garden of your imagination, to pause in that unhurried space, and to uncover delight, mystery, and wonder—and to see the possibilities of a different future take shape.

So we begin with an invitation to recover our childlike wonder. To daydream again. To imagine what could be. What are the fertile places your thoughts wander to? And might God meet you there? In the dance between the divine and the daydream, we unlock a world of heavenly possibilities.

Welcome to Your Secret Superpower

Here is our creative genesis—the recognition that your extraordinary imagination connects with the God who creates *bara* and who invites you to join with him in the *asah* of the world. Understanding the source and headwater of your spiritual DNA is fertile ground to unlocking the vast potential within you. In the chapters ahead, you'll learn to unlock your imagination and follow the dreams the Creator has gifted you with. You will have adventures and you will have failures. This journey will demand courage, risk, and a willingness to make space for the Creator to spark something new deep in your soul. The future is shaped by those who dare to dream. The kingdom of heaven belongs to those who make space for the Creator Spirit to ignite their imaginations for the glory of God.

Come, Creator Spirit

Back at the whiteboard, I am still standing, staring at the wall, pen in hand. I have nothing—no vision, no brainwaves, no solutions. Finally, in the desperate silence, I whisper a simple, ancient prayer under my breath: "Come, Creator Spirit." It's a cry that has echoed through the ages, a prayer to the original Creator, an acknowledgment that we can't do it on our own. We need to return to the source, to the author of life, and ask him to break into our imaginations with his holy newness, that *bara* creativity.

There is a pregnant pause.

Silence.

Stillness.

The nervous chewing of the pen lid.

The sound of the city—sirens in the distance.

And still, I wait, staring at the blank white space on the wall.

Then—a spark.

A holy pulse across some hidden synapse.

Slowly my imagination begins to fire, fuelled by a flicker of faith. Deep in my mind, dots begin to join together. Concepts coalesce, emerging from the brooding gloom. The tiniest flicker of an idea—a connection—starts to form. My imagination is coming alive. Here, in holy dreaming, all things are possible.

Spark! Quick as a flash, I reach out my arm.

Bang! It feels almost like an act of obedience—a leap of faith.

Wow! Tentatively the marker begins to squeak across the surface of the whiteboard.

A few scribbles. Just a word or two. But I am off. This is where all dreaming begins—the collision of human imagination and holy inspiration.

Come, Creator Spirit. Spark!

Come, O Creator Spirit, come,
and make within our heart thy home;
to us thy grace celestial give,
who of thy breathing move and live.
  —Veni Creator Spiritus, Ninth Century Hymn

SPARK CIRCLE

Circle back through this chapter of Spark.

Notice
What moment in the chapter awakened something in you? Did a phrase, story, or insight stir wonder, longing, or a sense of creative calling?

Name
Where have you shut down your imagination—through fear, cynicism, disappointment, or distraction?
How do you feel about the call to recover your childlike imagination?

Next Step
This week, invite the Creator to breathe on your imagination. Pray simply: "Come, Creator Spirit." Then give yourself space—journal, walk, or sit in stillness—and see what stirs. What do you sense the Creator awakening in you? Bring that into your Spark Circle.

CHAPTER 2

Ignite Your Imagination

> *At the back of our brains, so to speak, there is a forgotten blaze or burst of astonishment at our own existence. The object of the artistic and spiritual life is to dig for this submerged sunrise of wonder.*
> —G. K. Chesterton

Her voice quivers with emotion. Her tear-streaked cheeks are crisscrossed with anxiety. Barely twenty-five, she seems too young to be grappling with something so existential. But like so many today, she's facing a crisis no one could have predicted at the turn of the millennium. Despite being highly educated, talented, hard-working, and outwardly successful, something in her soul has reached a breaking point. Frustration has simmered to desperation, and now she can no longer contain it. The words spill out of her—part confession, part cry for help: "It's my imagination. It's gone. I've forgotten how to dream. I can't hear myself think anymore. And it's killing me."

This crisis of creative confidence is something I encounter with alarming frequency—a quiet malaise sweeping through the minds of so many people I meet in our ever-connected, never-dreaming world. It's subtle and invisible. It does not show up in CT scans or blood tests. It's difficult to diagnose and hard to name. Yet we can trace its shape through the silent psychological toll it takes on our lives. The great thinker Karl Barth saw this crisis coming and warned prophetically that we must "resist to the very last the peculiar habit of the modern Western mind that itself suffers above all from a chronic lack of imagination."[1]

We are a generation standing at the hinge of history—humanity's most technologically connected, informationally rich, digitally stimulated cohort. Hypnotised by flickering pixels. Anaesthetised by the constant drip, drip, drip of endless data points. Our imaginations are lulled into a state of dreamless slumber. The muscles of originality waste away, atrophying into apathy.

The Way to Wonderland

We have forgotten the way to the wonderland of imagination. Our sunsets are streamed, not seen. Our minds are never bored yet rarely satisfied. We trade contentment for content, existing vicariously through the filters of other people's online curation. And what little newness we find too often arrives pre-packaged in the echo chamber of an algorithm. We have outsourced the holy act of imagining to the priesthood of the pixel. And then one day—like the girl with the tear-streaked face—we come to the crashing realisation that we can't take it anymore. Something in us recoils, even rebels against it all. We know we must break free at all costs and escape the suffocating noise and make for the wide-open spaces of this wonderland, where we truly belong. We long for that magical place where our dreams take shape, the sunlit pastures of the soul where ideas ruminate. It is a realm where originality is oxygen and imagining is instinctive.

There is an urgency to all of this, because without imagination, nothing new is possible. Every breakthrough, invention, story, song, and symphony that has shaped our human experience flowed first from the imagination. Imagination is the wonderland of the soul—the place where nothing is impossible. It is the strings on which faith plays its symphony, the gentle melodic landscape where all things become possible. Your imagination is the deep water from which your heart and soul drink. If you want to solve a problem, create something new, change the world, or

IGNITE YOUR IMAGINATION

move the human heart, there is only one place to begin: this wonderland of imagination, this world of unlimited possibility.

So how do we find our way back to wonderland? How do we hack a system that feels so stacked against us? How do we make space in a noisy world for the sweet music of the imagination to sing? In this chapter, we're going to explore five hacks that will spark the power of your creative imagination—five simple, tangible habits that anyone can learn to build into their creative rhythm. Because creativity isn't just a gift; it's a muscle. And like any muscle, it needs to be stretched, strengthened, and awakened. You either use it or you lose it.

Hack 1: Pause

The year is 1787. A horse-drawn carriage rumbles along the rough road between Prague and Vienna, and slumped in the back, staring out of the window into the distance, is composer Wolfgang Amadeus Mozart. The carriage trundles through the rich Bavarian landscape with the rugged hills giving way to dense green forests. The landscape comes alive in the early summer sun, the mountain road occasionally entering lush green meadows bursting with life before plunging back into the darkness of the forest. There are glimpses of baroque churches and romantic castles until eventually the road winds down toward the Danube and the grandeur of Vienna's imperial architecture.

Mozart leans wearily on the window frame, yawning. The journey has been long, with melted spring snow leaving the road rutted in places. The frustratingly slow pace is an enforced pause in the hectic life of this feted young composer. It's his second full day of travelling. No piano to play, no quill and ink, no orchestra to conduct—just the rocking of the carriage, the rhythmic thud of the horses' hooves, the rising and falling of the forests and fields. He is beyond bored. Stuck in his carriage, unable to do anything, his mind begins to wander. As the carriage rumbles through the landscape, something begins to spark. Perhaps it was the sound of the hooves, the relentless:

IMAGINATION

Duh-dum-duh-duh-dum.
Duh-dum-duh-duh-dum.

Mozart finds himself entering the wonderland of the imagination. Gradually, notes begin to dance in his mind: Melodies and harmonies weave together in his subconscious as phrases start to form in his imagination.

In the music, you can almost hear the rhythm of the carriage, the drumbeat of the hooves, the symphony of the landscape's rolling swells. Take the famous Rondo from Horn Concerto No. 4:

Duh-dum-duh-duh-dum.
Duh-dum-duh-duh-dum.

Mozart later described in a letter to a friend how his most creative ideas flowed from his imagination in those moments—such as when travelling by carriage—writing, "It is on such occasions that my ideas flow best and most abundantly."[2]

Mozart knew the secret to our first hack: Ideas come in the gaps. Many of the greatest creative breakthroughs come in those liminal spaces between business and busyness, pressure and activity. Ironically, the best thing you often can do to nurture your imagination is to *do absolutely nothing*. Counterintuitive as it may seem, some of our most productive moments—when we need to solve problems, innovate, or create—come when we make space for the soul. Allowing yourself to be bored and your imagination to run free will break new ground. This is not just wishful thinking. There's good scientific basis for how intentionally pressing pause ignites your imagination and leads to greater creativity. To understand this, let's take a trip inside your head.

The Wonderland of the Brain

Your brain is a wonderland—a vast network of complex connections, each playing its part in your ability to imagine. The different parts of

IGNITE YOUR IMAGINATION

your brain all perform distinct functions that—thanks to advances in MRI and brain mapping—we can observe scientifically:

+ The temporal and parietal lobes act as a memory bank, drawing from past experiences and mental imagery.
+ The occipital lobes and your hippocampus handle visual processing and spatial navigation, shaping the way you see and move through both real and imagined worlds.
+ The amygdala infuses your imagination with emotion, adding depth, colour, and feeling to every thought, vision, and dream.
+ But the true epicentre of your imagination lies in what neuroscientists call the default mode network—a collection of brain regions that light up when your mind drifts into daydreaming, mind wandering, and introspection.

At the core of the default mode network are the prefrontal cortex and the posterior cingulate cortex. It's here, researchers have found, that the most essential functions of creative imagination take shape, the place where ideas spark, connections form, and innovation is born. This is the ground zero of creativity in your brain. Extraordinarily, the default mode network comes to life when the rest of your brain is at rest—when your mind is in neutral, unoccupied, doing nothing at all. This is the brain's white blank page, the open space from which creativity flows. Again, one of the most powerful ways to spark your imagination and cultivate this superpower is to do nothing.

If you get tired, learn to rest not quit.
—Banksy

My friend Dr. Jake Fairnie, who has a PhD in neuroscience with a particular focus on the creative power of the brain, explains how this works: "Giving your brain some space to do nothing can be one of the best things you can do for your creativity. When you're constantly focused on a task, it leaves little space for big-picture thinking. Taking a break

IMAGINATION

can reduce cognitive load, freeing up brainpower to explore new ideas, jump between concepts, and make creative connections that wouldn't necessarily emerge in a focused state."[3]

So how do we harness the creative power of pausing? Is it as simple—sometimes—as choosing to do nothing and allowing yourself to become bored? "Interestingly," Jake says, "when you stop focusing on a task, the default mode network kicks in. This network is most active when you're daydreaming, reflecting, or letting your mind wander. And that's when your brain starts connecting different ideas in ways it normally wouldn't, leading to those (sometimes big) moments of creative insight.

"On top of that," Jake adds, "constant work can lead to stress, which dampens creativity. Taking a break lowers stress hormones—like cortisol—and helps your brain function more efficiently, boosting problem-solving and innovative thinking. So yes, doing 'nothing' can actually be a key part of the creative process, giving space for fresh ideas to bubble up when you're not forcing them."

Take Agatha Christie—one of the best-selling authors of all time. The creator of Hercule Poirot and Miss Marple was no stranger to writer's block. When stuck for ideas, she wouldn't force inspiration at her desk. Instead, she would put down the pen, step away, and sink into a long, warm bath. For hours she would soak—not trying to be productive, just letting her mind drift, staring at the ceiling or out of the window. It was precisely in these moments of stillness that her most brilliant plot twists would surface. The clues, the red herrings, the ingenious whodunits—many of them were born not at her writing desk but in the bath.

Or picture Albert Einstein daydreaming on a tram in Bern, Switzerland, far from his library, laboratory, and lectures. As the tram crisscrosses the streets, sunlight streaming through the windows, his mind begins to wander. He imagines what it would be like to travel through space, riding on a beam of light. That moment of daydreaming—of letting his mind drift beyond the ordinary—became the spark that would ultimately lead to his revolutionary work on relativity, space, and time. To daydream is to step into a realm where all things are

IGNITE YOUR IMAGINATION

suddenly possible. Creativity is the discovery of truth, the stumbling into the sunlight of reality for the first time.

J. K. Rowling says it was on a train from Manchester to London, one that was severely delayed, that she dreamed up the world of Harry Potter. For hours the train didn't move. No pen. No paper. No laptop. Nothing to entertain her. Just time and space. Her mind began to wander. Over the course of that prolonged journey, the entire world of Harry Potter took shape in her imagination. The characters. The locations. The plotlines. The architecture of a whole magical universe. By the time her train reached London (Platform 9 ¾), she had mapped out the full arc and structure of the seven-book series. That enforced delay would spark the best-selling work of fiction of all time. The interruptions. The waiting. The inconveniences. These are not the enemies of imagination. They are often its best friends. (Remember that next time you're stuck, delayed, frustrated.)

Paul McCartney—fast asleep—is dreaming. In his dream, he hears a simple melody, brand-new, and then the lyrics, perfectly formed. It comes from nowhere, just appears—complete—in his dream. His resting body allows his mind to process and create, and his ideas play out in his dreams. As soon as he wakes up, he reaches for his notebook and pen and scribbles down what he can remember from what he's heard. The Beatles later recorded "Yesterday" pretty much as it was in Paul's dream.

Pablo Picasso—bored—is leaving his studio to walk the streets of Paris. Escaping the stagnant claustrophobia of his painter's garret, he wanders the city, restless. One day, searching for inspiration, he steps into a museum and finds himself captivated by a new exhibition of African art. The experience is transformative. Masks. Shapes. Geometric forms. Something about them speaks to him—the lines, angles, a new way of seeing. Picasso is overwhelmed. In his words, "I didn't leave. I stayed. I stayed."[4] This now famous encounter sparked a revolution, and a whole new creative direction began to take shape in his mind, one that would shatter artistic conventions. That moment—the chance encounter—became the genesis of Cubism, a movement that would radically transform art in the twentieth century.

IMAGINATION

You get the picture.

So often the most innovative breakthroughs don't come when we're straining to force creativity but when we allow our minds the space to declutter, dream, and wander. Rest is the root of revelation. In an always-on, overstimulated world, boredom is a gift.

So what if we cultivated boredom as a spiritual discipline? What if we saw making space as strategic—not wasted time but essential time? The deliberate breathing-in of your soul oxygenates the lifeblood of your imagination. Boredom is the birthplace of brilliance.

In chapter 1, we explored how God is the original dreamer, the Creator of all things. Humanity has always looked back at his creativity as the origin and source of all innovation. But in those first pages of the creation story, we find something deeply significant: Rest is built into the process. The first thing God did when his work of creation was complete was to stop and rest. Genesis tells us, "Then God blessed the seventh day and made it holy, because on it he rested from all the work of creating that he had done" (Genesis 2:3).

Rest is not an afterthought. It's part of the creative rhythm. There, in the original act of creation, God himself built into his own creative process the priority of pausing. In the same way, we are hardwired to do our best imagining when we operate from a place of rest. If we want to create from a place of deep inspiration, the starting point isn't striving; it's stopping.

Slow down.

Unplug.

Pause.

It may feel counter-intuitive, but it's profoundly effective.

When you slow down, pause, and disconnect, your imagination begins to awaken. You'll be retreating to advance, inhaling to exhale. Again, the psalmist encourages us to "be still before the LORD and wait patiently for him" (Psalm 37:7).

So, permission granted—close this book, unplug, take a walk, run a bath, have a nap, make a cup of coffee, or stare out the window. This may not come naturally, especially if you struggle to sit still or have bought into the myth that true productivity means relentless activity. But resist the urge to fill every moment. Instead, take a trip to your imagination—because you never know what might be waiting there for you.

> *The Christian is the one whose imagination should fly beyond the stars.*
> —Francis Schaeffer

Hack 2: Pray

C. S. Lewis was not the praying type. Belief in God wasn't part of his internal world. He would later describe himself as the most "reluctant convert in all England."[5] But for Lewis, the aha moment came while reading the works of writer George MacDonald.[6] Something in MacDonald's words stirred him not just intellectually but imaginatively. In his autobiographical work *Surprised by Joy*, Lewis described this awakening as nothing less than a baptism of the imagination—a moment when something deeper was unlocked, drawing him toward a truth he had long resisted. As he turned the pages, the words began to stir something deep within him, awakening his innermost being in a way he had never experienced before: "That night my imagination was, in a certain sense, baptized; the rest of me, not unnaturally, took longer."[7]

For Lewis, this moment was more than an intellectual shift, it was a spiritual awakening of the imagination. Alongside his friend and fellow author J. R. R. Tolkien, he would go on to shape worlds and stories that carried the redemptive power of imagination at their core. The world of Narnia, the epic landscapes of *The Lord of the Rings*, and many other tales that have inspired generations can all trace their genesis back to this spiritual connection where imagination and faith merged.

We're only just beginning to understand, scientifically, the deep connection between spiritual engagement and the imagination. It turns out that the human soul and the human imagination are far more intertwined than previously thought. This isn't wishful thinking or crackpot theory.

IMAGINATION

As technology advances, allowing us to better map the way thoughts are formed in the brain, researchers have begun to uncover an extraordinary synergy between spiritual connection and creative flow. And a crucial piece of this puzzle is our old friend, the default mode network.

In an attempt to unlock how our brains work, scientists have studied the brain's electromagnetic patterns across a wide range of human experiences. Different areas of the brain activate depending on the task: Sleep triggers one region, logic and reason another, memory retention another, and emotions—like love or attraction—yet another. But what they discovered was fascinating and unexpected: The same parts of your brain that power imagination and your creative flow also fire up in your moments of spiritual connection.

Studies have uncovered that the prefrontal cortex and posterior cingulate cortex—key components of the brain's default mode network, which become active when we're daydreaming, reflecting, and allowing our imaginations to roam free—also mysteriously light up during moments of prayer, worship, and deep spiritual engagement. In their book *How God Changes the Brain*, neuroscientists Andrew Newberg and Mark Robert Waldman describe the surprising discovery that the very regions of the brain "responsible for the greater imagination, creativity and originality" are also activated when we think about "the immaterial qualities of God."[8]

In other words, the very part of your brain responsible for creative insight is the same part that activates when you connect with God. The creative act is, at its core, a spiritual one. Creativity is prayer, and prayer is creativity.

Your soul is deeply creative, and when you pray, you tap into the life force at the heart of the universe—the Creator Spirit—that holy spark who not only gives life but continues igniting the power of your best ideas. Whether or not we believe in God, most of us pray, and not just when the plane is passing through turbulence. Prayer is not going out of fashion. Far from it. A recent study revealed that young people today are more likely to pray than their parents' generation.[9] In fact, the younger you are, the more likely you are to pray—even if you wouldn't call yourself religious. In this new era of artificial intelligence and digital determinism, we are waking up to the reality that we are not just collections of data but souls created for wonder. Prayer lifts our eyes beyond the horizon of our human experience to the endless possibility of eternity.

Sure, you can create without praying—but if there is a place where you can interface with your Creator, why wouldn't you? Your Creator is alive, present, and longing for connection, and encountering him will excite or even enhance your imagination. To pray is to light up the deepest parts of your soul, and spark your creativity with holy fire.

So next time you're stuck for an idea, instead of jumping online, try switching off your device and switching on your soul. Take a moment to be quiet. Slow down. Notice your breathing. Invite the Creator Spirit to fill you.

Your imagination is essential. It sees the unseen. It makes the impossible possible. Faith is the inner realm of dreaming, possibility, and hope, and it is the heart of the soul's inner life. And this kind of faith isn't possible without activating the imagination. It's the imagination that lifts the eyes of faith beyond the material and allows us to conceive of the eternal.

Feed your soul, and your imagination will come alive. Baptise your creativity in spiritual reality, and you'll tap into an unending source of life, inspiration, and creative power.

While this all sounds great, the truth is, most of us struggle with the spiritual stuff. Life is loud. We're overwhelmed, distracted, and pulled in a hundred directions. A great starting place is simply to step away—to carve out a moment each day to pause, breathe, and pray. Speak to God. Ask for inspiration. Practice gratitude. Share your anxieties. Be still and listen.

In the presence of God, our deepest dreams come to life. But to enable this, we must slow down and give God our fullest attention. "Attention is the rarest and purest form of generosity," wrote twentieth-century French philosopher Simone Weil, describing prayer as a kind of attention: "The soul empties itself of all its own contents in order to receive into itself the being it is looking at, just as he is, in all his truth. Only he who is capable of attention can do this."[10]

IMAGINATION

Prayer is about slowing down and creating space, and it has been shown to enhance divergent thinking, cultivate peace, and reduce stress. It activates neuroplasticity, the brain's ability to adapt, reorganise, and reprioritise itself. Beyond that, prayer fosters emotional connection and empathy, shaping us into people of greater understanding and compassion, even when our minds feel unfruitful, even when we find ourselves drifting. Because in those quiet spaces, something deeper is always at work. The poet and divine John Donne described the tension of prayer as a battle between blessing and boredom: "I throw myself down in my chamber, and I call in, and invite God, and His angels thither." But soon his mind began to drift: "I neglect God and His angels for the noise of a fly, for the rattling of a coach, for the whining of a door . . . and if God or His angels should ask me when I thought last of God in that prayer, I cannot tell."[11]

Ironically, this state of boredom and distraction, even when we are praying, is not our enemy. In fact, it's often in these moments—when the mind is in neutral—that the brain enters a meditative, almost sacred state. Here we unlock unexpected insight, creativity, and connection. The same is true when it comes to reading Scripture. Investing in your soul is also an investment in your ability to think creatively.

This isn't just a nice idea for the impossibly pious; compelling evidence links regular reading of Scripture with enhanced imagination and cognitive function. A scientific study published by the National Academy of Sciences found that consistent Scripture reading, combined with prayer, activates neural networks in the temporoparietal junction and the precuneus, regions of the brain involved in creative imagination.[12] As Jesus said, "The Spirit gives life; the flesh counts for nothing. The words I have spoken to you—they are full of the Spirit and life" (John 6:63).

> *Ever since my earliest youth, I have been fascinated with the Bible. . . . I have sought its reflection in life and art. The Bible is life, an echo of nature, and this is the secret I have endeavoured to transmit.*
> —Marc Chagall

IGNITE YOUR IMAGINATION

Reading the Bible can literally spark your imagination to life. All Scripture is God-breathed (2 Timothy 3:16), thick with the very breath of the Creator himself. The Bible is the Creator's handbook, the user manual for the human experience. These words, handed down through generations, are in themselves an art form—poetry, prose, songs, and prophetic imagining.

Following a spiritual rhythm in your daily life cultivates a rich and fertile inner world. Find your rhythm. Make space to reflect. Keep a journal where you can download thoughts, sketch ideas, and track where you're at.

Feed your soul.
Get outdoors.
Go on retreat.
Embrace silence.
Take a moment.
Pursue solitude.

This hack is like stretching the muscle of your creative soul. Learning to regularly connect with God will fuel your imagination. This divine connection has a prophetic quality: It's in prayer that we imagine different futures for the world. Theologian Walter Brueggemann described the connection between prayer and the power of the imagination as "the prophetic imagination," something with an almost sacramental quality. He added, "The people we later recognize as prophets are also poets. They reframe what is at stake in chaotic times." There is power in a prayer-infused, spiritual imagination. Brueggemann understood the dynamic force of a Spirit-filled imagination, noting: "Every totalitarian regime is frightened of the artist. It is the vocation of the prophet to keep alive the ministry of imagination."[13]

An awareness of God has shaped the experience of countless creatives throughout history. From Michelangelo, who "took great pleasure from the Holy Scriptures"[14] to musician Pharrell Williams, who when asked by producer Rick Rubin, "What do you do outside of your creative life that has the most impact on your creative life?" replied, "Pray!"[15] By allowing yourself space to encounter God on a regular basis, you are giving your creative soul permission to dream. And there is nothing more powerful for your imagination than that.

Hack 3: Play

> *Play is the highest form of research.*
> —Albert Einstein

When we were children, our imaginations joyfully ruled the world. We didn't need to be taught creativity, expression, or how to dream—it all came naturally. Original ideas poured out of us in a great stream of laughter, make-believe, adventure, and storytelling. We cared a little less and played a lot more. The act of play unlocked our imaginations, and the line between reality and imagination was porous. All things were possible. An old cardboard box became a fort. A few Lego blocks, a spaceship. A simple toy, the hero of a grand adventure unfolding in our minds. And no one ever had to teach us how to play because play was as natural to us as breathing.

But then—like Wendy in Peter Pan—we grew up and forgot the way to the Neverland of our imaginations. We forgot to fly. We forgot to dream. We forgot that play unlocked a world where all things were possible. Pablo Picasso put it like this: "Every child is an artist. The problem is how to remain an artist once we grow up."[16] Gradually, the realm of imagination slipped into the distance, hidden beyond the horizon of our lives by clouds of busyness, responsibility, pressures, and concerns. Our mature, time-poor, sensible, vexed, educated, and over-stimulated souls became, well . . . old.

> *We don't stop playing because we grow old;*
> *we grow old because we stop playing.*
> —George Bernard Shaw

IGNITE YOUR IMAGINATION

When we stop operating from a place of playfulness—the lightness of spirit that meets life's challenges with joyful curiosity—we begin to lose wonder. We swap the plastic, dynamic abilities of our imaginations for a more fixed, rigid way of thinking. Our ability to think outside the box diminishes, and we become trapped in habitual, linear patterns. Things stop being fun. We start taking ourselves too seriously. And our thoughts—once flexible and light—become stuck and heavy.

This is such a well-documented phenomenon that psychologists even have a name for it: *cognitive rigidity*. Over time this rigidity trains our brains to over-rely on the prefrontal cortex, the centre of logic and control, while diminishing neuroplasticity—the brain's ability to adapt, rewire, and make new connections. Our imaginations become trapped by functional fixedness, a state where we see only what is rather than what could be. Put simply, a mind that is too fixed stops being creative, and a life without imagination is a life without possibility.

Now here's the good news. That playfulness you so readily accessed as a child, the spark that fired up your imagination and opened a world of possibilities, is still there. In fact, it's fighting to get out. That instinct to tear up the rule book, stick it to the man, walk on the grass, let your hair down—that's not just rebellion or whimsy. That's your mind fighting to preserve the best parts of your brain function. You just need to choose to start using it again.

When we first started Renaissance, our gatherings of creatives in cities around the world, we made a deliberate decision: Every event would include intentional moments of hands-on interaction and lots of fun. We wanted people to make stuff. Try stuff. Taste stuff. Step outside their comfort zones. So, we started designing the programme to break the intensity, shake things up, and surprise people.

We invited guests to take part in spontaneous karaoke right in the middle of our main keynotes, embracing the joy, chaos, and laughter that followed. We took them outdoors to learn wild baking with one of the UK's best bakers, who didn't just teach them how to make dough but how to bake fresh, delicious bread over a charcoal fire. We even took

IMAGINATION

people to meet our bees in their hives—and guests learned how bees work together to survive, make honey, and bring flourishing to the whole ecosystem.

Time and time again at these Renaissance gatherings, it's not just the inspirational teaching or the outstanding contributors that leave the deepest impact; it's these moments of hands-on, sensory creativity. The moments when people get their hands messy with dough. The moments when they smell or taste something new. The moments when they step outside the ordinary and reawaken their imaginations. Because experience sparks creativity in a way that words alone cannot.

Next time you're trying to solve a problem or break new ground, choose to approach it with curiosity, playfulness, and fun. What you'll find is that play stimulates the flow of imagination. It increases your ability to think outside the box, solve problems, and even improve your mood. Playing even releases dopamine—the happy chemical—making us more engaged, adaptable, and open to new insight. A playful mind is a creative mind.

Do you remember the way to Narnia? It was little Lucy Pevensie, escaping from her brothers and sisters during a game of hide-and-seek, who pushed through the coats and stumbled into a whole new world on the other side of the wardrobe. Her playful curiosity was the key that unlocked a new reality. Worlds and wonders are waiting for us on the other side of our curiosity. And sometimes all we need to do is playfully push through the layers of grown-up concerns we've wrapped ourselves in and follow our childlike curiosity into new places. Biochemist and writer Isaac Asimov made a powerful point: "The most exciting phrase to hear in science, the one that heralds new discoveries, is not 'Eureka!' but 'That's funny.'"[17] Here's your assignment:

Play joyfully.

Laugh deeply.

Bring your curiosity.

Pay attention to "That's funny."

Pick at the frayed seams and loose stitches of your world, because beneath that fragile hem may lie a world of wonder.

Hack 4: People

You and I are not meant to create alone.

As powerful as our imaginations may be, we ignite our deepest creativity when we create alongside others. Yet ironically we live in a time when creativity is often confused with self-sufficiency. Our individualistic culture has made an idol of independence, and yet many creatives find themselves feeling isolated and unseen. We crave encouragement, affirmation, and love. This reliance on one another is part of what it means to be human—we're created to be in community, and so we create in community. This is creative interdependency—the truth that we create best when we create together.

Giant sequoias are some of the most extraordinary organisms on earth. These trees are among the oldest living things, with some surpassing three thousand years in age. They are also the tallest trees on the planet, growing to more than twice the height of the Statue of Liberty. Standing at the base of their six-meter-wide trunks is like standing next to a twenty-five-story skyscraper made of living wood. And that's just what's above the ground. What's below the surface is even more remarkable. For a tree that tall, you'd expect deep roots, anchoring them firmly into the earth. But surprisingly, the roots of a sequoia only reach about six to twelve feet—extraordinarily shallow for a tree of such massive scale.

So how do these towering structures remain upright for millennia—enduring earthquakes, fires, and storms? The secret of the sequoia is simple: They don't do it alone. These trees only survive where their root systems intertwine with those of their neighbours, creating an unbreakable network of support. Alone they fail. Together they stand strong. They anchor one another, providing the stability needed to endure across centuries. We, too, survive longer when we stand united. We grow taller when we share the sunlight and oxygen of encouragement. And we thrive when our creativity is strengthened by community.

Our creative interdependency should not come as a surprise to us because God is not a solo artist. The Creator exists in relationship—a divine community of love and commitment within Father, Son, and

IMAGINATION

Holy Spirit. Heavenly creativity flows from this relationship; it does not happen in isolation but as the fruit of divine communion. This is what Eastern Orthodox theologians describe as *perichoresis*—a dance at the heart of God in which Father, Son, and Spirit exist in perfect harmony, co-creating, co-existing, and moving together in love.

This is a big deal—if you think about it—for the creative process.

If the source of all creativity is relational, then it follows that our creativity flourishes most in community. And while God could certainly do it all on his own, as we will explore later in this book, God has chosen to do it in collaboration with us.

We get to do this together.

Our fourth hack is to create with people and to imagine together. There's a proverb that says, "As iron sharpens iron, so one person sharpens another" (Proverbs 27:17). When your life, your creativity, and your gifts are sharpening others, sparks will fly. Creatively, the more we work together, the braver we are, the stronger we become, and the more we can learn from one another.

Now, before the introverts reading this have a cardiac arrest, I don't mean to say that teamwork is always dream work. What I'm getting at is that for your soul to flourish creatively, you ultimately need love. And for love to flow, you need relationship. So please don't see yourself as a solo artist. Understand that you have been wired for community. Even if you find yourself working alone, let others into your mind, heart, and creative space. Practice sharing your work, collaborating, engaging and encouraging others in the creative process, and you'll find that your imagination will benefit from the connection.

To borrow from one great contemporary philosopher who, when finally face-to-face with her creator, pours out the heart cry of a generation:

> I want to be part of the people that make meaning. . . . I want to do the imagining.
> —Barbie

We could all take a leaf out of Barbie's book. Imagination thrives in collaboration. We all want to be part of communities that make meaning. Great ideas emerge from the meeting of minds. So next time you're tempted to lock yourself away and go it all alone, try to find moments to share your vision and dream with and encourage others. Because the truth is, when you look at the history of great creativity, while famous names pop up in the stories of the arts, innovation, sciences, and literature, behind every great creative moment or movement, there usually are groups of people spurring one another on, deeply rooted in relationship. As the famous African proverb says, "If you want to travel fast, travel alone. If you want to travel far, travel together."[18]

So let me ask you:

Who are your people?
Who are the voices sharpening your imagination?
Who can you turn to when the storms come?
How can you surround yourself with friends who will call you higher?

Build your creativity in relationship. Be rooted and established in love, and you'll find yourself growing in ways you never could have imagined.

Hack 5: Purpose

When David had served God's purpose in
his own generation, he fell asleep.
—Acts 13:36

Your imagination does its best work when sparked by a sense of purpose. Just as a plant naturally grows toward its source of energy—light—our imaginations are drawn toward whatever we have fixed our

IMAGINATION

hearts upon. Meaning is the magnet that propels creativity forward. So, our fifth hack is to continually refine our sense of purpose, to ask ourselves: "What's really driving me? What gets me out of bed in the morning? What makes me tick?" Because when our imaginations are aligned with our deepest sense of meaning and purpose, they don't just create; they come to life. Consider how all the great scientific, social, artistic, and technological breakthroughs in human history have emerged from the powerful combination of imagination and purpose. Everything you touch and use today—every innovation, every advancement—once existed only in the whirling ether of someone's imagination, fuelled by a sense of vision and the determination to bring it to life.

Steve Jobs, founder of Apple, was driven by a distinctive sense of purpose that infused his creativity. Under his leadership, Apple repeatedly produced game-changing designs and products, pushing the boundaries of technology and human experience. When asked what motivated him, Jobs would reply, "We're here to put a dent in the universe. Otherwise, why even be here?"[19]

Purpose is the rocket fuel of the imagination.

Jobs understood that creativity alone isn't enough—it takes a deep sense of purpose to sustain the commitment required to change the world. He once explained, "Your work is going to fill a large part of your life, and the only way to be truly satisfied is to do what you believe is great work."[20] For Jobs, purpose wasn't just about innovation—it was about impact.

I wonder: What would you consider the most important technological breakthrough of all time? Many sociologists and academics argue that one invention stands above the rest in terms of its impact on the human race.[21] Its arrival revolutionised learning, communication, science, theology, and the arts. It rewired the world, paving the way for the Enlightenment, the democratisation of knowledge, and the explosion of human innovation.[22] Without it, there would be no radio, no television, no computers, no internet, no artificial intelligence. And of course, without it, you wouldn't be reading these printed words on this page.

Johannes Gutenberg was a German goldsmith and inventor, but more

IGNITE YOUR IMAGINATION

than that, he was a man of deep faith. His desire was simple yet radical—that people might experience God's love personally. In Gutenberg's day, access to the Bible was controlled by the religious elites, who dictated who could understand the Scriptures.

Gutenberg had a vision: What if everyone could access the Scriptures for themselves, in their own language? What if people were free to experience a direct relationship with Jesus Christ? This longing ignited his imagination and gave him a driving sense of purpose.

In the early 1440s, Gutenberg began to experiment. Inspired by the mechanics of a winepress, he started developing a machine that could transfer ink onto paper with precision. It was painstaking work. He poured time, energy, and money into the project, often teetering on the brink of financial ruin. Many would have given up. But having a deep sense of purpose does something remarkable—it reinforces the imagination with the steel of longevity. Passions rise and fall.

Inspiration can be fleeting. But purpose turbocharges the imagination until breakthrough comes.

By 1450 Gutenberg had succeeded in building a working prototype press with movable type, and just five years later he printed his first Bible. His invention burst onto the scene with instant and revolutionary impact. The printing press coincided with the artistic and cultural explosion of the Renaissance. Books, once painstakingly copied by hand, could now be printed and shared, spreading knowledge and learning at an unprecedented scale. The ripple effects were enormous: The writings of Martin Luther would be mass-produced, igniting the Reformation. The Enlightenment, the communications revolution, and the information age can all be traced back to this single imaginative breakthrough.

Now, what's often missed—given the seismic impact of Gutenberg's invention—is just how crucial his sense of purpose was in motivating his imagination. Listen to how Gutenberg described what, until this point, had only existed in his imagination: "Yes, it is a press, certainly, but a press from which shall flow in inexhaustible streams, the most abundant and most marvellous liquor that has ever flowed to relieve the thirst of men! Through it, God will spread His Word. A spring of truth shall flow

IMAGINATION

from it: like a new star it shall scatter the darkness of ignorance, and cause a light heretofore unknown to shine amongst men."[23]

Gutenberg had purpose: to shine light. In doing so, he illuminated a key principle. Light is a better motivator than darkness. Love is more compelling than fear. Hope is more energising than despair. Creativity can be used for better or worse, but the ideas that truly stand the test of time are those made with love. Love outlasts hate. Altruism sustains where selfishness withers. Good is more powerful than evil. And here's why: Evil has no originality. Theologian David Bentley Hart describes evil as a parasitical wasting disease, something that cannot create life, only decay it. Evil is "a privation of the good, possessing no essence or nature of its own, a purely parasitic corruption of reality."[24] So, beware of a counterfeit creativity that has no power to build, imagine, or innovate but only denigrates and destroys.

Instead, true creativity is an act of love, and love creates what lasts. As we enter an age of algorithms, the purpose before us is clear: to make sure that the power, intelligence, and potential of the technologies we create are used for good, not evil. Out of our new creative and technological partnerships, we must shine truth, goodness, and beauty into the darkness.

Creativity is a profession for a few—but a purpose for all of us. There is something inherently good about creating. It's striking that when God created the world, he chose to define that creative act as "good." So, when you focus your creative energy on life, love, and hope, it is like connecting to the electricity grid—you turbocharge your imagination with heavenly power. The apostle Paul encouraged us toward this purpose when he wrote, "Whatever is true, whatever is noble, whatever is right, whatever is pure, whatever is lovely, whatever is admirable—if anything is excellent or praiseworthy—think about such things" (Philippians 4:8).

Welcome to Wonderland

When we build these hacks into our creative and spiritual rhythm, we begin to remember how to dream again. We wake up from the stupor

IGNITE YOUR IMAGINATION

we've been lulled into. The creative adrenaline courses once more through the veins of our souls.

So here's to embracing boredom and pressing pause, learning to step back and see with fresh eyes. Let me invite you to retrace your steps back to the garden of your creativity, where all things become new again. Here you will recover the joy of childlike play and break your imagination out of the prison of rigid rules. Here you'll make space to prayerfully renew your spiritual connection and fuel that creative fire that ignites your sense of purpose. And, as we'll see next, here is where you'll find the spark from heaven that will set your imagination ablaze.

Welcome home to wonderland.

SPARK CIRCLE

Circle back through this chapter of Spark.

Notice
Which of the five hacks—pause, pray, play, people, purpose—spoke most deeply to you?
Was there one that felt like a lost rhythm you want to reclaim? Which one?

Name
Name a moment, experience, or place that sparks wonder in you.
Can you describe what motivates you to create?

Next Step
Choose one of the five hacks to try out this week. Notice what shifts, and bring that story to your Spark Circle.

MOVEMENT TWO
Inspiration

CHAPTER 3

The Spark That Lights the Fire

*Consider what a great forest is set
on fire by a small spark.*
—James 3:5

*And every common bush afire with God:
But only he who sees, takes off his shoes,
The rest sit round it and pluck blackberries.*
—Elizabeth Barrett Browning

He first saw the spark out of the corner of his eye. Walking along the dried-up wadi in the heat of the early evening, a flicker caught his attention. A lone ember dancing against the twilight desert sky, twisting and floating until it disappeared into the dusk. As he drew near, he noticed a shimmering mirage of heat and then flames and smoke. He knew this could be dangerous under such dry conditions.

He moved carefully, scanning over his shoulder, mapping out an escape route. A brush fire could turn in an instant, cutting off the way out and trapping him in a deadly furnace. Rounding a sharp bend, he saw the source. A single, low scrub bush standing alone against the darkening sky—utterly ablaze.

He stopped. Stood still. Mesmerised.

INSPIRATION

Another spark flew upward, danced briefly in the quivering air, then drifted down, circling like a bird toward him. Without thinking, he held out his hand, as a child might catch a snowflake. The spark landed in the centre of his outstretched palm. For a moment, he stared. Then instinct kicked in and he swiped the burning ember away, expecting to feel its penetrating sting.

But the ember, pulsing red-hot, was cool as water on his skin. No searing pain. No burning flesh.

Only a slowly rising sense of wonder.

Suddenly the air felt heavy—thick with a presence unlike anything he had ever felt before. Something mysterious—even magical—was happening. Most would have turned and run. But he stood rooted to the spot, fascinated and intrigued, as if in a dream. And in that moment, deep in his soul, something caught fire. His imagination began to burn—and burn—and burn. The bush was not consumed, but he was.

A holy fire.

The unquenchable flame.

His heart strangely warmed.

Consuming fire.

And then, the voice—roaring like a furnace—he could never forget:

I am who I am.
You're on holy ground.
Take off your shoes.
I come down to rescue.
What's in your hand?
Go!

Moses would never be the same. In an instant, everything changed. The spark had ignited in his soul a holy calling and a vision of a new world, alive with possibility. In the twilight, he had met the God who answers with fire. The craziest collaboration had begun: Creator and created conspiring together to write a story way beyond Moses' wildest dreams.

THE SPARK THAT LIGHTS THE FIRE

Even the greatest fires start with a single spark. That's all it takes to change everything. And the same is true for your soul's creativity. Your imagination is a tinderbox, waiting for the spark that will set it on fire. But this inspiration isn't something we work up in our own strength. It's a gift, something received, not manufactured. Given, not grasped. What's in your hand?

It's hard to see the spark of divine creativity against the sunlight of success. Instead, the spark shines brighter against the dark night of our failures. It's here—empty-handed and dry as a desert—that we lift our eyes upward. We turn toward heaven and tap into the source of unlimited creativity. And yet, you have to know where to look.

Starlight

Stare at the sky on a starry night, and you'll notice something strange: If you look directly at a distant star, you'll struggle to see it. The light waves, having travelled millions of light-years across space, arrive in a form so faint that by the time they reach your eyes, the signal is almost imperceptible. This happens because the cells at the front of your retina—cone cells—are built for sharp detail and colour. They're looking for strong light, clear and defined, certainty, and precision. Right now, as you read this, you're relying mostly on them. But cone cells aren't great at picking up faint light like the far-off flickers of starlight.

To see the gentle light waves that have travelled across the universe, your eyes use a different set of sensors called rod cells. These are scattered around the edges of your retina, and they're designed for the shadows, attuned to the dim and the distant. They pick up movement at the margins, sensing things your direct vision cannot. That's why we say, "I saw something out of the corner of my eye." Because we did—literally—use the corners of our eyes.

So try this next time you're stargazing. Look slightly to the left or right of a far-off star, and you'll suddenly find you can see the starlight more clearly. You're using the corner of your eye, the edge of your perception. It's counter-intuitive, but real: Sometimes the best way to see is not to look directly but to look into the darkness to truly see the light.

The same is true of inspiration.

Open your eyes, and you will find that the world is alive with flickers of inspiration. But be sure to look to the edges, the margins, and the twilight of your vision, because the best creative ideas rarely arrive front and centre, in high definition and vivid colour. They come in the twilight and in the shadows at the edges of awareness. The spark is most visible at the margins. Inspiration often strikes at the periphery.

Your task is simple: Be ready. Ready to receive. Ready to respond. Ready to pay attention to that flicker of inspiration that sets fire to your imagination. Watch for the sparks, the tracers of glory, spinning and dancing through your life. Train your eyes of faith to learn to see the signs of the spark, and hold out your hand to receive.

Songwriter Leonard Cohen once described the artist's job not as one of creating but of receiving—that we're to see inspiration not as a task but as a gift. He said, "If I knew where the good songs came from, I'd go there more often."[1]

And sometimes—as I was soon to learn—that spark can come when you least expect it.

Sparks in the Dark

A few months into our adventure in Hackney, we attempted to launch a new Sunday service in the old church building that had become home to us. For weeks we had prepared, prayed, worked, and invited. That last week we kicked things off with a launch party. A few dozen interested people turned up, and for a moment it felt like momentum was building. But this week was different.

First, I had taken on the tragic funeral of a teenager: a gang killing. The murder had made national news—a totemic tragedy, tracing the story of a lost generation. We'd had police protection at the funeral as

THE SPARK THAT LIGHTS THE FIRE

hundreds of young people gathered at the graveside. To be honest, it knocked me sideways. The emotion. The pain. The sheer weight of it all. It was so bleak, I felt utterly helpless. How could we bring life to a generation so far from hope and so marked by death?

Then today—Sunday—things were supposed to be looking up. It was week two of our new service, and I stood at the door of the church, waiting to welcome back guests from last week. It was the kind of cold winter evening in London when the rain cuts right to the bone. Inside, the empty church felt like a fridge, the relentless damp dripping through every crack in the decaying ceiling.

Instead of being full, alive, and buzzing with conversation, only a handful of those who had come to the launch had returned. It felt like a disaster. I stood in the almost empty church, trying to lead a service with a brave face on. But as I spoke, a steady drip of water trickled from a hole in the roof, landing squarely on the back of my head. The quiet, relentless splash, splash, splash reminded me of how hopeless I felt. I went home that night with my spirits dampened.

This vision—this dream—felt impossible. We didn't have the energy or the imagination to resurrect a dying church in the middle of a grieving community where hope itself was in short supply. Even though we'd only just started, it seemed we were on a path to failure. For all our good intentions, passion, and vision, it felt like not all things were possible after all. How quickly the dream had faded.

It is harder to see the sparks of creativity against the sunlight of success, but they shine bright against the darkness of failure. Success makes you comfortable. It dulls the creative edge, shifting your focus to what is immediate, tangible, and rewarding. Ironically, the satisfaction of success can anesthetise the creative soul. Instead, it's when you feel like you have nothing left—when everything has failed, when hope has run dry—that your vision shifts. Suddenly, in the darkness, if you'll allow yourself, you'll begin to see little glimmers of something sparking at the edge of your imagination. Through the fog of failure, defeat, past hurts, and bruised dreams, something will inevitably catch your eye. And that divine spark will start to lighten the horizon of your hopes.

INSPIRATION

Flickering Lights

By the time I arrived home that evening, I was exhausted—drained in a way that went deeper than just tiredness. I slumped onto the sofa, utterly deflated: Today had been a complete failure. Thankfully, my wife Olivia is wise and kind, and she knew exactly what I needed. That great modern form of therapy:
 A fast-food delivery.
 While lying flat on the sofa.
 Watching TV.
 We call it "flickering lights" in our family. I'm convinced that someday a scientist will publish a study that will prove beyond doubt that lying motionless and staring at the comforting glow of a TV screen whilst eating a takeaway has deep therapeutic benefits. And they will win the Nobel Prize. Or maybe not.

So, there we were, stretched out on the couch, scrolling through Netflix, when we found ourselves watching a documentary called *Abstract*.[2] This documentary series is about human creativity, charting the lives and practices of some of the world's leading creative minds. And one episode in particular caught my attention.

Es Devlin is arguably the world's leading visual artist today, considering the scale and ambition of her work. If you've ever been wowed by a live experience—from U2 to the Olympics—it's likely to have been dreamed up by Es. She has collaborated with the greatest artists of our generation, a list as long as it is impressive: Beyoncé, U2, Billie Eilish, Kanye West, Adele, as well as the leading plays, operas, ballets, Super Bowl half-time shows, art installations, and spectacles of our time. Her work is bold, intelligent, and groundbreaking. She was awarded a CBE for her outstanding contribution to the arts.

But while her creative achievements are remarkable, one part of her story jumps out at me. When asked where it all began for her, she described visiting a small countryside church near her home as a teenager. Tudeley Church in Kent is an unassuming rural parish—except for one

THE SPARK THAT LIGHTS THE FIRE

extraordinary detail: It houses a stunning set of stained glass windows by artist Marc Chagall.

As a young girl, Es was captivated by these windows—the interplay of light and colour, the deep tones, the vivid figures floating within the glass. She experienced an epiphany. There, in that church—bathed in colour, light, and otherness—something ignited in Es: a creative spark that has burned through her work ever since.

Watching this story unfold before my tired eyes, something sparked at the periphery of my vision. Just a faint glimmer, a distant "what if?" Isn't this what the church is here to do? Aren't we supposed to be the spaces where people experience the spark for themselves? Why should young people only come into church to bury their friends? Why not to be inspired? Catch fire? Experience an everyday epiphany?

Holy ground.
Shoes off.
What's in your hand?
Eyes open in wonder.

These spiritual spaces should be the wonderland of creativity, the burning ground of holy potential, and the birthplace of brilliance. Here the Spirit of God can connect the dots of meaning and purpose, life and beauty, and inspire us to dream again. What if churches everywhere were places of everyday epiphanies where callings come alive, sparks fly, hearts are set on fire, and imaginations are ignited in blazes of wonder?

I reached for my laptop, my mind buzzing, and decided to write a short email:

Hi, I'm a vicar in East London.
I'm burying teenagers caught up in gang violence.
I'm moved by your story. Would you come and help us create some Chagall moments—moments that would restore hope and spark the creativity of a new generation?

Nothing ventured, nothing gained. I hit Send.

INSPIRATION

Shared Sky

I never expected a reply, but only hours later, to my amazement, Es graciously responded. A couple of days later, my wife, Olivia, and I were having a cup of tea with Es. We talked. We dreamed about what could be. What would it look like to create something beautiful for God—something that brings hope to the young people who walk into the church? We walked the familiar route through the churchyard, under the bullet-pocked glass above the front door, into the lobby of the church. As we wandered through the building, one space in particular captured Es's imagination—a small, dark chapel off the entrance. In the corner of her eye, it was an overlooked space, unloved and unkempt. There in the twilight, something sparked in Es's mind. In her words: "As soon as you enter, I felt this was a really important moment of engagement. Because when you walk into a church, you bring all sorts of preconceptions—what a church is, what a church should be."[3]

Even though the church was in ruins and the chapel itself was unloved, dingy, and cold, Es saw the potential. In a later conversation for Renaissance, Es Devlin reflected on the role of sacred spaces: "These buildings should be places where communities gather . . . where the art is allowed to tell a story in the way that stained glass windows always did . . . Why not advance with the times and allow the stained-glass windows of today?"

We discussed the Chagall windows and what the modern equivalent would be. What if these spaces could be places of inspiration, a modern-day take on a historic art form? Es continued, "The conversation between us here was—what is a contemporary correlative to a stained-glass window? . . . The screen itself has become such a ubiquitous form of storytelling. . . . So how do you retain and regain the magic and the poignancy of glimmering liquid crystal or glimmering light-emitting diodes? . . . The answer is sculpture."[4]

A few days later, a concept for a permanent installation began to take shape.

The piece—*Shared Sky*—was born.

THE SPARK THAT LIGHTS THE FIRE

The work is a modern stained-glass window. Instead of traditional panels, the floor and ceiling are made of video screen—displaying the sky over two different parts of the world. The viewer stands in the gap between them, inhabiting the space between. A pair of rotating skies create a liminal space. Each pairing maps the tension between the highest and the lowest, the most and the least. Places of pain and conflict. Places of hope and healing.

We have stood beneath the skies over Ukraine and Gaza. Over war zones, hotspots, the places on our hearts and in our prayers. Here we stand in the in-between. The now and the not yet. Between the most and the least. Between those in danger and those in safety. The point is powerful: Wherever we are in the world, we stand beneath the same shared sky. The space is filled with mist, incense-like, immersing the viewer in a bath of colour. It is glorious. Mysterious. Mystical.

Shared Sky has become a contemporary prayer chapel. A digital pilgrimage. A refuge for those who walk through the doors of the church. A place of intercession where people stand in the gap. And they pray.

> *We all live under the same sky.*
> *Yet we each see things differently.*
> —Es Devlin

I have learned so much from the *Shared Sky* journey. Not least, the importance of paying attention to the small sparks in life. To follow moments of inspiration. To watch for the things on the periphery of your attention that ignite something in your soul—a sense of calling, an echo of hope, a note that strikes a chord in your imagination. And often, as we'll see later, these experiences are deeply moving, awe-inspiring, reducing those of us who step inside those spaces to tears.

Look for the sparks.
Pay attention to your peripheral vision.
The embers floating in the wind.
Follow them to their source.

INSPIRATION

Let yourself be drawn in.
Pursue your curiosity.
Because you never know what you might find when you follow those dancing embers in the night.

The Spark Between Us

A spiritual big bang.
Angels. Colour. Clouds. Chaos.
Spinning explosion of creation.
Michelangelo's *The Creation of Adam* is iconic. Adorning the ceiling of the Sistine Chapel, this masterpiece is one of the most recognised works of art. The response when unveiled? Awestruck wonder. The great art critic Giorgio Vasari recorded, "The whole world came running when the vault was revealed, and the sight of it was enough to reduce them to stunned silence."[5]
The outstretched fingers.
The connection between heaven and earth.
The crackling energy. Pregnant with potential.
God in his glory, reaching out his hand, life-giving.
This essence of the moment.
That place of genesis.
The spark between God and us.
This, too, was the ground zero of the European Renaissance, with Vasari concluding that the scene restored "light to a world that for centuries had been plunged into darkness."[6] But look closely at the fingers in the famous image, and you'll notice a fascinating detail. There is a tiny gap between God's and Adam's fingers. Follow the anatomy of the fingers: God's hand is fully outstretched. Every sinew, every digit is reaching for Adam. Adam's fingers, however, are not fully extended. He's holding back.
Just one tiny movement, and we feel like sparks will fly. And yet the gap will only close the moment Adam reaches out. In fact, the way

Michelangelo depicted the fingers—anatomically—means it would take only the smallest motion from Adam's index finger to connect perfectly with the tip of God's outstretched hand. God doesn't ask us to move as much as to reach. It's not about changing your position, only your response.

Michelangelo was making a powerful point: All of us are just one stretch, a touch away from the source, the spark, the holy fire. But the Creator will never force himself into your creativity. You must choose receptivity. The gift is God's, but the choice to accept it is yours. Yours is the agency. The dignity. The decision.

God will never force his way into your imagination. The spark only lands on open hands, on outstretched hearts, on the "Here I am" (Exodus 3:4) of obedience.[7] But consider this: Just the smallest movement toward God can unlock immense creative power. God initiates—we simply have to respond. It takes only the slightest motion, a holy curiosity, the stretching out of our creative desire toward the very source of life. And in return, God is already there, longing to impart that spark to you at this moment. His arm is fully extended, reaching, and waiting for you to choose connection. And when you reach back, sparks fly.

All things become possible. Your creativity takes on a whole new dimension. Just as Jewish tradition holds that the spark of life is also the spark of creativity, in the same way God breathes into your life, fanning the spark into flame, and that breath is the breath of creativity.

Inspiration

When God breathes into Adam, he fills human lungs with his divine creativity—and that same breath lives in you today. The very word *inspiration* comes from the Latin *inspirare*, meaning "to breathe into." God's Holy Spirit is longing to breathe into your creativity the full force of his divine power.

Holy inspiration turbocharges human imagination. Understanding this changes our relationship with the creative process, because to unlock the potential of our creativity, we must learn to breathe in the breath—the *pneuma*—of the Creator. Sure, you could do it on your own. But why would you? Instead, learn to breathe deeply of the breath of heaven. Let the breath of God fill your lungs, your soul, your creativity.

Embers

Sometimes the flame of creativity dwindles until only embers remain. Perhaps you've felt this way—depleted, devoid of inspiration. Yet, even in such moments, those creative embers persist deep within your soul. The fire in you will not have gone out. In fact, it's precisely at these moments when we do well to bring our "Here I am" to God, because he loves to kindle those embers into a blazing fire.

The apostle Paul—a prolific writer, thinker, theologian, and pastor—mentored a young man named Timothy. In one of his letters to his protégé, Paul offered insight into how to nurture the gifts God has given us: "For this reason I remind you to fan into flame the gift of God, which is in you through the laying on of my hands" (2 Timothy 1:6). Paul understood that we must actively nurture our gifts, which includes our creativity. When only embers remain, ask the Creator to breathe on you and fan into flame the spark in you.

As the old English hymn by Edwin Hatch goes:

> Breathe on me, breath of God,
> Till I am wholly Thine,
> Until this earthly part of me
> Glows with Thy fire divine.[8]

God is longing to breathe the inspiration from heaven on the embers of your creativity. Throughout history this has been the experience of countless creative minds. Just when you think you've hit rock bottom, you turn your heart to heaven and feel the breath of God.

THE SPARK THAT LIGHTS THE FIRE

Handel's Hallelujah

Composer George Frideric Handel had reached a breaking point. His recent work had fallen flat, his career was faltering, and his health was rapidly declining. By 1741 he was in debt and facing prison, and in April he gave what he assumed would be his final concert. But on the verge of giving up, a charity gave him a grant to compose a new work that would encourage and lift the spirits of those who, like him, were caught up in debt. In August of that year, having turned to the Scriptures, something shifted in his soul. He immersed himself in prayer, and there in the ashes of his life, he felt a surge of divine inspiration, a spark that reignited his creativity.

What followed was a personal and spiritual renaissance. Handel was unable to eat during those days and would often be found in tears, caught up in a deep encounter with his Creator. Over just twenty-four days and nights, he poured his soul into a new composition, writing with an urgency like he'd never known. Later he would reflect, "Whether I was in my body or out of my body as I wrote it, I know not. God knows." He would describe seeing "all heaven before him" as he wrote.[9]

The finished work? The iconic *Messiah*, with the "Hallelujah Chorus" becoming one of the most celebrated pieces of music in history. To this day, to hear the "Hallelujah Chorus" is to be caught up into glory:

> King of Kings, and Lord of Lords,
> And He shall reign forever and ever. . . .
> Hallelujah! Hallelujah!

When King George II first heard the piece being performed, he was apparently so overcome with emotion that, breaking all convention—especially for an earthly monarch—he rose to his feet spontaneously in stunned reverence, starting a tradition that is followed by audiences to this day. And the next time you hear the famous "Hallelujah Chorus," remember that it rose from the ashes of a broken life set ablaze by the spark that lights the fire.

Like Handel, we can invite the Holy Spirit to meet us right now in our imagining, our dreaming, and our creativity. Let me encourage you, in this moment, to breathe in the breath of God—to receive that spark from heaven for yourself. Without dependence on the creative Spirit, our creativity can only take us so far. But with his breath inspiring us, all things become possible, for "the Spirit gives life" (John 6:63).

The Death Zone

In the world of high-altitude mountaineering, there's a point known as the death zone—the altitude above twenty-six thousand feet where the air is too thin to sustain human life. No amount of training, experience, or willpower can overcome this reality. After a short period of time, the body begins to shut down as hypoxia sets in. Without supplemental oxygen, survival is a race against time.

This is a striking picture of what can happen when we try to create without dependence on the Holy Spirit. We push. We strive. We rely on our talent, our discipline, and our ability to make things happen. But we're operating at an altitude we were never designed to endure alone. Without the breath of God, our creativity can't rise to its full potential.

The world celebrates self-sufficiency—this idea that if you just work harder, dig deeper, push through, you'll make it. But in the kingdom of God, self-reliance is not a virtue; it's a slow suffocation. We were never meant to create in isolation from the One who breathes life into all things. Above a certain point, human effort is not enough. Grit will only take you so far. Skill has limits. At some point, you either learn to rely on the Spirit or you run out of air.

To combat hypoxia, climbers carry supplemental oxygen—a lifeline that enables them to survive in the death zone. With it, their lungs absorb what was missing, and as a result they don't just endure—they thrive. They ascend the highest peaks, achieving what would have been impossible on their own.

In the same way, the way to combat spiritual hypoxia is full reliance on the breath of God when you create. When you step into the unknown, you will feel exposed, vulnerable, and unsure if you'll make it. Breathe in—the inspiration of the Holy Spirit—and you won't just survive; you will come alive.

The Day Everything Sparked to Life

The early church was a handful of broken believers, bruised and waiting in an upper room. And then, after days and nights of crying out, the spark in them ignited, as the Holy Spirit came. The wind—the breath of God—filled their lungs. In the book of Acts, we read that the Spirit came like "tongues of fire" (Acts 2:3) alighting on their heads, and a mighty wind swept through the place. Do you see what God was doing? Spark! Bang! Wow! God was igniting their lives with holy fire, blowing on the kindling of their souls with the breath of heaven. The impact? The birth of the most dynamic movement the world has ever seen.

The early church exploded out of the upper room with a creativity and impact unrivalled in human history. Despite persecution, death, and opposition, the church did not falter. It grew, and it continues to grow. To this day, across the world, the breath of God is still inspiring this divine mission—fuelling innovators and pioneers of the faith.

What is the church if not the homeland of human creativity? The incubator for divine newness? The place where God sparks the future of the world, making all things new? But to do this, we must have fire.

Pascal's Fire

The great mathematician, physicist, and philosopher Blaise Pascal was one of the most brilliant minds in history. His work in mathematics shaped probability theory, and his philosophical writings continue to inspire thinkers today. But one of the most fascinating insights into Pascal's story emerged only after his death. When Pascal died, his

INSPIRATION

belongings were carefully examined, and inside the lining of his jacket, a small, tattered piece of parchment was found. It had been sewn in there deliberately, and with each new coat, the parchment had been carefully restitched into the lining so that Pascal could carry it with him in secret throughout his academic career.

This was no ordinary note. It was a record of an encounter with God that Pascal had on the night of November 23, 1654, an experience so profound that he kept it hidden close to his heart, transferring it from jacket to jacket over the years. On this fragile piece of paper, written in Pascal's own hand, were these words:

> The year of grace 1654.
> From about 10:30 at night until about half past midnight
> —FIRE.
> God of Abraham,
> God of Isaac,
> God of Jacob—not of the philosophers and the learned.
> Certitude. Certitude. Feeling. Joy. Peace.
> God of Jesus Christ. My God and your God.
> "Thy God shall be my God."[10]

This was more than a reflection; it was a moment of divine encounter, a night when heaven broke through. Pascal, a man of logic and reason, had experienced something that transcended the limits of his knowledge. And he carried this defining moment with him, quite literally, for the rest of his life. It clothed his intellect and creative thinking. While his brilliance in science, mathematics, and philosophy made him famous, Pascal knew the true source behind it all—FIRE. The fact that he had this piece of paper sewn into the lining of his jacket reveals just how pivotal this encounter was to him. Beneath his creativity, inspiration, and groundbreaking innovations lay this sacred moment—the spark from heaven that ignited a fire in his mind and intellect.

So let me encourage you to receive this invitation today. The spark that lights the fire of your creativity is waiting for a simple invitation—a small action, a final extension of the fingertip toward a God who is already reaching out toward you with his hand fully extended. The extraordinary impact that follows could change your life forever—the striking of a holy match. There are two ways you can respond: You can either continue in your own creativity, in your own strength. Or you can decide to invite the Creator Spirit into your life and learn to call on the fire from heaven. Set your creativity on fire by inviting the Holy Spirit to fill you.

So let me invite you right now: As you sit reading this, stretch out your hands. Let the same fire that fell on the burning bush, that blazed in the upper room, fall in your life today. And know that all of heaven is cheering you on. The world is waiting to see the fire of his glory expressed through your creativity. Let the same breath that rushed through the upper room on the day of Pentecost fill your lungs right now. Catch the spark that is drifting down into your hand today and watch in awe of what God can do in the tinder box of your creative soul.

God's Grandeur

The world is charged with the grandeur of God.
    It will flame out, like shining from shook foil;
    It gathers to a greatness, like the ooze of oil
Crushed. Why do men then now not reck his rod?
Generations have trod, have trod, have trod;
    And all is seared with trade; bleared, smeared with toil;
    And wears man's smudge and shares man's smell: the soil
Is bare now, nor can foot feel, being shod.

And for all this, nature is never spent;
    There lives the dearest freshness deep down things;
And though the last lights off the black West went
    Oh, morning, at the brown brink eastward, springs—
Because the Holy Ghost over the bent
    World broods with warm breast and with ah! bright wings.
        —Gerard Manley Hopkins

SPARK CIRCLE

Circle back through this chapter of Spark.

Notice
Where did the idea of a spark connect with your story?
What sparks have you noticed on the margins of your life?

Name
Have you ever tried inviting the Holy Spirit to fill your creativity? What was the result?
What small action might you do to reach out to God?

Next Step
Take ten minutes this week to "remove your shoes." Find a quiet space. Pause. Acknowledge God's presence.

CHAPTER 4

Lightbulb Moments

> *The Spirit of God was moving (hovering,*
> *brooding) over the face of the waters.*
> *And God said, "Let there be light."*
> —Genesis 1:2–3 AMP

Have you ever had a moment when everything suddenly clicks? A flash of insight. One spark and everything changes. They're not called lightbulb moments for nothing. These epiphanies don't come from nowhere—they emerge from ideas that have been brewing, fermenting, taking shape in the depths of your imagination. In this chapter, we'll dive into these aha moments—those flashes of brilliance that often come when we least expect them. We'll explore how creativity is born in the dark and incubated in our souls, and how when we invite the Spirit of God to empower those inspirations, they can start a chain reaction that will impact our lives in profound and far-reaching ways.

The journey from a spark of imagination to concrete reality requires inspiration: the oxygenating of that initial idea until it is birthed into life. Inspiration is where divine creativity can really take root, growing and multiplying our thoughts and dreams into something altogether new. And learning to embrace this wonderful process is one of the secrets to unlocking the fullness of your creative potential.

I'll explain how to work with these lightbulb moments by borrowing from one of the natural world's most wonderful and hidden processes:

INSPIRATION

fermentation. Fermentation is a perfect example of creative transformation. It's a natural case study in how small ingredients, over time, transform into something far greater than the sum of their parts. Under the right conditions—balance, time, and patience—natural sugars are broken down and transformed into something new. Just like creativity, it requires the right environment, care, and patience for that spark to emerge. This is nature at its most creative, taking a few simple ingredients and producing something radically different. And fermentation gives us so many good things: yogurt, cheese, kimchi, sourdough, miso, soy sauce, beer, wine, kefir . . . the list goes on.

Creativity, like fermentation, takes time. Ideas need space to develop—love, patience, and the right care and conditions to turn something raw into something rich. The journey from idea to reality is long, full of highs and lows. It demands our passion, our mistakes, and our persistence—but it will be worth it.

And like fermentation, the presence of the Creator Spirit acts like an accelerant, bubbling away quietly in the secret places of our souls—and if we'll give enough time and love—it will gently transform what was raw and unformed into something rich and full of life. And the fruit will be full of wonder.

It's no coincidence that Jesus' first miracle—turning water into wine—was a sort of divine act of fermentation.[1] God takes the natural and infuses it with the supernatural. And this wasn't just any wine; it was the best wine, like turning bathwater into Chateau Lafite 1983. He wasn't messing around. And he wants to do the same with the water of our ideas: to help us move from imagination into reality. This process requires trial and error; the right ingredients; a careful blend of trust, skill, and care; and above all, patience. But we're in safe hands because if we'll let him, we'll discover that Jesus is a specialist in holy fermentation. He loves to work with us, taking and giving thanks for our bread and wine—the fruit of human creativity. As W. David O. Taylor says, "Jesus takes culture, blesses it, breaks it, and gives it to his friends."[2]

God sees your potential, and it's miraculous.

And so, he takes his time. That's why the fermentation of the creative soul can't be rushed. Your best ideas—the ones that will shift culture, shape the future, and change the landscape of your life—won't arrive fully formed. They require deep, consistent focus and work. This isn't just a spiritual principle: There's solid science behind it too. Your ideas deserve deliberate concentration, those times when you enter that magical space where you break from the distractions, the endless notifications, and the mindless scrolling. Here you enter a state of focused, concentrated creativity—*flow state*, the deep, immersive focus where time slows, the mind zooms in, and your creative ideas begin to ferment.

Perhaps you know that feeling—the hours disappear, the world fades, and the work pulls you in. The musician who plays and plays until her fingers are raw. The architect who is so caught up shaping and problem-solving that time seems to stand still. The writer who sits at his desk, lost in a world of words, surfacing hours later with pages he barely remembers writing. This is flow, the magical alchemy of creative work.

> *The best moments in our lives are not the passive, receptive, relaxing times. . . . The best moments usually occur if a person's body or mind is stretched to its limits in a voluntary effort to accomplish something difficult and worthwhile.*
> —Mihaly Csikszentmihalyi

Flow is mental fermentation. Just as in bread making yeast needs the deliberate and intentional mix of sugar, warmth, and time to work its magic, so the yeast of your creativity needs time, concentration, and the right conditions to come alive. When the environment is right, transformation happens, and the dough of an idea rises with inspiration.

Consequently, learning to protect and prioritise the moments of flow in your life is one of the most important creative tasks you face. You must learn to resist a world that is constantly interrupting you with notifications pinging, emails stacking up, and endless distractions pulling at your focus. Your single-mindedness is the oxygen your best ideas are waiting for. Take a lesson from that great builder Nehemiah. When he was rebuilding the walls of Jerusalem, people tried to pull him away, but he replied, "I am doing a great work and I cannot come down" (Nehemiah 6:3 ESV).

So, here are some questions I'd like you to consider before you read on:

+ When do you find it easiest to enter into a flow state?
+ What environment and ingredients help you get there?
+ Is it a time, a certain place, or a format of working?
+ What needs to change to enable you to prioritise entering into your flow state?

Alongside these, here are some broader questions to consider that will help your inspiration bubble up:

+ In what areas of your life do you feel like there's something brewing?
+ What ideas are floating around the edges of your imagination— ideas that will require care, patience, and the right conditions to allow fermentation to take place?
+ Make a list and think about what ingredients might be missing to let that natural fermentation process take off.
+ What prayer would you most like to see answered in this area?
+ What is it that you need the Holy Spirit to inspire?

The best way to tackle these questions is to talk them through with a friend. Let your soul pray those prayers bubbling with possibility, because it's here that a miraculous fermentation takes place.

The Brewery

Sometimes inspiration takes time to ferment. A passing thought. A quiet prayer. An idea bubbling beneath the surface until suddenly the conditions are right and something much bigger begins to take shape. And since we're already talking about miraculous fermentation, this might be a good time to tell you how that very process led, quite unexpectedly, to the birth of a church brewery.

Brewing was definitely never part of our plan. We set out to kickstart a new chapter for the parish church. My theological college had no training course on making beer (though, had it been an option, I suspect it would have been popular). Instead, one class I took was on starting new things, and it did give me some precious spiritual insights. Our tutor encouraged us to spend as much time as possible prayer walking—moving through the neighbourhood, praying, watching, and paying attention to what God was already doing. This turned out to be invaluable advice.

So that's what I did. I developed a habit of walking through the streets of East London, praying as I went. I found that when I walked and prayed—prayed and walked—I began to see things differently. The familiar became fresh again. The unnoticed became unavoidable. And sometimes what started as a simple act of faith fermented into something entirely unexpected.

Prayer is like yeast in the process of fermentation—it's the hidden enzyme of the soul that connects us with the great power of heaven and unlocks the potential of divine omnipotence in the everyday processes we're involved in. So, for inspiration, add a healthy dose of prayer. And prayer often leads us to the places God is at work. If our creative collaboration with God—this co-creating—is truly about repairing and renewing the world, then it can't just be confined to the shiny bits. It must lead us into the broken places, where God sparks our imaginations with ideas that don't just inspire but change lives. The kingdom of God isn't abstract; it's walked out in postcodes and worked out over decades. When you walk a neighbourhood, you begin to notice things. Walk through the streets of East London, and you'll see it all—the brilliant and the broken, colliding in a restless energy that defines this place.

The neighbourhoods of East London are densely populated by the emerging creative industries that make London the global cultural powerhouse it is. The borough of Hackney alone is host to more start-ups per square mile than anywhere else in Europe. The block known as "Silicon Roundabout" in Shoreditch is home to the largest cluster of tech companies outside of San Francisco. And yet, as is so often the case, our neighbourhood is a tale of two cities. We have some of the highest violent crime and child deprivation rates in the UK. Communities that have been pummelled by poverty and are struggling with addiction and homelessness. If creativity is to be meaningful—if it is to be truly kingdom creativity—then it must find its way here, into the spaces where renewal is not just a poetic ideal but an urgent, tangible need.

God inspires us to create redemptively, connecting the dots of hope, faith, and love. He wants to help us close the gap between those who need help and those who can help. This is where the most powerful magic of creativity happens: where purpose and passion collide. It's here that the lightbulb moments spark up the night.

The Wrong Funeral

Patrick was ex-army, and years of living homeless on the streets had worn him down. He was a prodigious drinker and someone whose presence was hard to ignore. I was first introduced to Patrick at a funeral I was conducting. He made quite the entrance. I was standing on the steps of the church with the mourners, watching as the coffin was solemnly loaded into the hearse. The air was thick with grief, quiet except for the murmur of conversation and the occasional rustle of movement. Then, just as the hearse was about to depart, Patrick—who had until this point been hiding in a bush—made a break for it. He launched himself from the crowd and threw himself onto the rear window of the hearse, fists pounding against the glass. Right there, in that hushed, dignified moment, he started his own eulogy: "Why, Lord? Why? He was a king among men! He was my friend!"

It was quite a touching scene, except for the minor detail that Patrick had got entirely the wrong funeral. The deceased was not one of Patrick's drinking buddies, but a young woman from Jamaica. One of the mourners stepped forward and kindly pointed this out to him with the immortal words: "Babe! Babe! Babe! He is actually a she."

To give him credit—despite being inebriated—Patrick was very quick to admit his mistake, which it turned out was entirely innocent. He was confused and genuinely thought it was one of his drinking friend's funerals. Repentant, he turned to address the crowd: "Sorry everyone, wrong funeral!"

Patrick then exited stage left, treating us to his own a cappella version of Frank Sinatra's "My Way" as he wobbled down the street.

As I got to know Patrick, I became very fond of him. Like so many people in his position, he was trapped in a cycle of addiction. We wanted to help, but beyond offering our time, tea, and sympathy, we didn't have the resources to provide a meaningful space to support Patrick—and his many friends I'd come across every day.

If we're to bring real hope, we need to harness the power of good creativity—ideas that don't just inspire but create change, light that can shine in the darkness. As I walked the neighbourhood praying, I kept noticing the same two realities side by side: people like Patrick drinking themselves to death on park benches and, at the same time, an emerging scene of young, independent microbreweries popping up all over East London.

It felt like a collision of worlds—one trapped in despair, the other bursting with new possibilities. And I started to wonder: *What if there is a way to close the gap? Surely that's what communities like churches are here to do. What if we existed in the space between, in the tension, and joined the dots?*

Just a flash of an idea: *Let's start a brewery.*

A flicker of the lightbulb.

I felt it. Something sparked.

What if we started a microbrewery—and used the profits to help those facing addiction?

Okay, look, I get it—there are a thousand reasons why this is a bad idea sheer madness. But the more I thought about it, the less outlandish it seemed. Of course, there is historic precedent for this. You can't ignore the old stories of the first missionaries who came to this country and established communities of prayer from the second century onward. In a pagan culture, in dark times, the first Christian missionaries to these isles set up monasteries and churches that served the people in the most imaginative ways. They brewed beer, kept bees, helped heal people, trained them, and built up the creativity of the culture. These innovations were not marketing; they were the mission: Jesus moved into the neighbourhood and made his dwelling among us.

God is the God who gets his hands dirty. The God of the incarnation. The God of fermentation and the honeybee. The God of glorious architecture and anointed music. Space and light and hope and beauty are the language of the creative soul. The result? Over time the people came, they listened, and they were led to encounter God.

No small beer, as they say.

The process of fermentation turned poor quality water into something good, safe, and nutritious with mild anti-bacterial properties. And to this day, the best beer in the world is made by monastic communities, such as the famous Trappist monks of Belgium. So there's a rich and deep heritage of the church being involved in brewing still to this day. Maybe, just maybe, a response to what I had been seeing on the streets wasn't going to be found in trying to impose some external programme or idea on the neighbourhood, but rather in letting something new ferment in the imagination, bubble up from the creative synergy all around us.

Our best ideas are formed in the tension, in the space between, in the chain reaction of joy that happens when good things emerge. And when we learn to unlock this kind of creativity, it has the power to change the world, little by little, bubble by bubble, as inspiration transforms the invisible into that which is visible. Inspired creativity is about making space for this magical chemistry to happen deep in our souls. It's here that the Holy Spirit will begin to join the dots.

It's what a friend of mine calls "the unfair advantage."

When we put our trust in Jesus, he promises to fill us with his Holy Spirit. The same creative force that made the universe makes his home in us, sparking creativity, enhancing and even anointing our lives. Then there should be a distinctive and dynamic power at play in our souls. Our imaginations come most alive when we invite God to inspire us.

For me, the story of the brewery all started with a throwaway prayer while walking down the street one day. I noticed again the homeless, the street drinkers—and at the same time, the makers, the creative talent and entrepreneurs who lived locally. What if the church could help join the dots? What if the energy, resources, income, and creativity of the neighbourhood could be harnessed for good?

When I got back to the church, I stood in front of the whiteboard and drew a little lightbulb and jotted down a few words: "Start brewery. Help people." Just a few scribbles, an idea barely formed. And there it stayed, just some writing on the wall. Hold that thought for a moment, because what I'm about to tell you is wild. But first I want to talk about how these lightbulb moments will happen in your life.

There's a lot going on in that brain of yours. Each day you will spend between 30 and 50 percent of your waking hours daydreaming, during which your cognitive function is in neutral. This is important because, like a muscle, your mind produces an average of six thousand distinct thoughts per day and needs moments to rest and reset.[3] Each day, among the thousands of thoughts and ideas your imagination is constantly generating, a few sparks of creative fire emerge. And you need to learn to identify and pay attention to these.

When we have lightbulb moments, it's tempting to switch them off or ignore them. As soon as we think of something crazy or fun or unpredictable, our internal risk management system kicks in and we self-edit. We start to tell ourselves the thousands of reasons why that new idea is a bad idea:

We'll fail.
We'll look stupid.
People will laugh at us.
They'll think we're mad.

INSPIRATION

And of course, much of the time, those reasons may hold true. But the future is rarely created by people who buy the lie that all ideas are bad ideas. At some point, you have to take the risk and be prepared to look foolish. Because sometimes, just sometimes—like once in thousands and thousands of bad ideas—you'll hit on something that is going to work. But honestly, you'll never know unless you learn to allow some of those crazy ideas to live for a while on the whiteboards of your wildest dreams. Those ideas must have somewhere they can ferment. Where they can mix with the Spirit's oxygen and enzymes and—in the darkness—start to fizzle and bubble away. It's here, in this hidden fermentation, that you'll begin to feel if the idea is a good idea or even a God idea.

Okay—back to the brewery.

The Email

About ten days after the lightbulb brewery moment, I opened my laptop to see a single unread email in my inbox. It was from a name I barely recognized, totally out of the blue. And the subject line is what made my heart skip a beat.

Subject: Anyone want to start a Brewery?

I froze. My mind spun. Then, heart pounding, I clicked. The email was from a guy named Reggie whom I'd only met a couple of times through a mutual friend in the US. Reggie was a titan in the tech business, having founded two digital companies that had become huge success stories. My fingers trembling, I scrolled down:

Hey Al,
I'm sure this is a long shot.
I'm looking to start a microbrewery in East London.
I'd like this to have a connection to the church.

LIGHTBULB MOMENTS

Do you know anyone who might be interested in helping?
Reggie

I stared at the screen.
Then back at the whiteboard.
Then back at the screen.
Then back at the whiteboard.
Then back at the screen.

A few days later, Reggie and I were sitting together, dreaming about what could be. The fermentation process had started. Three months later, we found a site in railway arches just a few hundred metres from the church. Six months on, I poured the first bag of grain into the brewing kettle and said a prayer to bless and dedicate the equipment. Nine months on, we were tasting the first beer. Most of it was undrinkable, but one or two of the test brews were really stunning. This thing was going to work. A year on, we opened the doors to a state-of-the-art brewery and tap house—a type of pub—and it became a place built not just for great beer but for community, connection, and renewal.

We decided to call it Hackney Church Brew Co. The venture heralded the beginning of the revitalisation of that part of the neighbourhood, with more local businesses springing up around it. What started as a brewery quickly became a hub for creativity. We launched Alpha courses there and grew the now legendary Beer and Carols event that shuts down the street every Christmas. More importantly, our community piled into the space—a bridge between the church and the culture, week in, week out.

People found it was sometimes easier to invite a friend for a drink at the local pub than to a church service. As a result, I have regularly met people at SAINT who came to the brewery first—drawn by the space, the conversations, the welcome—and then found their way into the church. The brewery began to employ local people, creating pathways into work.

As for Patrick, and many others like him, the partnership between the church and the brewery joined the dots and changed things. When the beer began to be sold, the real magic began to happen: The portion

INSPIRATION

of the income—the firstfruits—from the new business were donated by the investors to enable us to kick-start the dream of looking after the vulnerable, marginalised, and homeless on the streets. As the people of East London bought beer, the kingdom of God joined the dots—and we bought secondhand cookers and saucepans, crockery, and tables. A new venture—Lighthouse—was born. A story for another chapter.

The impact is still felt today when people walk through our neighbourhood. Like all adventures, there have been plenty of highs and lows. And now, a decade later, the brewery has grown up and left home. We've moved on from the day-to-day running of the place: It's now a thriving, stand-alone independent venture that has won several awards, including Brewery of the Year at the prestigious World Beer Awards.[4] What started as a scribble on a whiteboard didn't just become a reality; it became a blessing to hundreds of thousands of people in our city in the darkest time.

What did we learn? Well, just as a good beer requires skillful fermentation, bringing an idea from imagination to reality requires careful incubation. We learned that there's a magical common ground between entrepreneurs and the church—a shared space where vision, risk, and faith meet. There's a sweet spot for a kind of creative venture-philanthropy: entrepreneurialism that brings social impact. And when these factors align, they bring about extraordinary synergy and blessing for the community. We've never looked back, and we now try and make space in the life of SAINT to encourage and incubate new social enterprises, start-ups, and ventures.

Learning to brew your ideas is a key part of creativity. Allow your craziest dreams to ferment in the presence of your Creator. Look for the signs and sparks in your life that maybe—just maybe—point to the magical process by which the Spirit of God is fermenting your ideas into action.

And be careful what you pray for. Through this journey, I've become convinced that God is as interested in answering our big, audacious, crazy prayers as our more quotidian ones. We might have convinced ourselves that God is too busy or too distracted to care, but quite the opposite is true. The mountain-moving, city-shaping God is infinitely more interested in what we're cooking up and more willing to respond to our fragile prayers than we could ever imagine. There's nothing we can dream up, think up, or sketch up that will overwhelm him.

Life Starts in the Dark

So take courage even when things seem dark. Because life always starts in the dark. And here we learn an invaluable lesson about incubation: to invite God to brood over the unformed ideas in your creative soul. In the beginning, before anything takes shape, God hovers over the darkness. The void. The primordial deep—wild, raw, and brimming with potential. And here, in the thick of unformed nothingness, he broods. To the Jewish mind, this concept was huge. Deep waters meant chaos—the absence of light, the absence of life. The unknown. The uncontrollable. The untamed. And yet, this is where God chooses to hover. He doesn't recoil from the darkness. He doesn't step back from the disorder. He moves toward it. Present. Intentional. Seeing the creative potential where others would only see void.

> *When God began to create heaven and earth,*
> *and the earth then was welter and waste*
> *and darkness over the deep and*
> *God's breath hovering over the waters,*
> *God said, "Let there be light."*
> —Genesis 1:1, translated by Robert Alter

It's in the welter and waste that God speaks.
Then suddenly everything changes. This brooding gloom of the human soul is where creativity is born. Not from the perfect, polished, or pristine. But from the pain, the grit, the weight of the world pressing in under blood-red skies.

In *Heart of Darkness*, Joseph Conrad echoed the creation narrative in

INSPIRATION

his opening scene, describing the Thames estuary as thick with brooding tension. The sky burns red. The water stretches toward London, heavy with something unspoken yet undeniable. It's a world on the edge of transformation. Waiting. Like the primordial chaos before creation. Before the moment when light breaks in.

> *The air was dark above Gravesend, and farther back still seemed condensed into a mournful gloom, brooding motionless over the biggest, and the greatest, town on earth.*
> —Joseph Conrad, *Heart of Darkness*

It's foreboding, almost menacing—a darkness that presses in, waiting to be overcome by light. While *Heart of Darkness* is a journey into the depths of human depravity—our empires, our egos, our illusions of control—it mirrors a battle that isn't just confined to history. The battle plays out in the chaos of our cities, our cultures, our own souls. We short-change ourselves if we believe ideas are always born in pristine spaces—against the backdrop of whiteboards and miraculous emails from investors. The reality is far rawer.

So, when you feel you have nothing, you still have something: potential.

When you have chaos, that's the place God wants to work. When you feel empty and out of ideas, you're giving God his favourite canvas to display his glory: power made perfect in weakness. To bring an idea to life requires painful, patient brooding in the dark. It means wrestling with the unknown, sitting in the tension, letting something take shape in the shadows long before it ever sees the light.

In the Shadows

There's a cost to incubating ideas—one that's rarely counted. Those who shine the brightest often struggle with the depth of their shadow. It's no coincidence that some of the most creative minds have also been the most tortured.[5] A certain darkness frequently follows those who create, as if it were part and parcel of creative brilliance. Turning your dreams into reality can take a toll. Creativity comes with a cost: pressure, exhaustion, boredom, loneliness, stress. One study found that serious mental illness is significantly higher among those who identify as creative compared to the general population.[6] Among those working in the creative industries, 70 percent reported experiencing burnout in the last year.[7]

Creatives tend to suffer from higher rates of anxiety, poorer mental health, and increased levels of emotional pain.[8] One in five earns below the poverty line.[9] And consequently, a sobering statistic: Suicide rates among creatives are three times higher than average.[10]

Let that sink in.

Can I take a moment to encourage you with this brief but urgent plea for compassion and kindness? First, for yourself. Second, for your friends. The world needs your brilliance, but not at any cost. Be unusually and continually kind to yourself. Guard your soul. Don't be afraid to ask for help, even when things seem darkest. And if you're struggling, please let someone know.[11] Surround yourself with people who will weep with you in the depths of the night just as readily as they will stand with you in the spotlight of success.

When you find yourself in the shadowlands of creativity, under the weight of the gloom, remember: We're never alone. God draws close to the brokenhearted, overshadowing us with his presence. In the next chapter, we'll learn more about a man named Bezalel—the first person in the Bible to be filled with the Holy Spirit. But there's something interesting about Bezalel's name. It actually means "one who is in the shadow of God." This is no accident. Bezalel was a man hidden in the presence of the Creator Spirit—the Spirit brooded over his life, resting on him, empowering his creativity, helping inspire his imagination, and fermenting his ideas deep within his soul. He was available to God's plan.

The meaning of Bezalel's name also speaks to us: We are never alone in the darkness. God is often more tangible to our souls when we're under the shadow, not in the brilliance of success and sunlight. Bezalel was a man whose soul was ready to receive the spark from heaven. And the same is true of you today. You're not reading this by accident. You're reading this because you have a call on your life. You care about this because the Holy Spirit is hovering over your life, resting on you, empowering you to create for his glory.

So let me reassure you: There will be times when you feel like you're in the shadow, in the darkness, struggling to see the light. But the shadow is often where God meets us—so that we can recognise the spark of his glory when it comes. This twilight is often where the most precious creativity is birthed. In the tension. In the dark places. In the pain. It rises from the cry of the heart, the ache of longing, the gap between the now and the not yet. If you're incubating anything new—allowing inspiration to start to impact reality—it will be painful. It will take time. You will have to fight battles. There will be a hidden cost. And at times it will feel like you're alone and lost in the darkness. Your darkest moments as an artist, creator, or entrepreneur can be when God comes closest. The shadow isn't just a place of struggle. It's a place of covering. As Jun'ichirō Tanizaki reflected in his seminal essay *In Praise of Shadows*, "Were it not for shadows, there would be no beauty."[12]

There is beauty in the shadow. The shadow is the place where the Creator Spirit hovers over your life, brooding over the deep, birthing something new. So let me remind you of this truth—even when you find yourself in the shadow, you are still in the shelter of God's wings. The one who called you is faithful and will not let you go.

Ah! Bright Wings

If we go back to the very start, we find the Spirit of God brooding over the darkness. Notice the first few words of the creation story: "The Spirit of God was moving (hovering, brooding) over the face of the waters" (Genesis 1:2 AMP).

The image here is of a bird in motion—hovering, waiting, watching over the deep. The Spirit is not distant or detached. He is close, protective, alert to your needs. The Jewish word used here is *merachefet*, which means to brood over, to gently flutter—the way a bird hovers over its young, shielding, guarding, nurturing, encouraging life to break through. Gerard Manley Hopkins draws on this image in his celebrated poem "God's Grandeur":

> The Holy Ghost over the bent
> World broods with warm breast and with ah! bright wings.[13]

In the same way the Spirit hovered over the waters of Genesis, the Spirit of God now hovers over your imagination: incubating, nurturing, giving life. Just as the Spirit descended like a dove at Jesus' baptism, so too divine love broods over the baptism of your imagination. In this holy moment, a new *bara* heart is formed within you, with which you can see God. You don't need to remain trapped in darkness; instead, invite God to renew your mind and soul.

God's love is revolutionary for the creative soul because it frees us from the pressure to perform and allows us to shelter in the safety of his divine love. Jesus picked up this metaphor when speaking about his love for us. Looking over Jerusalem, he said, "How often I have longed to gather your children together, as a hen gathers her chicks under her wings" (Luke 13:34). Might you make space today to allow God to gather your imagination into the shelter of his love? You're not bothering him or disturbing him from running the universe. He longs to brood over your ideas—to sit with you and your sketch pad in the studio—simply because he loves you. He doesn't need your output or productivity; he just cares for you.

This is God's incubating warmth of heart for you—the lightbulb moment you are to pay most attention to. He is wanting to draw you close, to comfort, to console. And from that heart of nearness and covering, you will find that *bara* creativity flows. We can pray as the psalmist prayed, "Hide me in the shadow of your wings" (Psalm 17:8).

Overshadowed

Mary, the mother of Jesus, was just a young woman when the angel Gabriel appeared to her, announcing that she would give birth to the Saviour of the world. The whole story of the annunciation is a creation account—a holy mystery—dripping in the language of Genesis. The angel proclaimed, "The Holy Spirit will come on you, and the power of the Most High will overshadow you" (Luke 1:35). Mary would be in the shadow of God—the Creator Spirit brooding over her, and from that miracle, the author of life would step into the scene. In this way, Mary was a kind of Bezalel, chosen to create Jesus' dwelling place among us. And so—mystery of mysteries—Mary herself became a living tabernacle for God.

Giving life takes time. None of us entered the world in an instant. In the same way, ideas don't leap out of the imagination fully formed. They require gestation. They take shape in the waiting. Here's the point: Our creativity requires incubation. The creative soul becomes a kind of tabernacle—overshadowed by the Creator Spirit, incubated by his presence, and ready to bring the *bara* newness of God into the world. So, then, we wait, watching, for the ah! bright wings hovering over us.

When God Fills the Room

It's a Saturday night in November in East London. We're midway through the Renaissance London gathering—a thousand young creatives packed into the building. The plan is set: worship, interviews, a speaker, some fun moments. But halfway through worship, something shifts. Gently, almost imperceptibly at first, the atmosphere changes. A weight fills the room—not heavy but tangible. God is here. None of us knows what to do. The musicians can't carry on; they're on their faces on the stage. Across the room, people are encountering the love of Jesus in a way that defies explanation. God's presence moves like a cloud—thick, near, filling the space.

LIGHTBULB MOMENTS

People are overwhelmed. Kneeling. Weeping. Stunned. It's wonderful, holy, terrifying, and wow—all at once. This isn't business as usual. This isn't something you manufacture. It feels as though the Creator is brooding over the room, hovering over hearts like he once hovered over the waters. I venture nervously onto the platform and speak with the worship team. Despite having led all over the world and at many large gatherings, they are at a loss as to what to do. One worship leader leans in and whispers in my ear, "I'm terrified. I don't know where to go from here. God is here." All we can do is go low and wait for him. This is not hype; it's holy.

For hours, we stay there—under the shadow of God's presence. No one is leading the meeting, and yet a thousand young creative leaders remain, their faces pressed to the ground, their hearts on fire. The Creator Spirit rests on the gathering, filling people, bringing hope and freedom. It's a moment that marks people—a deep imprint of encounter, love, and power.

As I look out across the room, I wonder—what ideas will emerge?

What might God be incubating?

What might the Creator be fermenting in these hearts and lives?

What spark of wonder, what flash of creativity ignited by the Spirit of God?

Over and over again at these Renaissance gatherings, we thought we were coming into the room for a creative conference, but we've left overwhelmed by the sense of God's nearness. It's almost as if a gathering of modern-day Bezalels is irresistible to God. He understands the urgency, the hardship, the hunger we carry, and he is only too willing to respond by flooding these spaces with his overwhelming love and glory. And the fruit of these moments in God's presence emerges months, years, even decades later. People describe a sense of being marked by God—changed from the inside out, their natural creativity and gifting set alight by the spark of his divine presence. Moments like this are rare and extraordinary—and when they happen, you can feel it. The atmosphere shifts. Time slows. The whole room becomes immersed in God's presence.

INSPIRATION

Spiritual Flow

God's presence moving in lives, too, is flow. But not just creative flow—spiritual flow. A space where God pours out the river of his creative power into a specific time and place. A place of heavenly immersion where our imaginations are baptised afresh in the glory of God. David knew it when he danced before the ark, lost in worship. Isaiah knew it when he fell on his face, undone before the throne. Mary of Bethany knew it when she sat at Jesus' feet, pouring out her perfume. Here, in these moments, divine inspiration and human imagination collide. But you don't have to wait for a perfect moment. God will meet you wherever you are.

Like fermentation, creative flow requires certain conditions. It can't be forced, but it can be cultivated. It happens in the hidden places—where the raw ingredients of your soul are given time, space, warmth, and love. Where inspiration is nurtured, patience is forged, and transformation begins. And then—the spark.

The lightbulb moment doesn't happen in isolation. Just as yeast needs the right mix of sugar, warmth, and time to create something powerful, your imagination needs space, focus, and flow. The best artists, writers, and innovators don't stumble into creativity by accident. They create the conditions for it. That's why Jesus withdrew to quiet places—why monks and mystics through the ages practiced deep work in prayer and contemplation. It's why the most creative minds in history have carved out sacred, distraction-free spaces where imagination can be ignited by the divine. Because lightbulbs only light up when they're connected to a power source.

So, let me ask you: Where is your power source? Where can you step into a space that allows you to fully engage—to enter that creative flow state where God is at work through you? Let's get practical and determine what is going to work for you.

+ Maybe it's setting aside an hour—no distractions, no notifications.
+ Perhaps it's creating a space where prayer, worship, and creativity intertwine.

LIGHTBULB MOMENTS

+ Try building a daily rhythm—a regular practice that shuts out the noise and allows you to tune in to the Spirit.

Let me challenge you: How will you allow God to overshadow you? Maybe it's in quiet solitude or in collaboration with others. What if it's simply learning to be still long enough to hear his whisper. Even as you read this, what is the darkness in your life that you need to invite the Spirit of God to hover over? Because all your best lightbulb moments will begin the same way: with the brooding Spirit saying, "Let there be light." And don't be afraid of the darkness, because life always starts in the dark. Seeds of our best ideas take root beneath the soil of our faithfulness. The wine of creativity ferments in the hidden cellars of the soul. And our best God ideas are already being shaped in the pregnant potential of God's presence.

So make space.

Stay in the process.

Trust the fermentation.

Let love shelter you.

Because when the spark catches, everything changes.

Let there be light!

SPARK CIRCLE

Circle back through this chapter of Spark.

Notice
Was there a moment in this chapter that felt like a light turning on?
What story, idea, or Scripture helped you see something clearly for the first time?

Name
Have you ever felt like your creativity has been a struggle?
Share an experience when you've felt the Creator draw close to you.

Next Step
This week, train yourself to catch the light. Start each day by listening to some music, praying, and reading a short passage of Scripture, and simply ask, "What are you showing me, God?" Keep a notebook or note app with you—capture insights, nudges, or convictions as they come. Then bring your sharpest insight to your Spark Circle and reflect on how God is illuminating your path.

CHAPTER 5

The Priesthood of the Creative

Art is not a pastime but a priesthood.

—Jean Cocteau

Let's be honest: Creativity can be costly. Before moving to East London, we lived in another part of the city while I was still training as a vicar. It was a friendly neighbourhood, and after a couple of weeks, a neighbour invited us over for lunch—a big Sunday gathering with a dozen or so people from the street. Seated around a long table, people started to introduce themselves, sharing a little about their lives—jobs, families, hobbies.

So far, so good. But then came the inevitable question: "So, Al, what do you do?"

As a newly ordained priest, I'd quickly learned that dropping "man-of-the-cloth" into a conversation was the equivalent of hitting the fire alarm at a party: Nothing kills a vibe faster. Responses usually fall into three categories: polite disappointment, mild antagonism, or a desperate attempt to find common ground—"Oh, my aunt is a nun," or "I did Sunday school as a kid." So, I usually change the subject. But on this occasion, before I could, a woman at the far end of the table—who hadn't spoken much—suddenly piped up: "Well, everybody, I think I should let you know that Al isn't just a vicar. He's also a recording artist."

This was technically true. Before getting ordained, I'd recorded an

INSPIRATION

album of songs, though sales were not exactly astronomical. But still I felt a rush of pride. My ego swelled. After all, creating work, whatever the audience, is a labour of love. I'd spent years crafting those songs, months in the studio refining them, poring over arrangements, wrestling with lyrics. And when release day finally came, it felt like breathing life into something that had existed only in my imagination.

The woman continued, "Yeah, we listen to Al's album *Future Sound* all the time. On repeat."

The creative process is hard. But every now and then, you get those golden glimpses of glory—when the sunlight of success seems to break through the dull drizzle of self-doubt. Moments when your efforts actually seem to connect make all the hard work of the creative process feel worth it. And this was going to be one of those days. I could feel it in my bones. The mood shifted. People suddenly looked interested. A whiff of glamour descended over the roast beef and Yorkshire pudding. Side conversations hushed. I saw a flicker of intrigue in their eyes. *Maybe he's a big deal after all. Perhaps we're in the presence of greatness.*

I was very happy to roll with the illusion. While we Brits love a bit of self-deprecation, we'll also willingly take the wins. But then—just as my head was inflating beyond repair—the lady's husband (unhelpfully) decided to add some context: "Yeah," he said with a faint smirk on his face, "the reason we listen to your album all the time is because it's the only CD we have."

The room went quiet. "Last week our car got broken into. The thieves stole everything—our entire CD collection." Pause. "But apparently they weren't fans of yours, because they carefully put your CD back on the front seat." Silence. And then roars of laughter. Just like that my ego was obliterated. One minute I was high on the oxygen of recognition. The next I was choking on my pride.

No one warns you about the highs and lows. About how costly the creative process really is. This was not the first time I'd tasted rejection— apparently even car thieves have standards—nor would it be the last. It's not just the risk of putting a part of yourself out there—it's the time, the effort, the sacrifice. The emotional and spiritual personal investment in creating. You pour your heart, ideas, and imagination into the fragile vessel of your creative work, shaping it with care, only to watch it crack, slip through your fingers, and be cast aside.

Creativity costs. The requisite vulnerability can leave you exposed to pain. And we all bear the scars. Disappointment. Demoralisation. Disillusionment. The rejection letters. The frustration when your work is misunderstood. The ghosting from the casting agent. The door slammed in your face. The client who just does not get it.

And we convince ourselves that the long hours and the heartbreak must be the price we pay for following our dreams. And yet, despite all of this, something in us refuses to stop creating. Over the years, in every corner of the world, I've heard the same cry emerge—the pain, the cost, the misunderstanding. The burden of creative expression. The financial strain. The sacrifices no one sees. The long days. The late nights. The hidden battles.

The weight of carrying a creative calling in a world that worships utility is almost universal. The frustration of always having to justify your creativity, watching it take second place to financial realities, career pressures, and the relentless demands of everyday life. And here's the part that stings the most: Sometimes, the pain you feel comes from the church community: the one place that should be cheering you on. Instead of being nurtured, the creativity of all believers is often ignored, dismissed, or—at worst—actively discouraged. The creative gift is seen as a commodity to be coopted and controlled. And the result can be heartache, burnout, and breakdown. Please hear me: If that's been your story, you need to know it was not God's plan. Let me take this moment to apologise: I'm sorry if that has been your experience. The past does not get to write your future. In fact, now is the time for you to recover your creative purpose, because it's never been more critical than now.

The Death of Originality

Look around the culture and you'll notice an alarming pattern emerging. The contemporary creative landscape has undergone a profound

INSPIRATION

transformation, one marked by a deep crisis of originality. Everywhere you look, the world is dominated by a handful of giant brands, voices, and industries. Like juggernauts, they roll through culture, flattening everything in their path under their immense weight. Instead of innovation, we get imitation. Instead of originality, we get replication. Instead of the new, we get the old, recycled over and over.

A generation is emerging without the confidence to truly create—only to consume. And the tools we increasingly depend on—the algorithms, the endless feedback loops of social media—aren't helping. If anything, they're amplifying the problem. The rise of streaming platforms and social media promised to democratise content. But instead, algorithms have created an echo chamber, prioritising formula over originality, virality over depth, and familiarity over innovation. Creativity is no longer measured by boldness or artistic vision—it's about what will keep people scrolling.

The result is a flattening of creative expression—compressing difference, dulling originality, mimicking success—rather than breaking the new ground of wonder. As educationalist Andy Hargreaves warns, "There is no algorithm for creativity."[1] Instead of reaching for the stars, we settle for the pedestrian and the predictable.

Take the pressures the music industry faces. The temptation is to default to manufactured, algorithm-friendly artists who are carefully curated, tested, and polished to fit whatever the streaming services decide is trending that week. Where is the room for wacky and weird? For gloriously experimental? For the frankly eccentric? As the inimitable musical iconoclast Frank Zappa lamented, "All the good music has already been written by people with wigs and stuff."[2]

A recent study analysing the UK pop charts over the last few decades reveals a startling trend: the near extinction of original bands. Think about it: Name one new band that has conquered the world in the last decade. Coldplay? 2000. BTS? 2013. In the early 1980s, bands made up more than 60 percent of chart placements. By 2021 that figure had collapsed to just 7 percent.[3] We are in danger of losing the unique chemistry of collective creative expression as it's replaced with standardisation. Which leaves the world, well, less weird and wonderful.

The same is true of the communications industry. In the early eighties, fifty corporations controlled the majority of American media, creating a landscape of diversity, competition, and innovation.[4] By 2011 that number had shrunk to just six mega-corporations, consolidating control over nearly everything we watch, read, and consume.[5] We are witnessing the slow death of originality.

Even the idea of the creative has become a paradox—both ubiquitous and yet out of reach. Everyone is now a content creator, and yet true originality feels more missing than ever before. Rather than embracing the creativity of all believers, we've created an elite. The secret sauce of innovation has been outsourced to a select few, while the rest of us are left waiting for permission.

We're drowning in imitation. Sameness everywhere. Clicks and likes reward familiarity rather than originality. Copy-paste culture. And beneath it all, a nagging ache. A sense we were made for something more. That there has to be something deeper. Something real. Nick Cave—in an interview with the *New Yorker*—summed this up perfectly: "AI may very well save the world, but it can't save our souls. That's what true art is for."[6] How do we return to a deeper understanding of the creative soul where art is a sacrament, beauty redemptive, and innovation a holy thing? To recapture this, we have to rewind back to a time of true originals.

The God Colors

Did you know that until a few generations ago, the idea of the Creative with a capital *C* didn't really exist? The pre-modern world understood creativity as an activity, not an identity. People weren't *creatives*; they were artists, makers, craftsmen, inventors, thinkers, and storytellers. Creativity was an activity, not an identity—something you did, not something you were. As the great art critic and thinker John Ruskin put it, "All great art is the expression of man's delight in God's work, not his own."[7]

While God creates *ex nihilo*, we create *ex materia*. God creates with divine *bara* newness, we make with *asah* creativity. Only God says,

INSPIRATION

"Let there be light" (Genesis 1:3). Human creativity is working in that refracted light and "bringing out the God-colors in the world."[8] We are co-creators, or as J. R. R. Tolkien understood it, sub-creators. Tolkien used the analogy of white light being divided by a prism into many different colours to illustrate how God's original creative spark is displayed through the soul's creativity:

> Man, Sub-creator, the refracted light
> through whom is splintered from a single White
> to many hues, and endlessly combined
> in living shapes that move from mind to mind.[9]

God's creative life illuminates the world of the artist, the designer, the dreamer, the storyteller, revealing for the first time a world in Technicolor. New dimensions open up, ones we never knew existed. It's as if we'd been working in 2D all along, trapped by finite human limitation, until suddenly we begin to see in 3D, our vision shaped by the eternal perspective of divine *bara* creativity and gloriously purposeful *asah* creativity. And of course the discovery of new perspective is what lies at the heart of all true creative renaissances.

When we lay down the idol of having to be the master Creative and recalculate our lives around the eternal Creator, we uncover a world far more mysterious and wonderful than we could imagine. Here is true creativity: where triumph is found in sacrifice, where power flows from self-giving love, and where the deepest source of inspiration isn't human brilliance but divine grace. Because in the end, it's not about us. It never was. It's about him.

Trevor Hart says, "God alone is uncreated and God alone creates."[10] We don't need to be the source of originality. The pressure is off. And this truth really, really can set us free. We can stop trying to play God and lift our eyes to the source of all true beauty. We can stop striving to create in our own strength and begin to see our creativity as a gift—freely given, freely received—with its potential fully ignited when offered back to God.

THE PRIESTHOOD OF THE CREATIVE

The Mission from God

If we want to know how God remakes the world—if we want to see what making all things new really looks like—we can look at Jesus on the cross. There we see a life laid down, love woven into every broken fibre. There we see power flowing not from ego but from sacrifice. The rescue from sin offered by the cross is divine newness—pure *bara*. But it's also an invitation to creative *asah*—to be made new. And when we see this—when we let it reshape our posture toward creativity—something shifts.

We become resurrection people. "If anyone is in Christ, the new creation has come" (2 Corinthians 5:17). We are liberated. Freed from the pressure to be god-like geniuses. Freed from the need to prove, define, or justify our worth through what we create. Instead, we're free to remake the world as we were meant to: for the other, for love, for beauty. But creation doesn't stop there. In fact, this is where the work of redeeming creation begins.

You don't need me to tell you that we live in a broken world. And creativity—like everything else—has fallen from the grace of God and desperately needs redeeming. God wants to save your creativity.

Let me explain. In Genesis 1 when God gave his evaluation of creation with his final "It was very good" (Genesis 1:31) before he rested, it wasn't a full stop—it was a comma. The work of creation wasn't finished in those opening pages of Genesis. In fact, God was only just getting started. And your creativity is part of that.

Ultimately, it was only when Jesus hung on the cross—reconciling the world, defeating sin and darkness—that he made his final pronouncement: "It is finished" (John 19:30). The creation was finally complete, redeemed: the waste and welter of chaos and sin and darkness and pain finally overcome.

This full stop—like the old bullet hole in the glass above the front door—is the marker that punctuates the end of the old and beginning of the new. It is the starting gun of the new creation, the moment from which everything is being remade. The old, decaying, crumbling relic

INSPIRATION

is being resurrected. At the cross, your creativity is fully redeemed. From that point on, Jesus is in the business of making everything new—remaking, redeeming, re-enchanting all things. Including your creative life.

Now we move from a brand-new kind of new that only God does, to being caught up in remaking, rescuing, restoring with an old-made-new kind of new. This is the greatest adventure of all: that we get to be collaborators with God in the great redeeming of all things. Suddenly our creativity, vision, ideas, imagination, and courage have meaning beyond our wildest dreams. With every space you design, every stroke of the paintbrush, every word you craft, and every note you sing, you are building that which will endure into eternity. For the first time, we understand the creative act for what it truly is—smouldering with holiness.[11] And so, as Jake and Elwood discover in *The Blues Brothers*, we find to our astonishment that "we're on a mission from God."[12]

1. Calling

God is full of surprises. When it comes to the first human being to be filled with the Holy Spirit, God's choice is ... unexpected. A king? A holy priest? A wild prophet? Maybe one of the heroes of the faith—Abraham, Moses? Or a mighty warrior like David or Samson?

No. The first person filled with the Spirit was Bezalel—an artist. Bezalel's grandfather, Hur, had once held up Moses' hands during battle, an act of quiet strength that turned the tide of victory. Perhaps Bezalel grew up believing that serving God by empowering others with his gifts was a calling worth giving his life to. Rabbinic tradition also holds that Hur was killed opposing the making of the golden calf, refusing to let worship be misdirected. Maybe there was something in his very DNA, something that stood for the power of creativity rightly directed toward heaven. Because when the Spirit of God filled Bezalel, it was not to preach, prophesy, or go to war. It was to create.

THE PRIESTHOOD OF THE CREATIVE

> *See, I have chosen Bezalel son of Uri, the son of Hur, of the tribe of Judah, and I have filled him with the Spirit of God, with wisdom, with understanding, with knowledge and with all kinds of skills—to make artistic designs for work in gold, silver and bronze, to cut and set stones, to work in wood, and to engage in all kinds of crafts.*
> —Exodus 31:2–5

Bezalel's mission is specific. He is tasked with building a dwelling place for the presence of God—and not just any design, but one that follows God's exact blueprint. People say the devil is in the details, but the opposite is true: God is in the details. He knows the number of hairs on your head. He sees every creative decision you make—every colour choice, every metaphor, every idea that flows through you. And while God could have built the tabernacle himself—just as he spoke the universe into being—he chose to call Bezalel, working through his human hands. And this wasn't just a random decision.

This tells us something crucial about creativity: It is a divine calling. When you create, you are involved in something holy. Matter matters to God. Beauty is important. Creativity is sacred.

The Creative Anointing

The good news is that you don't have to do this alone. God wants to help you. He has given you this task, and he will pour out his Spirit on your life, just as he did on Bezalel. The way God empowers creatively is through what the Bible calls anointing.

After Jacob's vision of the ladder to heaven, he anointed that place with oil. Priests and kings would follow in this pattern, being set apart by anointing. Even today, when a King or Queen of England is crowned, oil from the Holy Land is used—echoing that ancient tradition of anointing. The concept of anointing is sometimes described as functional novelty—a divine activation for a specific purpose. The oil of anointing points to a

INSPIRATION

deeper spiritual reality—the outpouring of the Spirit to empower a life for dynamic creative potential to remake and initiate. It marks a life set apart, infused with divine creativity, filled with the Spirit for a purpose.

If you want to create work that truly lasts—work that outlives you, that echoes into eternity—you need anointing. Without it, even the best innovation is fleeting. But with God, it carries the weight of the eternal. When God pours out his Spirit, it's not just to bless. It's to commission. To innovate. To empower. To create. To build. To change.

You are anointed with this same priestly calling: for a purpose. The priesthood of all believers means that when creativity is activated by the outpouring of the Spirit, it becomes more than self-expression. It takes on a holy quality. This is the priesthood of the creative—where your work becomes an offering. Where your craft becomes a sacred act. Where your creativity becomes a bridge between heaven and earth. You step into your Father's work: the remaking of the world. Or as Iris Murdoch said, "The world is not given to us 'on a plate,' it is given to us as a creative task.... We work, and 'make something of it.' We help it to be."[13]

Your role in the world is to make something of it—not as a split between sacred and secular, but as a seamless flow of God's Spirit at work in you. When he pours out his Spirit, everything can become holy. This is why creativity isn't just an outlet. Or a passion project. It's a priestly calling. And not just some vague, general calling. It's specific. God is calling you. Right now. Your creative calling matters because the world is full of places where the divine presence has been forgotten. Your work can make it seen again.

Creativity is priestly, a mediation, standing in the gap between heaven and earth. So, expect God to meet you in your work. In the casting studio. In the songwriting session. In the design sprint. In the boardroom. In the client presentation. In the code you write. He's already there. We talk about an artist's output as their work—a work on paper, a work on canvas. A filmmaker screens their work. An actor is praised for their work.

In Hebrew the word *avodah* (עבודה) is used to describe work in Exodus 34:21: "Six days you shall *avodah* (labor), but on the seventh day you shall rest." But here's the twist—the same word is also used for worship. In Joshua 24:15, we read: "As for me and my household, we will *avodah* (serve [worship]) the LORD." For the people of God, work and worship aren't separate categories—they are one and the same. And that means your creativity—the things you make, the ideas, inventions, and innovations that flow from you—are not just an outlet or a job. They are an offering. They are not a waste of time. They are worship.

When you create, you draw closer to heaven—offering the fruit of your hands as a sacrifice of praise. Put like this, suddenly all of human history—culture, the arts, the sciences—takes on a new dimension. Every breakthrough, every discovery, every piece of art, film, music, or literature that stirs the soul is a collaboration between human effort and divine spark.

Creativity is a sacred calling. The spark in each of us that dreams, imagines, and creates is a telltale sign that we are made to make. That the act of initiating something new, of turning inspiration into action, is, at its core, a holy act. The making and forming and shaping of the world through your creativity is not just something nice we do to pass the time, it's the core calling of all who believe. As N. T. Wright puts it,

> What you do in the present—by painting, preaching, singing, sewing, praying, teaching, building hospitals, digging wells, campaigning for justice, writing poems, caring for the needy, loving your neighbor as yourself—will last into God's future. These activities are not simply ways of making the present life a little less beastly, a little more bearable, until the day when we leave it behind altogether. . . . They are part of what we may call building for God's kingdom.[14]

2. Collaboration

Adam had barely drawn his first breath when God handed him his first assignment: the naming of the animals:

INSPIRATION

> *Now the* LORD *God had formed out of the ground all the wild animals and all the birds in the sky. He brought them to the man to see what he would name them; and whatever the man called each living creature, that was its name.*
> —Genesis 2:19

I mean, where would you even begin?

Aardvark.
Anteater.
Antelope.
Badger.
Bison.
Bumblebee.
Cat.
Clam.
Cockerel.

And so on. And so forth.

I imagine Adam hesitated at first—but soon he found his rhythm. And I imagine it was fun—with a few exceptions, perhaps.

Tapeworm.
Cockroach.
Leech.
(Yuck.)

And then what about the really scary animals? The ones with the big teeth and bad tempers? That must've been awkward:

Crocodile.
Tiger.
Lion.
(Yikes.)

THE PRIESTHOOD OF THE CREATIVE

Adam wasn't just following orders, he was collaborating with God. He was shaping identity, calling out purpose, helping the world make sense. In that way, his work wasn't merely functional, it was priestly. In the naming, he conferred identity. Each act of creativity is an echo of that first task. Your creativity is like the naming of the animals. As T. S. Eliot put it, "Each venture is a new beginning, a raid on the inarticulate."[15] And thus Adam—in his creative calling—was doing something uniquely priestly: He was bridging the gap between Creator and creation. And notice how God didn't micromanage the process. He didn't dictate the names. He didn't interfere. He didn't interrupt with suggestions. Instead, whatever Adam decided to name each animal, God went with.

What I love about this story is it's the first human creative act, but it's also a collab. Think about this for a moment because this is a big deal. God actually enjoys working alongside you. That's what collaboration literally means. The word *collaborate* comes from *collaborare*, which combines *com-* ("together") and *laborare* ("to work"), meaning to work together. When you collaborate, you're not just creating, you're co-labouring, co-creating, together.

Just to be clear: God is perfectly capable of going it alone. But he likes the company. So, you and I don't have to do this work alone. Every creative act, every stretch, every risk, every step of faith—God is right there with us. He walks alongside us. He is, according to Trevor Hart, "a God whose creative work is ultimately achieved per *collaborationi*."[16] Here is where the best creativity happens—in community. You weren't created to be alone, and likewise, you don't create alone.

The music producer Brian Eno—famous for his work with David Bowie, U2, Talking Heads, and Coldplay—describes the power of collaboration: "It's through conversation and collaboration with other people that you really develop your own ideas. Until you put them in front of other people and see how they work when they're no longer under your control, you don't know what the value of those ideas is."[17]

Our creativity gets stronger when we do it together. This is not just good sense; it's God sense: There's a spiritual synergy that takes place when we collaborate. "For we are co-workers in God's service"

INSPIRATION

(1 Corinthians 3:9). Interestingly, the word used here in the Greek is συνεργοί (*synergoi*), from which we get the word *synergy*, the dynamic ability to create more together than we could on our own. Extraordinary things can happen when we work collaboratively.

I have the great joy of getting to work with some amazingly talented people. I think of Dr. Deborah Pritchard, an award-winning British contemporary composer who over the years has become a friend. Her work has been premiered by, among others, the London Symphony Orchestra and the BBC Symphony Orchestra, and she has collaborated with artist Maggi Hambling and poet Sir Ben Okri. Deborah has partnered with the Renaissance team to create some original compositions, including a piece inspired by the Chagall windows in Tudeley Church, the same windows that influenced Es Devlin's chapel at SAINT. Experiencing these two works together is mind-blowing. But what I especially love about Deb is her extraordinary ability to weave together different creative elements, colours, and instruments.

Every time I listen to Deb's work, I'm struck by the synergy that comes from the instruments. If you've ever listened closely to a string quartet, you'll know the sound is rich, deep, and powerful. Each instrument carries its own unique timbre, and while each alone can be stunning, something magical happens when they blend. The collaboration of sounds, frequencies, rhythms, and tones becomes more than the sum of its parts.

Creativity isn't a solo act—it's a symphony. Innovation thrives in collaboration. The sparks fly when ideas collide, when different perspectives meet, when creativity is shared rather than hoarded. So, here's the invitation: Don't create alone; co-create with God. He brings the raw materials of the world to us—like he once brought the animals to Adam—and says, "What will you name them?" He is intrigued by what you'll create. He is interested in your output. He is excited for your ideas. And trust me, that is a game changer: You are a co-creator.

The Prophetic and the Practical

Let's get practical. How does your creative calling move from inspiration to reality? How do ideas become something tangible—something

THE PRIESTHOOD OF THE CREATIVE

that matters in the real world? Well, it's one thing to dream. It's another to build. Creativity is about ideation, but innovation is the execution—the process of bringing an idea to reality.[18]

Creativity is the spark, the divine moment of insight. Innovation is the fire, the process of shaping that insight into something real. Creativity imagines, and innovation implements. And this is exactly why your creative calling is priestly. Because it isn't just about seeing something new; it's about bringing it into being. There's a prophetic edge to creativity—the dreamer sees what isn't there yet and, through the Spirit's inspiration, brings it into being.

Isaiah saw, then responded.

Jeremiah listened, then spoke.

Ezekiel dreamed, then acted.

John the Baptist called, then prepared.

All creativity starts in the swirl of ideas, the deep waters of your soul where God hovers. Your creativity is prophetic. You're collaborating with the Spirit to imagine what could be. Creativity without action is just daydreaming, just as faith without works is dead. It's not enough to imagine—we have to build. Bezalel didn't just dream up the tabernacle; he crafted it with his hands. Solomon didn't just envision the temple; he made it a reality. Nehemiah didn't just have a vision of a rebuilt Jerusalem; he picked up bricks. Paul didn't just believe the good news would spread; he planted churches. Creativity imagines the future. Innovation builds it. And so prophetic vision needs practical execution. One without the other is incomplete.

This collaboration isn't just about making you feel good or look good. It has a purpose. There's a mission to your creativity. We see this in the life of Jesus, who said to his Father in John 17:4, "I have brought you glory on earth by finishing the work you gave me to do." The work God has given you has a purpose and a time frame.

Here's an exercise to consider: Think about the things you're doing—the work, your to-do list, your passions, your projects. Now ask yourself: "Which of these align most closely with the dream God has placed in me, the call of God on my life? Which will spark life and hope? Which will have the greatest impact—not just on me, but on the world around me?" Identify those things. Make a list. Then invite the Creator Spirit into that space. Start praying about the items on your list. Because when your creativity aligns with heaven's mission, it isn't just productive—it's transformative.

The purpose of creativity isn't just to make better things; it's to make things better.

Creativity isn't an end in itself; it's a means of illumination, of transformation. God anoints people with creativity not so they can turn the gift inward but so they can turn it outward, to shine light into the world. This collaboration isn't just about expression; it's about impact. God wants you to be his hands and feet in the mission of remaking the world. And that changes everything. It means your work isn't just important; it's essential.

So, learn to see your work as purposeful. Your collaboration with heaven is a mission, not just a mandate. When you turn ideas into action, you're stepping into God's great plan of renewal. And this is not just a calling and an invitation to collaboration, but add these two together, and you and I get to experience something hugely powerful: the spiritual connection.

3. Connection

We live in an age of unprecedented connection. The media industry is the most powerful and far-reaching commercial enterprise on earth today. Trillions of pounds are spent each year on storytelling, filmmaking, television, and digital marketing. Hundreds of millions of people earn a living in this space, across every country on the planet. At its core, humanity is in the business of connecting and communicating.

We speak, write, create, and share—our words and images shaping culture, commerce, and connection. Every kind of media through which human creativity is expressed has the potential to become infused with a sacramental quality. The word *media* is interesting in itself. It comes from

THE PRIESTHOOD OF THE CREATIVE

the Latin *medius*, meaning "middle" or "in between." It's the same root from which we get *mediate*—the act of standing in the gap, bridging two sides, and bringing reconciliation. At its heart, all media is about connection. Good media stands between the creator and the audience, the storyteller and the listener, the artist and the world. Whether through words, images, sound, movement, performance, physical space, or digital form, media becomes the conduit through which ideas travel, culture is shaped, and meaning is made.

In the same way, the priestly calling is a calling to mediation between heaven and earth, a call to reconcile God and his people. The point is this: When you create and communicate vision, when you innovate and push at the boundaries of what is, you are engaging in something profound. You are mediating between what is and what could be—between reality and a future yet to be created. You are called to stand in the gap—your creativity both a ladder and a lifeline—connecting the present and the possible, the temporal and the eternal.

The Ladder to Heaven

A few days after my eighteenth birthday, I came to know Jesus. Around the same time, my father—a sculptor—had a spiritual awakening of his own. He began to express his faith in Jesus in his work. He would pour his soul into his work, crafting beauty from raw material.

And then, when I was nineteen, tragedy struck. One evening while he was alone in the house, my father collapsed. A heart attack. No warning. The medics did all they could to save him, but he died there on our kitchen floor. Gone.

I was devastated. Numb. Hurting. Nothing prepares you for a moment like this, especially as a teenager. The next day, the house was eerily quiet. I wandered through it in a daze, unsure of what to do. Across the garden stood my father's sculpture studio. He'd spent the entire day working there before he died. I crossed the garden and stepped inside, hesitantly, into the empty space he'd left behind.

Everything was untouched—his tools still resting where he left them. And there, on a stand, under a shroud was a new work of clay. His last piece. I gently lifted the cloth, studying the form beneath my hands. His fingerprints were still wet on the clay. I traced the shape of them with my fingers, silent tears falling down my cheeks. Although the work was only beginning to take shape, it became clear that it was a human figure with a ladder running up the figure's back. My mind spun. Where had I seen this before? Was it a Greek myth or ancient legend?

And then I remembered. Suddenly it became clear: The day my father died, he was working on a sculpture of Christ as Jacob's ladder from that moment in John's gospel when Jesus says, "Very truly I tell you, you will see 'heaven open, and the angels of God ascending and descending on' the Son of Man" (John 1:51). Jacob, the Old Testament character, had seen a vision of a ladder to heaven mediating between God and humankind. Jesus would point to himself as this ladder, reconciling earth and heaven. Jesus is the Way to heaven, the Truth, and the Life. And to know Jesus is to know the ladder to heaven, the one who bridges and reconciles. So, when we are caught up in the creative act, in a sense we are closer to the reality of heaven than at any other moment in this life.

Your creativity is sacred ground.

It has a sacramental quality.

It is a connection between heaven and earth.

It is a ladder between the seen and the unseen.

It is a place where the presence of God moves.

When you imagine, make, dream, step out, create, and shape, you're stepping onto the ladder that connects heaven and earth. You're stepping into the presence of a God who bridges, reconciles. It's not just his nature—the Creator—it's also where we find God at work: making all things new.

Babel Cancelled

God doesn't do typos. But on the day of Pentecost, in Peter's first sermon to the early church, Peter seemed to misquote Scripture. The fire had fallen. The spark had lit the early church with flames resting on every head. A wind had rushed through the upper room, creating a firestorm of divine energy that would reach the ends of the earth. The once-terrified disciples were now proclaiming God's story in languages they'd never learned. The same Spirit that hovered over the waters at the dawn of time was now brooding over the people—filling them, sending them.

And Peter stood to speak—like Adam naming the first animals—framing the moment. "Your young men will see visions, your old men will dream dreams" (Acts 2:17). But hang on—something was not quite right. That's not how Joel wrote it. Joel said, "Your old men will dream dreams, your young men will see visions" (Joel 2:28). The order seems to have changed. Something had shifted. Had Peter reversed it intentionally? Or is this just an innocent typo? Surely, if we believe that all Scripture is God-breathed, then there must be divine intention behind this apparent edit. What was going on here? Why had the order changed?

God's Creative Presence

Before the Spirit is poured out, dreaming leads to vision. But after the Spirit is poured out, vision leads to dreaming. In other words, the by-product of the vision the Spirit imparts into the church is dreaming, imagination, creativity. When the Holy Spirit comes, old men recover their childlike wonder and learn to dream again. Creativity and innovation are no longer just about function, execution, and building vision. Instead, the Spirit fuels a new kind of holy imagination. On the day of Pentecost, something shifted. The supernatural connection of all believers was restored. The Spirit of the Creator came to live within all who believe. A new spiritual language was given. Division turned to unity. Babel was cancelled. And from that day onward, the Spirit has empowered every generation to remake the world.

In a single moment, God restores a supernatural connection between Creator and creature. Innovation takes on a whole new meaning and purpose. Without this, creativity is just a cold survival mechanism. But with the empowering presence of God, human creativity takes on an eternal quality. It has the capacity for extraordinary goodness. It carries the weight of glory.

Consequently, the source of all originality is coursing through your soul with life and newness. You're walking in the footsteps of Bezalel.

INSPIRATION

The vision is now the call to recover your childlike dreaming again. In a world that grows jaded and old, God is eternally young. G. K. Chesterton described the freshness of God's creativity, saying, "Our Father is younger than we."[19] As a result, there's a novelty—a renewal—flowing through your veins.

The Holy Spirit restores originality, mystery, and wonder in a world that trades everything down for familiarity and banality. The spark of the Spirit lifts your eyes beyond the horizon of the possible. It is this divine connection that gives you permission to scale the heights of glory and plumb the depths of human experience with awe.

We live in an age starved of wonder. But the Spirit—the Wonderful Counsellor—comes to reconnect us. And so "the job of the artist," as the painter Francis Bacon is quoted as saying, "is always to deepen the mystery."[20] The Holy Spirit drives our souls into the wild places of God's imagination, to worlds yet to be created, to stories yet to be told. To innovate with the Spirit is to step beyond the limits of human reasoning and into the infinite possibilities of divine creativity. To connect with the Holy Spirit is to be filled with bravery—to step beyond the small, safe confines the world would box you into. To experiment. To dream. To break the mould. To do things differently.

This work is urgent. If the church is going to be a place where heavenly innovation thrives, we need to find the courage not to just maintain what was, but to build what could be. In their book *God Is Back*, sociologists John Micklethwait and Adrian Wooldridge coin the phrase "the pastorpreneur"—a kind of pastoral leadership that shepherds with both spiritual vision and creative, entrepreneurial instinct. They argue that in the coming decades, leaders in every sphere—creativity, church, business, culture—will need to think both pastorally and entrepreneurially to navigate a world that won't stand still. The most successful religious leaders will be those who think like entrepreneurs—building movements, taking risks, and embracing innovation.[21]

William Booth was one of those leaders—a true original. In Victorian Britain, Booth witnessed the emergence of the urban poor, people trapped in terrible housing, crippled by ill health, and devoid

THE PRIESTHOOD OF THE CREATIVE

of hope. While the traditional church stood disconnected and distant, Booth innovated. He took the drinking songs from local pubs and reworked them, filling them with lyrics that made God's love accessible to everyday people. It was Booth who famously asked, "Why should the devil have all the best tunes?"

This wasn't clever marketing; it was innovation driven by a calling and empowered by collaboration with the Holy Spirit. It was creativity flowing directly from his connection to God. Great spiritual innovation always begins with a sacred calling, Spirit-led collaboration, and supernatural connection. And that connection to heaven—that intimate partnership with the Creator Spirit—is exactly how William Booth's greatest innovations began.

Prior to this great period in his life, he would often escape London for the country, where he spent days lost in thought—praying and wrestling with the challenges he saw. One weekend a guest arrived to visit him, but Booth was nowhere to be found. Eventually a lone figure was spotted wandering the garden at the rear of the house, pacing among the flower beds, deep in thought. For hours the guest waited, watching as Booth walked back and forth, lost in his ideas. Eventually unable to contain his curiosity, the guest ventured into the garden to ask what Booth was doing. Booth stopped, turned to him with a glint in his eye, and simply said: "I'm working on a plan that will be a blessing to the whole world."[22]

That plan would of course eventually become the Salvation Army. As a consequence, hundreds of thousands came to faith. Millions more were impacted. God has done it before, and he'll do it again. Your creativity matters. Your imagination counts. Your voice is needed. God wants to collaborate with you in this great adventure. He wants to fill you with his Holy Spirit, igniting your imagination, unlocking potential you never thought possible. He's inviting you into the divine story of renewal—not as a spectator but as a participant, a partner, a co-creator.

You carry heaven's blueprint within you. You hold the raw materials of redemption. And you're here—at this very moment—to breathe life, beauty, and wonder into a weary world. So step forward boldly.

INSPIRATION

Take a deep breath. Lift your eyes. And allow God to set you apart for this task. You're invited into the great adventure, the holy partnership, the divine collab.

And here's the best part: The same Spirit who hovered over the deep waters of creation is hovering over you now, ready to empower, inspire, ignite. So create. Innovate. Dream. Risk. Remake. And as you do, know this: All of heaven is leaning in, watching closely, cheering you on. Because through your hands, God is continuing to make all things new.

Are you ready?

SPARK CIRCLE

Circle back through this chapter of Spark.

Notice
Where in this chapter did something shift in how you view your creativity?
Did a moment or phrase reframe how you see your work or calling?

Name
How do you feel about the idea of seeing your creativity as a calling?
What small creative act could become holy if you offered it back to God?
Name a time when you have collaborated with others. What did you learn?

Next Step
Choose one creative act—writing, planning, designing, cooking, dreaming—and intentionally dedicate it to God this week. Afterward ask, *"What changed when I offered my creativity as worship, not performance?"*
Bring that reflection to your Spark Circle.

MOVEMENT THREE
Innovation

CHAPTER 6

Courageous Creativity

Creativity takes courage.
—Henri Matisse

Have you ever tried skydiving? My first and only jump was when I was eighteen years old. I was over a military airfield in the West of England. I had agreed to do a parachute jump for charity with a group of friends. It had seemed like a brilliant idea at the time. We'd throw ourselves out of a plane, hopefully raising thousands of pounds for a good cause. "What could possibly go wrong?" I said to myself.

In preparation I watched the training videos, read the manual, and spent hours trying to imagine the feeling of falling from the plane door, plummeting through the sky. However, actually making the leap into the ether was something altogether different. The door of the plane slid open. The wind roared in. My legs turned to jelly. My bowels somersaulted. There, on the edge of the blue abyss, I was deeply regretting my decision. What if something went wrong? What if the parachute didn't work? But by this point it was too late. I was already dangling out the side door of a single-engine plane at fifteen thousand feet.

And besides, by this stage, my options were limited, because it was a tandem jump. In other words, I was strapped to the front of a very burly mustachioed man named Simon, who was ex-special forces, in something

INNOVATION

a bit like one of those sling baby carriers. And Simon—probably more used to hostage extraction—was definitely not the kind of guy you started negotiating with at fifteen thousand feet.

In that moment, things moved pretty quickly from theory to reality, from imagination to, well, sheer terror. Simon gave me the thumbs-up, and closing my eyes, I responded, plucking up all my courage. I didn't want to jump, but we'd come this far, and it was too late to turn around now. It was time to take the leap of faith.

Three. Two. One. The rush of the air. The screaming. The perspective. The adrenaline. The laughter. Nothing could prepare me for how exhilarating it was. By the time I reached the ground safely—thanks to my mustachioed bodyguard—I was beaming. It was the best feeling. I wanted to go again.

You know where we're going with this, right?

Turning your ideas into reality is a lot like skydiving: There comes a point when you must choose to make a leap of faith. A moment in your creative journey when you must overcome your fears, be brave, and throw yourself into the unknown. *What if I fail? What if I'm ridiculed? What if I crash and burn?* We feel terrified that we'll look stupid, that our best efforts won't be enough. That others will do it better. That our ideas will be dismissed as irrelevant or ignored. What if it all goes horribly wrong and our critics are proved right? How do we overcome failure to launch? How do we take the leap of faith, throw ourselves into the great creative unknown?

Let's talk about creative courage. Why? Because you're going to need it. Without courage all your best ideas will stay stuck to your biggest fears. You'll miss the rush, the wonder, the joy of bringing something new into being. You won't fail to launch, but harnessed to courage, you'll learn how to fly. How? In this chapter, we're going to look at five practices that will change your creative game. These are not natural talents or innate endowments; they're practices, meaning you grow them by doing them. And they will develop over time. Decide to exercise them at every opportunity—live them out—and watch what happens. And these practices also won't happen overnight, but they're going to help you build up the muscle of courage. And, if you decide to put time in with them, they will change your creative game for good. So, ready to begin?

Practice 1: Be Brave

Creativity Requires Boldness

In his memoir *Just Mercy*, lawyer and activist Bryan Stevenson recounts meeting his hero, the civil rights legend Rosa Parks. As he shared his vision for exonerating wrongfully convicted death row prisoners and challenging systemic racism in the US justice system, Parks listened intently. Then Stevenson received this winsome advice: "Ooooh, honey, all that's going to make you is tired, tired, tired. . . . That's why you've got to be brave, brave, brave."[1]

You'll need to be brave—brave enough to push through opposition, brave enough to face down your self-doubt, brave enough to keep going when you're exhausted. Brave, brave, brave. And that will take boldness. So, ask yourself honestly: "What's stopping me? Is it the fear of failing, or is it the fear of looking foolish? Is it the nagging voice of self-doubt that erodes my confidence? Is it the relentless inner critic that silences inspiration?" Here's the truth about bravery: You can't be brave without feeling afraid. If you look through the story of people who have changed things, you'll notice something surprising: Everyone has had to overcome opposition, fear, and doubt with huge courage.

> *Creativity is a path for the brave, yes, but it is not a path for the fearless, and it's important to recognise the distinction.*
> —Elizabeth Gilbert

Joshua, of Jericho and promised land fame, started out terrified he could never fill Moses' shoes. Otherwise, why would God have spoken to him so directly and repeatedly? "Be strong and courageous. Do not be afraid; do not be discouraged, for the LORD your God will be with you wherever you go" (Joshua 1:9).

The mighty warrior Gideon struggled with chronic low self-esteem. When God called him, he pushed back. He informed God that he came from the smallest tribe, the weakest clan. He listed all the reasons why he was the wrong guy for the job. He was a nobody, the least in his family. He'd written himself off before he even got started. But Gideon turned out to be a brilliant tactician and bold leader.

God is not put off by the limitations you speak over your life. Your ceilings are the platforms on which God will build your courage. He sees past the labels others have put on you. He sees the potential in your creative soul and delights to put his courage in you. Of course, that's what to *en-courage* literally means. Fear is part of the creative process. It's not a sign that you're on the wrong path; it's proof that you're stepping into something significant. Creativity requires boldness. It demands that you put yourself out there, risk rejection, and keep going even when doubt creeps in.

CHALLENGE

Here's your first challenge to help you practice being just a little bit braver:

What fear is holding you back creatively? Name it.

Decide—right now—to take one small step of bravery toward overcoming that fear. A practical action, however small, that requires courage. Start the project. Send the email. Share the idea. Pick up the brush, the pen, the camera. Start small. But know that it will have a big impact.

Practice 2: Take Risks

Creativity Involves Risk

You cannot swim for new horizons until you have courage to lose sight of the shore.
—William Faulkner

You can't innovate without risk. You can't create without stepping into the unknown. You can't change the world without the chance of failure. Believing in the potential of an idea means embracing uncertainty, and stepping into that uncertainty always takes faith. The pastor and founder of the Vineyard movement, John Wimber, used to say that faith is spelled r-i-s-k. The same is true of the kind of faith required in creativity. Sometimes the biggest creative breakthroughs happen when we take a risk, letting go of what's safe and comfortable, allowing something new to emerge. When you step out creatively, you have to leave behind the security of what worked yesterday.

A story is told of an experiment by scientists to explore how fleas respond to artificial limitations.[2] Fleas are naturally remarkable jumpers, able to leap distances up to two hundred times their own body height—equivalent to a human jumping over the Empire State Building. In the study, a group of fleas were placed inside a small glass box with a clear ceiling set at a specific height. After weeks of repeatedly hitting the ceiling, the fleas adapted. They began jumping just below the ceiling to avoid hitting it. Then, one day, the researchers removed the ceiling. Remarkably, the fleas continued to jump only to the height at which the ceiling had previously been. They'd grown so used to their constraints that they'd forgotten what they were truly capable of. They were now trapped by limitations that no longer existed.

What are the ceilings you've put on your soul's creativity? I bet they're not really there. But you'll never know without taking a risk. Great creativity demands risk. No risk, no gain.

INNOVATION

Let's look at how this worked in the determination Nehemiah demonstrated. His vision to rebuild the walls of Jerusalem seemed to be an impossible challenge. With no guarantees, he faced constant danger and relentless opposition. Yet he stepped out in faith. Risking everything, he boldly asked the occupying king for permission to rebuild his city: "If it pleases the king... let him send me to the city in Judah where my ancestors are buried so that I can rebuild it" (Nehemiah 2:5). It was a crazy idea, seemingly impossible. When the work began, his enemies mocked him: "What are those feeble Jews doing?" (4:2). And such was the opposition and intimidation that "those who carried materials did their work with one hand and held a weapon in the other" (4:17). Distractions came thick and fast. The threats mounted. And even his own people wavered. But Nehemiah stood firm: "I am carrying on" (6:3). And in just over seven weeks, despite the odds, the risk paid off and those old walls were rebuilt.

Some of the most impossible tasks you face might be achievable, but you'll never know if you don't take that first step and risk it. So, let me ask you—how comfortable are you with risk? Some of us thrive on stepping out in faith. Others lean toward caution. Neither is better than the other. But here's the thing: Your aptitude, your ability, your personality type—they're not the deciding factors. What matters is this: Will you trust the Creator to meet you in the leaps of faith you take?

Perhaps there have been moments in our story as a team when we took wild risks—when things felt impossible. But when you step into the thin air of faith, when you exercise the muscle of creative risk, when you're willing to put yourself out there, even at the cost of looking foolish, that's when God meets you. That's when breakthrough happens. Miracles don't tend to show up in the safety zone. They happen when we stretch in faith.

The Restoration of St John-at-Hackney

The restoration of St John-at-Hackney was a crazy risk. Built in 1792 but now a crumbling relic, the church was no longer fit for purpose.

But the truth? As a community, we didn't have the resources to make anything happen. We didn't have the capacity. We lacked the funds. We had no idea how we were going to pull it off.

Early on, we made a crucial call: We wouldn't play it safe. We'd take a risk and set the vision at a world-class level, because God isn't glorified by our settling for second best. He isn't reflected in mediocrity or the lowest common denominator. He deserves our best—our creativity, our ideas, our innovation. Sometimes I hear people say, "Oh, we mustn't make an idol out of excellence." And they're right. But I fear that we sometimes settle for making an idol out of mediocrity instead. You were created to reflect the glory of God. Don't settle for playing it safe.

So, aiming high, we started by making a list of world-class architects. And the top name on all our lists, the one we kept coming back to, was the renowned designer John Pawson CBE. John's work is iconic. He has been described by the *New York Times* as the father of modern architectural minimalism.[3] His stripped-back style has influenced everything from the aesthetic of the contemporary gallery to the design of Apple Stores. His influence runs deep, and his work includes London's Design Museum and the breathtaking Nový Dvůr monastery in Bohemia.[4] Any student of architecture knows his work. His books line the shelves of every serious architecture bookshop. His approach—distilling space to its purest form—has shaped a generation of design thinking. However, engaging John Pawson felt impossible. He was one of the most in-demand designers in the world, across multiple high-profile projects, with no reason to take notice of our little church restoration. What were the chances?

But we'd been learning to take a risk, to roll the dice of faith. Because when God is in the mix, the dice always seem to be loaded toward the miraculous. We took the plunge and sent an email, and to our surprise, John responded positively.

A few days later, we were walking through the interior of the crumbling church. John was silent, thoughtful, taking it all in. His team fired off questions, but he just observed. I couldn't determine if he had already decided we were a lost cause or not. Walking to the train station, I plucked up my courage and stopped to ask him whether he was interested in taking on the project and whether he thought it could work. As we walked down the hill, I turned to him and asked, "John, what do you think? Can we work with this?"

He stopped and simply said graciously, "Yes."

I pushed a little further. "And when do you think you might want to start?"

He looked at me with a twinkle in his eye and said, "I already have."

John would later reflect on that moment, saying, "I'm used to seeing the potential from the beginning, from the get-go."[5] Creativity demands that you take risks—because there's always the chance things might not work out as you imagined. But the alternative is far worse: settling for what's safe, predictable, and familiar.

Because if we've learned anything over the years, it's this: Keep a few wild ideas on the back burner. The kind that, if they ever came off, would make you laugh and laugh and laugh. Like the time we brought in a tattoo artist to give out free tattoos at the Renaissance London gathering. Right up until the night of the event, I was convinced it would be a disaster. People would think we'd lost the plot. The complaints would roll in. But as it turned out, several hundred people ended up getting tattoos, and it was a highlight. And in case you're wondering, I don't have any tattoos. I'm too afraid of the needle.

CHALLENGE

Here's your second bit of homework:

Where have you been playing it too safe?

Be honest. Make a list.

Practice 3: Make the Ask

There Is Power in Asking for Help

> *Ask and it will be given to you.*
> —Matthew 7:7

Your ideas have great potential—if you're willing to step out of your comfort zone, pluck up your courage, and communicate them with others. This is because great creativity has a unique ability to mobilise the human heart. The spark within you is one of the most powerful forces for good, but if you keep it hidden inside, it will never impact the world around you. So be brave. Collaborate. Ask for help. Talk to your heroes.

Apple founder Steve Jobs was twelve years old when he first started building computers. Rather than saving up and scraping together a few components, he decided to find the telephone number for Bill Hewlett, the founder of Hewlett-Packard. Jobs tells the story:

> I called up Bill Hewlett when I was 12 years old. He lived in Palo Alto. His number was still in the phonebook. And he answered the phone himself.

> He could have been ignored or dismissed, but Steve Jobs was thinking big.

> He said, "Yes?" And I said, "Hi, I'm Steve Jobs. I'm 12 years old. I'm a student in high school, and I want to build a frequency counter. And I was wondering if you had any spare parts I could have."

Bill Hewlett was so impressed with Steve's courage that he didn't just agree to give him the parts he needed for his project; he gave him a break that would change the future of personal computing.

INNOVATION

> He gave me a job that summer at Hewlett-Packard, working on the assembly line, putting nuts and bolts together on frequency counters. He got me a job in the place that built them.

Plucking up the courage to make that one phone call led to something bigger than Steve ever expected. Jobs learned the power of thinking big:

> I've never found anyone who said no or hung up the phone when I called. I just asked. Most people never pick up the phone and call. Most people never ask. And that's what separates, sometimes, the people that do things from the people that just dream about them. You gotta act.[6]

Sometimes you have to think big and make the ask. Every great pioneer I've ever met knows how to communicate their ideas, cast vision, and invite people to get on board. For some this comes naturally. For others it takes practice. But for all of us, it requires stepping beyond our comfort zone, opening our mouths, and making the ask. As James 4:2 reminds us, "You do not have because you do not ask."

It's time to step out with courage. Make the ask.

CHALLENGE

Think of one person you need to ask for help, advice, or collaboration.

Reach out.

Practice 4: Think Big

Shooting for the Moon Can Glorify God

*Shoot for the moon. Even if you miss,
you'll land among the stars.*
—Norman Vincent Peale

We decided to shoot for the moon with the rebuilding of St John-at-Hackney. When we took on the project, on paper there were a thousand reasons why it was impossible. When the church was a ruin, I used to go and sit in the balcony and pray. One verse in particular kept popping into my imagination, which became a promise that defined the project: "I will surely gather all of you, Jacob; I will surely bring together the remnant of Israel. I will bring them together like sheep in a pen, like a flock in its pasture; the place will throng with people" (Micah 2:12).

This was the promise we hung on to. Even though the building was mostly empty and falling in on itself, one day the place would be bursting with people. So early on we made the decision to aim to build something bigger than we needed and aimed to make it an exceptional space because we felt the community deserved something that truly pointed to the Creator's creativity and the greater glory of God. We built in faith. We'd chosen to set the bar high on the project: We wanted to create a cathedral of creativity, a huge, open space where everyone would be welcome. And we wanted to make sure it was calm, honouring to God, and beautiful.

John Pawson explained, "A church is spiritual, sacred, and is very different from anything else." The goal was simplicity: And yet, the building also needed to function as a busy working church, a highly complex live music and broadcast space that could go from hosting funerals one day to hosting some of the world's most creative musicians and artists another, all while delivering Sunday services week in and week out. In design terms, we kept on layering more complexity, more requirements.

And then we watched John Pawson's genius kick in: Everything was to be hidden, simple, spacious, and calm. Observing the world-class design

INNOVATION

team at work was an extraordinary lesson in thinking outside of the box in problem-solving and never settling for average. John described the process as, "a long, careful, painstaking business: ideas and reviewing them and then paring things back. I like things to be very logical. Of course, you have inspiration, and then you have things which you try, which are new, but generally, it's hard work and a constant review of the idea that you've had."[7]

We worked with more than five hundred extraordinarily talented craftsmen, designers, and architects who quietly poured over the design of the interior for hours with us. It took hours and hours of love and care: two hundred weeks of design and planning time. Eighty-four weeks of construction—with a pandemic thrown into the middle of it. The materials were sourced from all over the world, with items manufactured in the UK, USA, Italy, Germany, France, Denmark, China, India, Japan, and a dozen other countries. The glass windowpanes came from Mexico, the pendant lights from craftsmen just outside of Venice in Italy, and the chairs were custom designed and built in Denmark.

The finished church included two miles of sustainably sourced oak batons, seventy-five thousand screws and fixings, sixty miles of hidden cables, half a million lightbulbs—most of them hidden—and one metric ton of white paint. The line array of speakers was designed in a customized colour that the architect had specified. The attention to detail was mind-blowing. John revealed the extraordinary thinking required to enable this to happen: "The simplicity here is deceptive," he explained. "There is some magic I suppose, but mostly it's hard work. And trying to rationally see the basics of trying to create a space which will be conducive to being sacred. There are no guarantees. You can get the proportions right, if you can get the light right, the restriction of ornament right, the colours, and yet you can fail."[8]

Early on we decided to try to build something great—and we never looked back. This informed the little decisions and the big decisions. At the time, the whole thing seemed impossible, the challenges were too large, the obstacles impassable. Every penny had to be raised—a combination of sacrificial goodwill, huge support from heritage and public bodies, and endless miracles of provision. And looking back, despite all the battles we faced, it was worth it in the end. Now, hundreds of thousands of people have come through the doors of the re-opened church, and the place is alive with hope. Underneath all of this was a big idea that drove the decisions we made: decisions to execute the creative to the highest standard, to value space, honour God, work hard, and shoot for the moon.

Now when you walk into the church, you no longer enter under glass punctuated by a bullet hole. Instead, you pass a couple of plaques on the wall: one commemorating the restoration project, which ends with that verse from Micah 2:12, because now the place is bursting with people. And the second plaque is a memorial to the man who completed the original building of the church in 1797: John James Watson. His memorial simply says at the end, *"Soli Deo Gloria"*—to God alone be the glory. In the end, God—the God of the immeasurably more—gets all the glory for our best endeavours, our moonshots, our crazy ideas.

CHALLENGE

What's the biggest, most audacious idea you have?

Map out the first step.

Practice 5: Have More Ideas
Volume Creates Breakthrough

> *The best way to have a good idea*
> *is to have lots of ideas.*
> —Linus Pauling

The next practice of courageous creativity is to have lots and lots and lots of ideas. Most of them will be terrible. Most will never see the light of day. But the only way to find a great idea is to push through the bad ones—to generate, discard, refine, and keep going. The Bible is full of encouragement and stories that teach this principle. Zechariah 4:10 reminds us not to despise the day of small beginnings. Elijah's servant, in 1 Kings 18:44, saw only "a cloud as small as a man's hand" rising from the sea—just a hint of what would become a mighty downpour. The seeds of new creative life are sown in fragile ground, sprouting as green shoots of small ideas. Rarely do breakthrough ideas arrive fully formed. Most of the time they require the courage to allow lots and lots of them to surface—to give them space, to test, to refine.

Think of the parable of the sower. Jesus described a farmer scattering seed generously, lavishly, knowing that some would take root and bear fruit, while others would not. The same should be true of your approach to creativity. If you truly want to innovate, you must be prepared to have lots and lots of ideas—without fear, without hesitation, without holding back. Scatter the seed generously.

You see this principle at play in the lives of many of the great creatives. Take Pablo Picasso, for example. While he is widely known for a body of around a thousand major works, this represents only 2 percent of his total creative output. Over his lifetime, he produced an estimated fifty thousand works—including paintings, sculptures, drawings, ceramics, and prints—demonstrating the sheer scale of his relentless creativity.

Volume

The secret here is to start wide—don't overthink it. Volume creates breakthrough. Start a list of ideas. Fill your sketchbook, sticky notes, voice memos—whatever works for you. Cover the whiteboard of your imagination with raw material. Let the Holy Spirit inspire idea after idea, without rushing to judge them. To do this, you're going to need to turn down the perfectionism dial. Too often we shut off our ideas before they've even had a chance to be heard. Instead, get comfortable with allowing bad ideas to exist in your creative process. Give yourself permission to incubate ideas that may, in time, turn out to be brilliant. Or that may turn out to be terrible.

David Bayles and Ted Orland, authors of *Art & Fear*, tell a story about a photography class at the University of Florida.[9] On the first day of the term, the professor split the students into two groups. The first group was told that their work would be graded purely on the number of photos they produced. The more they submitted, the higher their grade. The second group, however, had to submit just one image for the entire term—but it had to be flawless. By the end of the term, something surprising had happened. Every single one of the highest-graded photos came from the quantity group—not the quality group. By focusing on volume, they learned through trial and error, experimenting with different lighting, composition, and techniques. Meanwhile, the quality group spent the term theorising about perfection. But in the end, they had very little to show for it. The single image they produced was often mediocre, and none of them made the top marks. The win is not quality at this stage, it's quantity.

Refining

Next comes the hard work of refining. A great way to do this is what I like to call "napkin time." Can you write the idea on the back of a napkin and explain it to someone? Will it make sense? Start sketching it out. Refine, simplify, and test. Ideas need space to breathe, but at some point, they also need shaping. I once spoke with a celebrated music producer about the process of creating a hit song. He explained, "Out of a hundred song ideas I hear, about ninety go straight in the bin."

That might sound harsh, but you still need those hundred ideas to get to the gold. From the remaining ten he keeps, he works with them—turning them around in his head, playing with the melodies and lyrics, rearranging them, investing time in them. And out of those ten, there might be one or two that truly stand out—songs worth developing further. That's when the real work begins. Those final few enter a much clearer process of investment. Serious time is spent refining, shaping, and getting them right. If you step back and think about that return rate, it's a hundred to one. Yet, so often we settle for just one idea and expect it to be the breakthrough.

INNOVATION

Instead, think of the creative process like a funnel. When you pour liquid into a funnel, it starts wide at the top, allowing for plenty of room. But as it moves downward, it gradually narrows, refining and focusing until it passes through into the container in a concentrated flow. Your creative process needs to work the same way: Start wide, generate volume, and filter the best ideas. For every thousand ideas, you might funnel down to refining a hundred. Out of those, maybe ten will see the light of day. And be prepared—nine out of ten may ultimately fail. But that one? The one that makes it could change everything.

Malcolm Gladwell explored this in his study of genius, not as some innate talent, but as something shaped through time, effort, and persistence. He famously described the ten thousand–hour rule—the idea that mastery comes from working, refining, and practicing over time.[10] But perhaps another way to think about it is that real breakthrough happens when you've refined ten thousand ideas.

Again, God is no stranger to this process. The Bible describes how God tests the heart, using the analogy of the crucible for silver and the furnace for gold (Proverbs 17:3). The skilled jeweller who works with metal will tell you the refining removes all the impurities, revealing the weaknesses, and brings them to the surface so they can be removed. The refining process is painful. It requires a lot of energy. But it's also the only way to produce pure gold. The same is true creatively.

Date Your Dreams

The final stage of selecting your best ideas is what we might call *dating your dreams*. Once you feel like you've landed on something really good, don't rush too quickly to execute. Instead, sit with the idea. Take it out for dinner. Go dancing. Have fun. Introduce it to your friends and family. Let it live through the highs and lows of your day. Come back to it again and again. Bringing a great idea to life is a little like falling in love—it takes time, attention, and investment. So, have lots of ideas. Refine them. Date your dreams. And then, when you find something that really works—when you strike gold—double down. Jesus used this very principle when he described a merchant searching for fine pearls:

"When he found one of great value, he went away and sold everything he had and bought it" (Matthew 13:45–46).

Then, after hundreds or even thousands of ideas, you will strike something that feels like a pearl of great price. When that happens, drop everything.

CHALLENGE

Do you have a system for collecting your ideas?

Start one now.

Pause and Recap

So, let's recap our five habits for growing your creative courage:

Practice 1: Be Brave—Creativity Requires Boldness
Practice 2: Take Risks—Creativity Involves Risk
Practice 3: Make the Ask—There Is Power in Asking for Help
Practice 4: Think Big—Shooting for the Moon Can Glorify God
Practice 5: Have More Ideas—Volume Creates Breakthrough

Take stock. Pause for a moment.

What's jumping out at you? Which practice resonates most? Have you begun putting any of these into action? Are there concrete changes you're planning to make? If you've already started stepping out, chances are you're encountering some frustration.

Maybe you've hit a brick wall, stepped out courageously, and found yourself flat on your face. Let me assure you: You're not alone. It's a core part of the creative process.

INNOVATION

So, here's what we're going to do: We're going to talk honestly about when things go wrong—because hidden inside these setbacks are the seeds of your greatest breakthroughs. As Brené Brown says, "There is no innovation and creativity without failure. Period."[11]

So, what do we do if it all goes wrong?

Well, it's high time we talked about failure.

SPARK CIRCLE

Circle back through this chapter of Spark.

Notice
Think of a time when your creativity required courage. Which practice stood out the most to you?

Name
If you could ask anyone to collaborate, who would you ask? Work back through each of the challenge sections in this chapter: Which might you try?

Next Step
What would dating your dreams look like in the week ahead? Provide feedback to your Spark Circle.

CHAPTER 7

Make Friends with Failure

Do not fear mistakes. There are none.
—Miles Davis

Panic-cooking frozen turkey, as it turns out, is never a good idea. The first sign that something had gone badly wrong was when people started vomiting in the middle of the night. The day before, we had rushed to defrost a batch of frozen turkey to feed our homeless guests at the newly launched shelter. The result? Mass food poisoning—affecting some of the most vulnerable people in our community. Most of the members of our little staff team were violently ill for the next forty-eight hours. It was brutal.

Clearly, we needed serious help in the food department. We wanted our homeless drop-in to be a banquet, not a crime scene. So, we gave up trying to cater ourselves and started looking for a better way forward. We started praying for a divine intervention: a food miracle. After all, God has a good track record on these.

A week later, the miracle came. I was in a conversation with a group of local business leaders when a gentle voice spoke up: "I think we can help you." A few days later, Olivia and I sat down for tea with Sam Clark.

Sam, along with her husband, also called Sam, had started the acclaimed East London restaurant MORO twenty years earlier. As chefs, they had reached the top of the food world: cookbooks, accolades, a reputation as culinary pioneers. They were legends in the London food scene.

MAKE FRIENDS WITH FAILURE

Over a cup of tea, we talked about the power of good food and how food brings people together. As with so many people I've met at the top of their game, there was a generosity to Sam and Sam's way of thinking that was inspiring. "We'd love to help: We want to make a difference," they said.

Just like that, a plan was born. We would bring the homeless, the cold, the hungry, the vulnerable; we would open our doors to those in need in the neighbourhood. Sam and Sam would open their kitchen and cook. A few weeks later, that plan became reality. That morning, as I stood outside the church, I watched a London taxi turn the corner. Inside was Sam Clark, who had come straight from the restaurant, with several huge vats of the most delicious lamb tagine you've ever tasted. This was a fabulous dish, one of the stars of their award-winning menu. Melt-in-the-mouth lamb, slow-cooked in Middle-Eastern spices, served on a bed of couscous and roasted tomatoes. I can still taste it now.

That day the homeless of Hackney ate the same meal as the diners fighting for a table at MORO. But there was more: I remember looking across the room as dozens of hungry men and women feasted. There, behind the makeshift kitchen counter of our drop-in was Sam Clark, serving our guests with the same care and passion as she would do from behind the counter of her award-winning restaurant.

Needless to say, nobody died of food poisoning. And everybody came back the next week. The drop-in—Lighthouse—went on to serve half a million meals across East London during the dark years of the pandemic. When the pandemic hit and the city ground to a halt, Lighthouse was able to step into the gap where other local agencies—and even the state—couldn't. And to this day, it has helped thousands get back on their feet—offering not just food, but hope, encouragement, and connection.

Failure Is Your Best Teacher

That day we learned an invaluable lesson: Failure is a far better teacher than success. Had we stuck with rubbery, mediocre defrosted turkey,

INNOVATION

Lighthouse would have been fine. We'd have muddled through. But the catastrophic—almost terminal—beginnings of Lighthouse forced us to rethink, to adapt, to get better. It taught us to make friends with failure, because failure is where real growth happens.

I didn't set out to write a chapter on failure. But recently a friend said to me, "It all sounds like it's been brilliant. But have there been things that were hard? Have there been any failures?" The question caught me off guard. Because of course, when you experience failure, those moments sit deep within you. They're painful. Humiliating. Embarrassing. You don't forget them. But we don't tend to boast about them either. It's tempting to focus only on our successes—the trophies on the mantelpiece, the highlights on our CV, the wins we showcase on LinkedIn.

I've had the huge privilege of working with Nicky and Pippa Gumbel for the past twenty-five years. They've been great friends, mentors, bosses, and encouragers. Time and time again, especially when I was a young leader, Nicky created space for me to take risks and step out in courage. And sometimes things went badly wrong. Projects flopped. Initiatives failed. I made terrible mistakes—too many to list here.

On one particularly humbling occasion, I was apologetically explaining to Nicky what had happened. Most bosses would have been rightly irritated. Instead, he smiled gently and said, "It's fine. Don't worry. At least you're moving—having a go." Then he added something I've never forgotten: *"You can steer a ship that's moving."*

I felt so relieved. But more than that, his words shifted my whole perspective on failure. I stopped seeing it as something to fear. Failure, I realised, is proof that you're trying. It's a necessary companion on the road to growth.

Here's the point:
Failure is your friend.
Failure is your best teacher.
If you're not failing, you're not learning.
If you're not failing, you're not growing.
Consider your greatest failures. The ones that still make you wince.

MAKE FRIENDS WITH FAILURE

The ones that, hopefully, you can laugh about now. Some will still feel raw. That's okay. Have the courage to sit with that discomfort for a moment. Ask yourself, "What did I learn?" Because the creative life is a school of hard knocks. We're not meant to be superheroes. Yes, creativity might feel like our secret superpower—but we don't need to be invincible. As Paul reminded us in 2 Corinthians 4:7: "We have this treasure in jars of clay to show that this all-surpassing power is from God and not from us."

The Original Lightbulb Moment

Thomas Edison's invention of the lightbulb is one of history's most famous lessons in failure. The year was 1878, and Edison and his team were deep in the challenge of creating an incandescent lamp. Every attempt ended in failure. He tested thousands of materials for the filament—plant fibres, cardboard, even strands of hair. Nothing worked. Eventually he discovered that carbonised bamboo showed some promise. With painstaking precision, he built a prototype—only for it to fail. He adjusted the design. That version failed too. The third? Another failure. And so it continued, again and again, until, famously, he had created ten thousand versions of the bulb—all of which had failed. "I have not failed," he insisted. "I've just found ten thousand ways that won't work."[1]

Edison never saw failure as a negative, but as a positive and essential part of the innovation process. He lived by the rule that, in his words, "the real measure of success is the number of experiments that can be crowded into twenty-four hours."[2] Eventually the trial and error paid off. But have you considered this? Edison's real lightbulb moment wasn't the success of finally inventing something that worked. The failures are what refined his process. The true breakthroughs weren't in the final glowing filament but in the thousands of ways that didn't work.

Without failure, you can't grow. Without failure, you'll never know how to make something better. The worst thing you can do creatively is settle for early success. The most powerful thing you can do is embrace the things that go wrong and ask, "How can I get better?" This is the story of every entrepreneurial breakthrough. Every innovator and pioneer knows the secret: If you want to make a difference, you have to be okay with failure. Rather than seeing failure as your enemy, you have to treat it as your friend. "Creative geniuses don't succeed by avoiding failure. They succeed by experimenting often, accepting failure as an essential step toward innovation." This is the conclusion of Tom and David Kelley in their book *Creative Confidence*. They assert that failure, when analysed and understood, becomes a tool for refinement, shaping stronger and more innovative creative outcomes.[3]

Failure helps lay the foundation for future fruitfulness. If necessity is the mother of invention and boredom is the mother of brilliance, then failure is the mother of fruitfulness. This has been the experience of so many of the great creative minds. The Beatles were turned down by four record labels before finally being signed. Steven Spielberg was rejected by three film schools. Picasso made thousands of works of art before the world recognised his genius. Failure is not the end; it's part of the process.

For some of us, learning to fail will mean letting go of the idol of success and giving ourselves permission to try, even if things go wrong. You need bad to make good. Your first song will be bad. Your first short story. Your first idea. Your first business. Your first attempt at something new. Failure isn't the enemy; it's the process. Your hundredth idea might be the one that breaks through. But you'll never get there without ninety-nine failures first. Creativity expert Sir Ken Robinson says, "If you're not prepared to be wrong, you'll never come up with anything original."[4]

I've shared things that have gone well—the lessons we've learned, the moments of breakthrough. But for every success story, there have been multiple failures. Things that didn't work. Ideas that flopped. I could write a whole book just on those—it would certainly be entertaining. But then sometimes failures force you to get better, to improve.

MAKE FRIENDS WITH FAILURE

> I've missed more than nine thousand shots in my career.
> I've lost almost three hundred games.
> Twenty-six times I've been trusted to take the game-winning shot and missed.
> I've failed over and over and over again in my life.
> And that is why I succeed.
>
> —Michael Jordan

The Million-Pound Letter

Let me tell you the story of the first music show I ever hosted at SAINT. It was the early days—back when the building was still crumbling and we were just beginning to experiment with opening up the church for music events. As a community, we had a vision: to see our church become a cathedral of creativity. And so we started exploring how we could collaborate with brilliant creatives to host extraordinary events in the space. The first of these was with one of the tech giants that was launching its flagship streaming service. The company wanted to kick it off with a gig at the church featuring the most successful British solo artist in UK chart history—Robbie Williams.[5]

Robbie Williams was used to playing stadiums, not small churches. And yet, somehow, this was happening. The tickets sold out in seconds. The buzz was huge. The production was on a massive scale—weeks of planning, cutting-edge visuals. A team had 3D-mapped the entire interior of the church. Custom laser projections were ready to light up the walls. Camera crews were everywhere, scoping the sight lines. It was shaping up to be something incredible.

Then disaster struck.

Just days before the event, the health and safety adviser I'd brought in dropped the bombshell: The fire capacity for the building was significantly lower than the number of tickets that had sold. Cue an awkward conversation with one of the world's largest and most powerful companies, which had just invested hundreds of thousands of pounds on

INNOVATION

planning, creative, and marketing for this show. Understandably, they were not thrilled. And then came the letter, which politely outlined that because the church had apparently shrunk in size overnight, meaning the show was unlikely to be able to go ahead, this whole situation was our responsibility. And that, as a result, it seemed we might be liable for the cost of the entire event. My blood ran cold. We had made a huge error: We had booked an event, signed a contract, and sold tickets for a show that we'd not thought through properly. It was devastating. I wasn't quite sure what vicars were supposed to do when their churches went bankrupt. I must have missed that chapter in theological training. But life is a great teacher, and in that moment I was about to learn on the job.

Thankfully, we found a way through. The solution? What appeared to be the largest number of portable fire extinguishers ever assembled in one place, and every family member and friend we could rope in, all wearing high-vis vests as makeshift fire marshals. It worked. The fire capacity restriction was lifted. We did the show. It was so much fun. But it's not a situation I'd want to repeat.

And Robbie Williams, sitting backstage—or rather, in my little office, since that was the closest thing we had to backstage—was genuinely intrigued by the idea that we'd opened up the space to collaborate: the church, the vision, the idea of hosting artists in spaces like this. Time and time again, when we host music events, artists comment on their experience visiting SAINT. They talk about what an extraordinary environment it is—how different it feels from the usual sticky-carpet, plastic-sofa type of venues they spend their lives in. There's something about the rhythm of prayer and community that makes a space precious.

That day we learned two things: First, you can never have enough fire extinguishers. Second, your mistakes are a better teacher than your successes. Success is comfortable. Mistakes make you work. In the aftermath of the million-pound letter, we started the urgent work of redesigning and rethinking the church space that led us to rebuild St John-at-Hackney with John Pawson. The lessons we learned in the early days became the teachers that informed how we designed the future church.

MAKE FRIENDS WITH FAILURE

Here's another example of what this looked like: Working with John Pawson's team, there was one particular design challenge that demanded an enormous amount of time and energy to solve. It wasn't hiding the cables—though there were sixty miles of them, threading through the building like arteries. That was complex, but at least there was a clear way to approach it. The real challenge was the sanctuary itself: how to create a space that could seamlessly transition between different uses—a funeral one moment, a school assembly the next, then a Sunday service, then a gig.

The mission was ambitious. The vision was bold. And working with world-class creatives, we set out to make something magical happen in the space. From Saturday night, hosting some of the biggest bands on the planet, to Sunday morning, transforming the space back into a sacred setting for worship, was a constant shift. One night Coldplay might be on stage; the next morning the church doors would open for a traditional service, complete with robes, incense, and people who had been attending services in the building for decades. The congregants weren't particularly fazed by who had been there the night before—they just wanted their church to feel like church.

The stage itself became one of the biggest design challenges. It needed to function as a gig-ready, flat-fronted performance stage while also seamlessly transforming into something more intimate for worship without creating a sense of separation. We spent weeks, months even, experimenting with different models. We started with retractable steps, but they didn't quite work. Then we tested different heights of staging, looking for the perfect balance. These were problematic from a safety point of view. On and on this conversation went, and dozens of iterations and designs were produced until finally we landed on the solution that you see today: a beautiful rounded stage with steps that spin magically in on themselves to create a flat-fronted stage in seconds.

Today the stage looks like it was designed instinctively, like it's always been there. In reality it represents hours and hours and weeks and weeks of back-and-forth hard work of imagination. But none of this would have happened were it not for the million-pound letter, which forced us to work hard before the breakthrough came. Mistakes make you better.

INNOVATION

Failure isn't fatal. It's formational. Failure shapes character and grows humility. And humility is a hallmark of creative excellence. The most groundbreaking creatives I've met know this. They have this combination of a quiet hunger and humility: They're always open to learning, always challenging, never resting on their laurels. They're constantly asking questions like, "How can we learn? How can we grow? What feedback can we take on board?" Dieter Rams, the renowned German designer behind Braun and Vitsœ, put it like this: "Good design is thorough down to the last detail. Nothing must be arbitrary or left to chance. Care and accuracy in the design process show respect."[6]

The point is this: It's always worth pushing. Through some of the events we've hosted at SAINT, we've had the privilege of observing some of the world's most talented creative teams at work. Watching them close up, again and again I've noticed that the best teams don't coast: They sharpen one another, stretch themselves, and refuse to settle for mediocrity or the easy way out. They care enough about the work, and about one another, to make sure it's done as well as it possibly can be. They turn over the problems in their minds with delicate persistence and humility.

> *Matter matters.*
> *You have to have a place to help you with the spiritual . . .*
> *to be closer to God.*
> —John Pawson

In Praise of Ignorance

> *The magic is not in the analysing or the understanding.*
> *The magic lives in the wonder of what we do not know.*
> —Rick Rubin

Let's face it, no one likes to look stupid. Sometimes the fear of not being an expert holds us back. We are afraid of creating something new because we feel like we don't know enough. We're afraid we'll get it wrong, that we haven't fully understood, that we're stepping out in ignorance. But here's the thing: You really don't have to have it all figured out before you begin. It's okay to be ignorant about things. In fact, I think it's sometimes essential. And, before you write me off as even more of a world-class ignoramus, I'm not alone in this view. I have good friends in my corner on this one.

Plato, in his *Apology*, captured a pivotal moment where Socrates revealed that true wisdom begins with recognising one's own ignorance: "I do not think I know what I do not know."[7] This approach runs through the thought life of Socratic wisdom, classical philosophy, Christian theology, and scientific enquiry right to you and me sitting here today scratching our heads. Socrates had been told by the oracle of Delphi that he was the wisest man in all of Athens. But Socrates was not quite so sure the oracle had it right, so he investigated and, as we might expect, discovered that other people knew things he did not know. And moreover, knowing that he didn't know everything was actually vital. Socrates put it like this: "I am wiser than this man; for neither of us appears to know anything great and good; but he fancies he knows something, although he knows nothing, whereas I do not know anything, so I do not fancy I do."[8]

Curiosity is the base camp we climb from if we want to ascend the mountain of creativity. When we admit that we don't know, our ideas become open terrain, ready to be explored. A healthy dose of humility is essential if we're to truly approach our challenges with clarity and grace. Knowing that we don't know keeps us inquisitive. It keeps us exploring, and then we can learn and grow. If you look around the world today, you'll find many of the really stupid things that go down happen because people have stopped listening and learning and, as a consequence, assume they know it all.

The implication of this? Knowing we don't know it all means there is no such thing as a bad idea. We're freed to imagine, innovate, risk, try, explore, fail, and learn every step of the way. When people say, "There's no such thing as a bad idea," it's usually in that semi-reassuring but mostly patronising tone that really means "Your idea sucks." We've all been in a meeting where someone just said something really out there and now we're all awkwardly staring at the floor as silence fills the room. "There's no such thing as a bad idea," we repeat, while tumbleweed blows through the conversation.

The more we think we know about a subject, the less room our brains have for noticing new ideas, perspectives, and information, and we stop learning. We stop being curious, and we dampen our creativity. Sustaining deep creativity, however, requires a degree of open-mindedness—a willingness to step beyond what you think you know and explore what might be possible. If we're going to innovate, we need to constantly make space for curiosity, experimentation, and mystery.

An interesting body of research describes this as "cognitive entrenchment," suggesting that the more we know about something, the less room our brains have for flexible thinking and creativity.[9] Too much information can be a creativity killer. Of course research and understanding are vital. It's just that we create most fluidly when we don't let the fear of the unknown stifle our creative flow.[10]

There's another danger lurking here: that we feel we need to be experts before making a start. Don't let a lack of knowledge stop you from being interested, experimental, or alive to creative curiosity. In fact, it's often *that* attitude—a growth mindset rather than a fixed one—that fuels great innovation. The intrigued willingness to ask questions, pick at things, explore ideas, and risk looking foolish is often what leads to the most groundbreaking ideas. This openness is a key ingredient in discovering the things that truly spark to life. And then sometimes the fire of failure contains the seeds of success. Our best ideas rise phoenix-like from the ashes of defeat. We are resurrection people, after all.

The Lego Story

When I was a kid, I was obsessed with Lego. I always had the little blocks in my pockets, and a familiar sound in our household was the agonising scream of an unsuspecting adult after stepping on one of those tiny plastic bricks. Few things are more painful than stepping on a rogue Lego piece.

MAKE FRIENDS WITH FAILURE

Years later I was fascinated to learn the story of how Lego came to be. It's a story of faith overcoming failure and pain—and it all started with a man named Ole Kirk Christiansen. He was a carpenter from the Danish town of Billund in the 1930s. After tragically losing his wife, he was left to raise his four young sons on his own. With little money to spare, he began crafting simple wooden toys for his boys. They were beautifully made and soon caught the attention of others. Before long, people started asking if they could buy them, but scaling up was a struggle, and after a few years Christiansen's business collapsed. Rather than calling it a day, he picked himself up, learned from his failures, and decided his venture needed a fresh start. He rebranded, choosing the name Lego—a name he later discovered, quite fittingly, means "to put together" in Latin.

Christiansen had strong faith, and when life hit him hardest—loss, failure, facing destitution—he had an encounter with the Creator Spirit. Jesus made himself known in that moment of despair, and Christiansen had a vision. "I saw, as if in a vision, a large factory where busy people hurried in and out, where raw materials were brought in, and finished products were dispatched," he later recalled.

At the time, Lego was still making wooden toys. Then, in 1942, disaster struck once more. Christiansen's entire factory burned to the ground. Everything was lost. Again, he could have given up and let failure have the final word. But out of the ashes of that disaster, something new was born. Instead of rebuilding exactly as before, Christiansen pivoted. He started experimenting with a new technology—moulded plastic. It was a risk. A step into the unknown. But it led to the iconic Lego brick we know today.

As of today, over a trillion LEGO pieces have been produced, and the business is valued at $13 billion. It's still in the hands of Christiansen's family. Reflecting on his father's life, Godtfred Christiansen said, "I am convinced that Father's faith in God, which was evident in everything he did, helped carry him through his grief and the difficulties that followed. His faith made him an active man. It gave him the courage and solace that enabled him to take on new responsibilities—and the strength to see a job through despite hardship."[11]

Constraints Make You Interesting

Failure and hardship focus the mind, test the mettle of your calling, and refine you. So often, it's the moments of greatest inconvenience and interruption that force us to think differently.

In the summer of 1665, twenty-two-year-old Isaac Newton found himself in an unexpected lockdown. A severe outbreak of plague had shut down Cambridge University, forcing students into rural isolation. Frustrated and cut off from his library, Newton returned to his family home—Woolsthorpe Manor, a quiet sheep farm in Lincolnshire—unable to continue the formal studies he had planned.

Our constraints contain the seeds of our greatest innovations. For Newton, what began as disruption became one of the most groundbreaking periods of discovery in scientific history.

With no lectures to attend, Newton threw himself into independent research. In what became known as his *annus mirabilis*—his "year of wonders"—he made some of the most important breakthroughs in science. It was here, in the quiet of forced exile, that he developed his theories of motion, calculus, and optics.

And yes, it was here that he sat thinking beneath his now-famous apple tree, the one that sparked his revelation about the theory of gravity. That apple tree is still there in that garden—and as a rather wonderful side note, centuries later, a cutting from that very same tree travelled into space on a NASA mission, defying the very force it helped define.[12]

What invisible force is keeping you back? What is constraining you? Is it time, resources, finances, permission, or confidence? Perhaps you're stuck in a job that doesn't ignite your passion or your time is stretched thin by family commitments. But what if these constraints weren't ceilings? What if, instead, they were the very conditions that could force you to think more creatively?

Creativity doesn't die in constraint—it's born there. Constraints make you interesting. They push your mind to find solutions you wouldn't have considered otherwise. Some of your best work will emerge not in unlimited freedom but in the creative tension of limitation. Ask any artist preparing for a show—the frantic burst of energy in those final days, the urgency of finishing those last pieces, often unlocks something new. The same is true for writers facing a deadline. Pressure forces focus. Deadlines sharpen ideas. And constraints? They don't just limit you—they shape you. As the great composer Igor Stravinsky noted, "The more constraints one imposes, the more one frees oneself of the chains that shackle the spirit."[13]

What have you learned from your mistakes? Are there failures you'd rather not confront—failures that might, in fact, hold lessons for your future success? Don't get too comfortable. Keep pushing yourself beyond what feels safe. Growth happens at the edge of your comfort zone.

Allow discomfort to grow you. Push yourself. Learn new things. Be inquisitive, be curious, experiment—and you'll grow far more than if you play it safe. Sure, you'll get things wrong. But that's part of the journey. If you're not making mistakes, you're probably not growing. If you're not getting things wrong, you're not trying new things. If you want your creativity to have an impact, push beyond your comfort zone. Overcome your fear of failure, and you'll find there's no limit to what you can achieve.

And then, let's be honest—sometimes things happen that are completely out of your control. There's no lesson to learn, no silver lining. They're just really hard. This chapter on failure isn't meant to be a pep talk. It's supposed to be a reality check. When you risk everything—when you step out in faith, hope, and love—there will be moments that test you. Moments of deep disappointment, of loss, of sadness.

Then there are the moments when none of it makes sense. The glorious miracles but also the unanswered prayers: the tears in the night, the unexpected grief. My friend Reggie—co-founder of our brewery—had grown to become a mentor and encourager through the early days of the SAINT story. Tragically, he passed away from cancer in the prime of his life. He was taken far too soon, and I still mourn that we didn't get more time to do more fun things. When you build something new with friends, the road isn't always smooth. It's marked with the potholes of pain, challenge, opposition, and discouragement.

INNOVATION

We will experience sorrow. There will be disappointments, heartache, and pain. It's impossible to do anything new or bring about change without facing these things. But what we can do is choose—to keep loving, to keep going, to keep the faith, to hold fast, to take heart.

Death Threats

There have also been times of genuine opposition at SAINT. The first I heard about my imminent death was from one of our regular street drinkers who was sitting on a bench at the front of the church. He said, "Oh, Priest, nice to see you. Glad you're still alive. I guess they didn't get you after all." When I questioned the man about this strange statement, I learned there had been a discussion in the criminal underworld as to whether it might be better for me to be removed from my post, and a local drug gang had hatched a plan to go to my house and execute me.

The backstory is that the churchyard is the largest green space in Hackney Central and consequently is a place where much of the area's hard drug trade happens. When the police swoop in to break up one of these drug gangs, because the land is linked to the church, the gangs sometimes assume that we are involved in the police operation. This is not exactly ideal when dealing with organised crime. Writing this a few years later, I realise that not all organised crime is, well, that organised, and thankfully not all creative ideation leads to literal execution. Praise God, I'm still here. But for a while, I was definitely looking over my shoulder.

A few months after I learned of the plot to take me out, I saw one of the guys who would normally be hanging out in the gardens stirring up mischief show up at a service. He was sitting at the back of the church, looking angry, and he spent the whole service pointing at me. At the end, he found me in the crowd and confronted me, clearly unhappy with the growth and life of the church. He got heated, jabbing his finger into my chest, his frustration spilling over. A small crowd gathered, like ringside spectators at a boxing match, waiting to see if my opponent would land a punch squarely on my nose. And it looked like he just might.

So, I started praying under my breath, *Lord, help me.* In that moment, something sparked in my imagination—a little nudge from the Holy Spirit: *Pray for his hip.*

I hesitated for a second, then plucked up the courage.

"Can I stop you there?" I said.

He looked a little shocked, mid-rant.

"I don't mean to interrupt you," I continued, "but do you have something wrong with your hip? And if so, would you mind if I prayed for it to be healed?"

There was a long pause, and I could feel the eyes of the crowd drilling into me. This was about to be a miracle moment, a breaking in of the kingdom of God. This was going to be a moment we'd tell our grandchildren about.

The little crowd waited in hushed expectancy.

Finally, the guy opened his mouth and said, "No, there's nothing wrong with my hip."

I was left feeling like a spiritual fraud, but at least the moment broke his angry chain of thought, and I was grateful when he turned around and stormed out the doors. Later that day, I was crossing the churchyard with my youngest child when I saw him standing with a group of men. They shouted across the ground, "We see you. We won't get you now because you've got your kid with you, but we'll get you later." I took a different route back to the church that evening, and for the next few weeks, I prayed every time I left the house.

Then, after a couple of weeks, I turned the corner down the side alley near the church and found myself bumping into the man physically. There was no escape. I started to pray under my breath, fearing the worst. But he stopped me with a smile on his face, looking intrigued. He said, "Priest, how did you know I had something wrong with my hip?" Shocked, I told him I had felt the Holy Spirit say to me that I needed to pray for his hip. He looked at me and said, "Well, the truth is, I've had a bad hip for two years. The pain is killing me, but

INNOVATION

I've never told anyone." Then, sheepishly, he added, "Priest, would you pray for me?" I placed a hand on his shoulder and said a simple prayer, asking God to heal him, before making excuses and heading off as quickly as I could.

About a week later, I bumped into him again in the same spot. This time he stopped me with a big grin on his face, and he was with two friends. He said excitedly, "Priest, Priest, you know we prayed for my hip? It's better! What's happened?" I said to him, "Well, here's the deal," and I found myself saying, "It's like this: Jesus loves you. I don't know why [as I said the second part of that phrase, I regretted it]. But he seems to have a soft spot for you. That's why he's healed you."

He turned to his friends and said, "Did you hear that, boys? God's got a soft spot for me!" He was absolutely delighted. Then the two guys he was with asked me to pray for them—one of them needed prayer to get a job. The next time I saw them, his friend had apparently got a job the next day, and now he wanted me to pray for his other three friends who needed jobs. A chain reaction of grace had started.

The point is this: Sometimes the situations that feel scariest and most desperate are the places where God will meet you most powerfully. When things are darkest, the light will shine brightest. You're going to face failures, opposition, setbacks, and sadness, but the real test will be how you approach these challenges. Will you be able to pick yourself up and turn your eyes to heaven, or will you give up at the first sign of opposition? Great breakthroughs happen when we bring our brokenness, not our brilliance, before God.

It's often our failures and weaknesses—the moments of desperation—that draw us closer to the loving hands of our Creator. When we try to do everything in our own strength, with no need for God, we miss the opportunity for him to work deeply in us. But when we are brought to our knees, God is able to begin his deep work in our souls. While God is the Creator and we are made in his image as co-creators, his great work—his primary mission in our lives—is to shape us to become more like him so that we become "conformed to the image of his Son" (Romans 8:29).

MAKE FRIENDS WITH FAILURE

The Giant

If there's one work of art that defines the Renaissance, it's a sculpture that has become one of the most instantly recognisable in the world. But like much creativity, the genesis of great work can be slow and painful. If you'd visited Florence, Italy, in 1501 you'd have seen a curious sight on the grounds of the Duomo, the city's great cathedral. There, lying on its side, covered in moss and dirt, was a massive lump of marble known as "The Giant." This block of marble, quarried from the famous Fantiscritti quarry in Carrara in 1464, had been intended for a supersized sculpture of a biblical figure. Carrara's quarry was renowned for producing flawless, pure white marble, but when sculptors began working on the piece, they found the stone too difficult to carve.

First, the artist Agostino began to shape the marble, but upon finding the stone to be of poor quality, he refused to continue. The cathedral then turned to Rossellino, who also attempted to work with it, but again, he was unable to make progress. The marble had too many veins; it was brittle and full of pinholes that made creating a smooth surface impossible. Eventually the material was abandoned and the giant was left discarded, gathering moss in the cathedral gardens, where it languished for the rest of the century.

Then in 1501 a new artist persuaded the cathedral to let him work on the giant. Despite the failures of others, he saw potential in the marble. This sculptor crafted his own tools and developed a brand-new technique for working with the flaws in the marble. His skill as an artist allowed him to incorporate the imperfections in the stone, turning what others saw as weaknesses into a fundamental part of his design. What others considered flaws, he used to build the structure of the sculpture. The work was hard, but it was also groundbreaking.

Michelangelo's *David* was completed in 1504 and remains one of the great masterpieces of Renaissance art. The work is iconic, but few people know that its journey was not smooth. It passed through the hands of three different artists, each overcoming challenges, abandonment, and rejection. Decades passed before someone had the ability to believe in its potential and bring it to life. It was this deliberate act of faith, choosing to see past the imperfections, that transformed the situation. This vision and belief in what could be is ultimately what enabled Michelangelo to achieve his greatness. The art critic Giorgio Vasari, a contemporary of Michelangelo's, noted that he "performed a miracle in restoring to life a block of marble left for dead."[14]

A tale is told of a visitor to Michelangelo's studio. Watching the sculptor chip away at a block of marble, he asked what he was doing. Michelangelo responded by asking the visitor what he saw. "I see a lump of marble," the man replied. "Ah," said Michelangelo, "but I see a hero trapped inside. And I'm chipping away at everything that is not David."

God is the great artist. Will you allow him to chip away at everything that is not who you were created to be? Will you embrace failure, not as an enemy but as a friend, here to teach, sharpen, and stretch you? Will you let the Holy Spirit do the same in you? Perhaps your imagination has been bruised, your ideas rejected, your dreams discarded. Maybe you're afraid to try again. But hear this: God meets you on the reject pile of life. And with patience and love, he begins to chip away, not in judgment but in care, revealing the beauty and potential within. He lifts you from the ashes and roots you—like the seeds of Newton's old apple tree—in the rich soil of his love.

When you make friends with failure, learn from your mistakes, find the courage to keep going, and live from the inside out—your creativity will begin to bear fruit in ways that you cannot even imagine. And some of those seeds may even defy gravity and carry your creativity to places beyond your wildest dreams.

You are chosen.

You are loved.

You have nothing to prove.

You are free to fail.

SPARK CIRCLE

Circle back through this chapter of Spark.

Notice
What part of the chapter helped you reframe failure from enemy to companion?
Which story gave you fresh permission to embrace failure?

Name
Think of a time when you experienced failure. What did you learn?
How might your constraints help your creativity?

Next Step
Pick one unfinished idea, rejected project, or creative endeavour you abandoned out of fear—what would it look like to give it another go?
Share this with your Spark Circle.

CHAPTER 8

Start the Work

Start the work and don't let anything stop you.
1 Chronicles 28:20 GNT

My friend Tom Herbert is a baker. But he's not just any old baker—his family has been baking bread for generations in rural Gloucestershire. Their family business, Hobbs House Bakery, is well known across the UK. He and his brother even had a TV show, *The Fabulous Baker Brothers*, sharing their passion for flour, fire, and food with the nation.

Often when I see Tom, he brings me a jar of his special sourdough starter. He'll take a small pot of bubbling brownish-grey gunk out of his rucksack, and inside will be something alive—a living culture of yeast and organic life that has been carefully nurtured for the best part of a hundred years, diligently passed down through generations of his family.

Every day the bakers at Hobbs House feed this sourdough culture, keeping it alive in a giant vat in the bakery. Just a small spoonful of this starter, when mixed with flour and water, can magically transform into a dough that rises beautifully before baking into the most incredible bread—flavourful, textured, and wonderfully delicious.

Tom often speaks at Renaissance gatherings, where he bakes bread live on stage, using this very sourdough starter. As he kneads and stretches the dough, he talks about how making bread is a lot like creativity.

"You need community," he says as he waves his sticky hands in the air. "Things might get messy. A little water, a little yeast—just the right ingredients. And then lots of hard work. It takes time, energy, effort." He kneads the dough some more. "Keep going, even if your hands hurt a bit. And as you do this, something magical will happen."

Tom always finishes by cooking the bread live on stage in a frying pan. Then, with a grin, he flings the frisbee-like flat sourdough into the crowd. It's always a moment of pure joy. Even when the bread disk smacked the pastor of a rather large and influential church in America firmly in the face. He'd been looking the other way at exactly the wrong moment. We all feared the worst, but he looked absolutely thrilled and later described it as the highlight of the event. He even kept the bread.

Failure to Launch

Inspired by Tom, I tried making my own bread. I followed the recipe to the letter, carefully measuring out the ingredients. I added the sourdough starter, the sticky yeast clinging to my fingers as I worked it into the mixture. I loaded the dough into a basket and lovingly baked my creation at the specific temperature. An hour later, I opened the oven door. To my horror, instead of a glorious sourdough, the finished product resembled a small clay brick. Something had gone horribly wrong. The loaf was so dense that it had the consistency of concrete. Needless to say, it was inedible. The subsequent post-mortem revealed multiple failures: I'd rushed the process, skimped on kneading, skipped the final rise. Frustrated by my failure, I gave up. The jar of sourdough starter was banished to the back of the fridge, where it eventually died and was thrown out. My sourdough dreams went stale—a textbook case of failure to launch.

Failure to launch is a well-documented phenomenon that haunts many creative journeys. So many of us struggle when it comes to turning a creative idea into reality. Innovation sounds great in theory, but when we actually try to make something happen, we never quite get off the ground. When our early attempts go wrong, we give up. Afraid of repeating our mistakes, we lose heart. Sometimes it's perfectionism that traps us—we're terrified of falling short of the unrealistic expectations we've set for ourselves. We practise failure avoidance to protect our image, concerned we'll look foolish. We self-censor when we're not excelling. We become our own worst critics.

And so, paralysed by fear, we end up doing nothing at all. We make excuses, procrastinate, play it safe. We tell ourselves, "One day I'll get round to this." Yet despite our best intentions, we are stuck at the conceptual stage. Ideas flow freely but never solidify into meaningful action. Experts call this "creative inertia."[1] And the impact is stark: Nearly 75 percent of new creative ventures never get off the ground. They simply fail to launch.[2]

The good news is that there's a way to overcome failure to launch. Watch a skilled baker at work, and you'll see a principle that applies just as much to innovation: No matter how brilliant the ingredients or how well the fermentation has gone, there's no short-cut for hard work. The dough must be kneaded, the yeast worked through until it reaches every part. It has to rise slowly and be shaped with care. It takes time, repetition, and commitment. And while it's tempting to cut corners, the truth is that the new thing you're trying to bring to life will reach its potential only through persistent, determined effort.

The Ingredients of Innovation

Let's get really practical: We're going to explore the hard work of overcoming failure to launch by taking an idea and actually bringing it to life. To do this, let's explore a recipe for creative innovation with five essential elements that together will help you truly make things happen. Stick to these ingredients, and you'll be well on your way to baking innovation into your creative process.

1. Execution

Make a Start

Vision without execution is hallucination.
—Thomas Edison

Our first ingredient is execution: Innovation requires a commitment to ruthlessly execute your ideas. Ideas don't fail for lack of imagination or vision; they fail for lack of execution. For innovation to happen, inspiration must find you willing to put in hard work. A creative idea is a little like the yeast in baking. Your job is to work it into the dough. The reason bakers call yeast the sourdough *starter* is because it makes a start. Execution is working your ideas into action. Knead the dough. Put in the hours. Don't cut corners. The biggest threat to your creative endeavours won't be a shortage of ideas; it will be your ability to execute.

Fashion designer Rick Owens describes the process of bringing a new collection into the world as being 5 percent creativity and 95 percent execution: "There's a lot of people that could be designers, a lot of people have great ideas, but it's the execution. It's easy to have inspiration and have a vision and an aesthetic, but if you don't have the execution and you don't get it out there properly and on time, it doesn't matter. It'll sink."[3]

The simplest way to start is to start simply. Don't delay. Don't wait for a better moment. Ideas alone are never enough. The difference between dreamers and doers isn't the quality of their imaginations but their ability to follow through and make things happen. So start right now because more often than not, the things you think are holding you back are only illusions. The obstacles you see in front of you might not be as immovable as they seem.

Something happens when you step out in obedience. You discover that God is already there, waiting for you to begin. There's a moment recorded in 1 Chronicles when King David spoke to his son Solomon, urging him to start building the temple. By any measure, it was a daunting task. There were a thousand reasons why it wasn't the right time. But in the end, David revealed a key principle for courageous innovation: "Be confident and determined. Start the work and don't let anything stop you. The Lord God, whom I serve, will be with you. He will not abandon you, but he will stay with you until you finish the work" (1 Chronicles 28:20 GNT).

Step out bravely and start executing your ideas for you're not on your own. Yes, it may be hard. Yes, it may take time. Yes, you may fail. But be confident of this: God is with you.

Daily Bread

I'll share with you a story about something that took a long time to get off the ground. It was frustrating. At times it felt demoralising. But in the end, the idea came to life—not because we waited for the perfect moment but because we took a deep breath and decided to make a start.

One day my baker friend Tom Herbert and I were hanging out. Because Tom is obsessed with bread (and I mean *obsessed*), literally every conversation ends up gravitating back to the mighty loaf. We ended up talking about how bread is woven right into the heart of Jesus' ministry. Every Sunday we break bread in church, remembering the Last Supper when Jesus took bread and broke it, saying, "This is my body given for you" (Luke 22:19). And as we were talking, we stumbled across an idea: What if we created a loaf called Daily Bread as a nod to the Lord's Prayer: "Give us this day our daily bread"? And when a person bought that loaf, it paid for another loaf to be given away through Lighthouse, our ministry to the vulnerable, to those who are hungry and in need. Instead of buy one *get* one free, it would be buy one *give* one free.

Tom was adamant that it should be good quality: sustaining, beautifully made, and delicious. Sometimes all it takes is a little bit of yeast—the yeast of courageous creativity—for ideas to rise and come to life. But even when we have all the ingredients for a creative idea, turning that vision into action requires execution. The truth is, it took a really, really long time to get Daily Bread off the ground.

For five years we half-heartedly pursued the idea. And for five years nothing happened: It stayed stubbornly stuck on the whiteboard. We

START THE WORK

just couldn't find the right solution. No one could see how we could do it. The business model didn't work. We failed to launch again and again. We'd explored working with different people to develop the idea, but we didn't get anywhere. In the end, we had to decide either to abandon it or to strain every sinew and properly execute the idea. We learned that getting serious about execution is the antidote to inertia.

It took my friend Zac Lloyd, a veritable master baker when it comes to making things happen, to push the idea over the line. He managed to arrange a meeting with the best bakery in East London—the legendary E5 Bakehouse, described by Time Out as "London's high temple of sourdough."[4] It's funny how often the people at the top of their game are the most willing to help. Some of the most brilliant minds have a generosity of spirit, a willingness to take risks and try new things, because they understand the power of collaborative innovation.

Happily, they were open to the collaboration, and we set to work together—problem-solving, testing recipes, figuring out the economics. It took time, but after a few months of making a start, I found myself sitting at my kitchen table, staring at a small, perfectly formed loaf of Daily Bread. It was delicious. But the best bit was that every time someone bought a loaf of Daily Bread, its twin was delivered to our Lighthouse project and handed to someone who was hungry. Witnessing the look on someone's face when they receive something crafted with love and care, the best bread, is incredible.

We launched the bread locally, and bit by bit people started buying it. Today you can even buy a loaf on a Sunday at the back of the church. The project is still in its early days, but as I write this, we're a few thousand loaves in. An idea that suffered from failure to launch is now flying. In the end, what made the difference? Choosing to make a start.

Your favourite sneaker brand has it right: Just do it. Really, just do it. Make it happen. Don't delay. Don't fail to launch. Because when you step out and act on the divine creativity that God has placed in your imagination, the Lord will be with you. Colossians 3:23 reminds us, "Whatever you do, work at it with all your heart, as working for the Lord." Your ability to turn ideas into action is not just a skill—it's holy.

INNOVATION

Start the work with heart and soul invested. Don't hide any longer under the comfort blanket of insecurity or the excuse of waiting for the right moment. You were created to realize the ideas God has placed in your soul; settling for anything less is short-changing your calling. The road to hell, after all, is paved with good intentions—or as novelist Philip Roth put it, with works in progress.[5] Don't delay—start today.

CHALLENGE

1. Write down your three best ideas.
2. Next to each idea, write the first step you need to take to move it forward.
3. Make a start today.

2. Dedication

Knead the Dough

Inspiration exists, but it has to find you working.
—Pablo Picasso

The next ingredient of innovation is hard work. Hard work is like the kneading of the dough. If you skip this stage of the process, your ideas will never rise to their full potential. Whatever God sparks in your imagination through the power of the Holy Spirit—whatever inspiration flows from your pen, your words, your mind—the truth is this: All great creative innovation requires blood, sweat, and tears. I've yet to meet a groundbreaking creative who didn't, behind the scenes, work extremely hard. Don't be fooled by the laconic tone or the laid-back exterior—great creativity requires intense focus and relentless dedication. I've seen this time and time again with the creatives I've had the privilege of working with. In musicians, filmmakers, writers, designers across every discipline, there's a common thread: a commitment to really hard work.

Now, understand this, I'm not saying you should burn yourself out on the altar of creativity. Rather, you need to identify what will help turn your idea into reality and then invest your best creative and intellectual energy into it. That means prioritizing time, attention, and focus, pouring them into the ideas that truly matter.

John Pawson shared a story with Renaissance about a creative breakthrough moment working with fashion designer Calvin Klein. At the time Calvin Klein was one of the most famous names in the creative industry globally. But what impressed John the most was Klein's extraordinary work ethic and relentless attention to detail. John recalled,

> We worked through for twelve hours, discussing a window frame detail. Seeing one of these people close up and realizing the drive that people who are hugely successful have: the singlemindedness, the obsession, it changes everything. That level of precision and detail, and the energy to take time to focus on the detail, that's a common thread that runs through all those hugely successful people.[6]

So our second ingredient of innovation is dedication. I wonder what this will look like in your creative discipline. Note that disciplines are called "disciplines" for a reason—they require hard work. Entrepreneurs, be prepared to stick with that idea you believe in even when everyone tells you it won't work. Writers, keep making room each day to put a few words on the page. Artists, keep working, observing, sketching. Musicians, put in the hours honing your craft, even when it's hard.

A famous story is told of the eminent violinist Mischa Elman, who was walking away from Carnegie Hall after a particularly frustrating rehearsal. As he made his way down the street, violin case in hand, a tourist spotted him and asked, "Excuse me, sir, how do you get to Carnegie Hall?" Without looking up, Elman simply replied, "Practice."[7] It's a simple truth: Creativity isn't just about talent or flashes of inspiration;

it's about discipline, persistence, and showing up again and again to do the work. Or as Thomas Edison said, "Inspiration is perspiration."[8]

Creating requires hard work and dedication, but here's the good news: You have it in you. You've come this far, and the dough of your ideas will eventually rise to form something wonderful.

CHALLENGE

Where do you do your best work?

How has hard work shaped you in the past?

3. Disruption

Add the Salt

No one pours new wine into old wineskins. Otherwise, the wine will burst the skins.
—Mark 2:22

To create something new requires being prepared to disrupt things. Adding a generous pinch of disruption is like salt in dough—it will make all the difference. Be prepared to become iconoclastic, unafraid to break the idols of unhealthy tradition, pointless continuity, and over-reliance on past successes, even when it's painful. Because the most meaningful way to honour the past is to build an extraordinary future upon the foundation it provides.

There's a fear I see all the time: That disruptive innovation dishonours the past. That to build something new is to reject those who came before us. But the opposite is true. The single best way to honour the past is not to preserve it unchanged, but to build upon it, stretch it, and take it somewhere extraordinary. The only things that don't grow in the garden are things that are dead. If we want to grow creatively, we must be willing to embrace disruption—even if it's uncomfortable.

The wisdom of the Scriptures teaches us to embrace a mould-breaking attitude toward life. Think of Romans 12:2: "Do not conform to the pattern of this world, but be transformed by the renewing of your mind." If we apply this to our creativity, God is urging us not to be confined by the patterns we've inherited but to be transformed, renewed, and courageous—to see things differently, to think bigger, and to create boldly. In doing this, you're going to upset some people. And that's okay.

You're not setting out to offend or create conflict, but the reality is that true innovation always meets resistance. If you spend all your energy trying to manage resistance, you'll have nothing left to forge the new. You will have to handle external critics—learning from them when necessary, ignoring them when needed. But just as importantly, you have to silence the internal critic, that voice whispering, *You can't do this. You can't change things. You can't create something new.* That voice is lying. The most important narrative to disrupt is that of the internal critic. Unless you're prepared to be audacious and defiant, you won't have to worry about innovation because all you'll be left with is decline.

But that's not going to be your story. God has filled you with divine creativity and sparked your imagination so that you might be bold and courageous and break new ground—even when it's uncomfortable. Without this, you'll stagnate. If you don't push yourself to keep challenging how you do things and growing in your creative practice, you'll just turn out the same old ideas. You're better than that. Great creativity requires you to refuse to settle. Let the beauty of the past propel you into a glorious future. Even if that means sprinkling your creative practice with the salt of disruption.

Keep Changing the Menu

I recently took our creative team from SAINT to have lunch with Sam and Sam Clark at MORO. Over piles of flatbread, lamb chops, and fish stew, we talked about creative leadership. I asked Sam how she stays fresh

INNOVATION

creatively after two decades of running one of London's top restaurants. Her answer fascinated me. She explained a practice they follow as a team. Rather than relying on past successes—like a band endlessly playing its greatest hits—the team at MORO commits to changing the menu every month. Just when they've mastered a set of dishes, when everything is running smoothly, they switch it up and start again. I was shocked.

Sam explained the logic behind this, revealing that if they don't force themselves to grow, stretch, and change, the kitchen team starts to stagnate and get bored. It takes about a week for a good chef to learn the new menu. That first week is stressful—they're pushed out of their comfort zone—but it's also exciting. They grow. Then, for the next three weeks, everything runs like clockwork. The kitchen is in rhythm. But by the fourth week, the team starts to get too familiar with the dishes. They are no longer being challenged. The energy fades. And so, at the end of each month, they reinvent their award-winning menu.

Sam's job as a creative leader and head chef is constantly to seek out new dishes—to travel, to scout, to let new flavours influence the menu. This creative rhythm may sound like hard work, but it's the secret to their success. They never settle for comfort. They stretch, push, sharpen, and learn. And the result? After two decades, MORO remains one of the best kitchens in London. Many of their chefs have gone on to great things, trained under the careful, watchful eye of a team that is constantly innovating.

Keep reinventing, refining, and pushing forward with courage, especially when it's hard. This isn't just theory: It's the story of many great creative breakthroughs. Be courageous and allow the creative spark in you to smash the mould.

CHALLENGE

Where have you accepted limits that might not be real?

Smash them.

4. Refining

Shape the Loaf

> *[My Father] cuts off every branch in me that bears no fruit, while every branch that does bear fruit he prunes so that it will be even more fruitful.*
> —John 15:2

The next ingredient of innovation is refining: the shaping, cutting back of your ideas. Just as a loaf is shaped, excess and unneeded dough trimmed away, and cuts made to the bread, so we have to learn to refine our ideas. This courage to prune, to discard without sentimentalism, lies at the heart of all good innovation. Editors do it, shaping and crafting the text. Musicians ruthlessly prioritise what to leave out of an arrangement. To borrow from Debussy, the real music is the space between the notes. Sculptors do it, chipping away all that is not needed. Engineers do it, refining away all that is not structurally essential.

Innovation requires you to be ruthlessly unsentimental with your ideas. British writer and literary critic Sir Arthur Quiller-Couch encouraged would-be writers to eliminate the self-indulgent and unnecessary from their work: "Whenever you feel an impulse to perpetrate a piece of exceptionally fine writing, obey it—wholeheartedly—and delete it before sending your manuscript to press. Murder your darlings."[9]

Don't settle for the safety of your past successes, which ultimately leads to creative stagnation. You often see this settling in the creative industries. Take, for instance, the difficult second album. A band keeps recycling the same sound that made them famous with their first hit instead of pressing forward and pushing into new creative territory. Or think of the stale film franchise that sticks to safe formulas instead of taking risks and breaking new ground.

The old adage is true: "Nothing kills success like success." The thing no one tells you about success is that it can make you lazy. Here's how it works: We all like to succeed, so when something works, the temptation

INNOVATION

is to keep going back to that familiar formula. Instead, when you see success, be on your guard, because our natural inclination is to double down instead of push forward.

Innovation requires the courage to trim the excess, to keep refining and reinventing. Many creatives land on their first good idea and get stuck there, content to stay in that pleasant land. All the while, just beyond the horizon, there's a whole new world of creative potential. The way to get there? Be willing to kill your darlings. Don't let success hold you back.

Ron Moore was a massive *Star Trek* fan. As a kid, it was his favourite TV show. He knew everything: every scene, every episode. And out of all the characters, Captain Kirk, the hero of the series, was his idol. Growing up in California, Moore dreamed of working in film and TV. He got his foot in the door of the industry, eventually becoming a writer—but then, one day, he got his big break. He couldn't believe it: He landed a job writing for *Star Trek*. Reflecting on that moment, he said, "When I started at *Star Trek*, it really was the fulfilment of a lifelong dream. I was a very serious Trekkie as a kid. I loved the old show."[10]

Nevertheless, Ron Moore was about to kill his darlings in a way that exemplifies this characteristic perfectly. When the *Star Trek* series made the leap to the big screen with its feature-length film *Star Trek: Generations*, Moore made the bravest creative decision of his life. He did the unthinkable. In his words: "I killed Kirk."

The move stunned hardcore *Star Trek* fans around the world. Moore confessed, "I killed my childhood hero. I wept when I wrote it. It still moves me when I think about it." The decision was deeply controversial, but *Star Trek: Generations* went on to be a box office success, netting three times its budget worldwide.

Refine. Prune. Trim. Cut. Reinvent. Don't rest on your laurels.

CHALLENGE

What needs to be left behind so you can move forward?

Let it go.

5. Resilience

Water the Dough

But blessed is the one who trusts in the LORD,
whose confidence is in him.
They will be like a tree planted by the water
that sends out its roots by the stream.
It does not fear when heat comes;
its leaves are always green.
It has no worries in a year of drought
and never fails to bear fruit.
—Jeremiah 17:7–8

Innovation requires resilience, without which our creativity will simply shrivel up and die. Like water in a good dough, resilience will keep us stretchy, alive, and able to rise in the heat of life. To turn our ideas and dreams into reality—to take action and bring them to life—we'll need plenty of this ingredient because we will face challenges, setbacks, and disappointments.

No Surrender!

I was turned down from my role at SAINT before I'd even started. It was 2016, and the parish of Hackney had no Rector. My boss at the time, the Bishop of London, was passionate about the potential of the parish and had encouraged me to apply for the position. And while it was a long shot—a church with a very different tradition from what I was used to—he wrote a generous letter of support. When the application period closed, there was only one applicant: me.

But as it turned out, the trustees making the decision weren't ready for change. They rejected my application. I was devastated. I felt like I had been fired before even getting the job. I wanted to give up. I drafted my resignation letter to the Church of England. And then, at my lowest point, an email landed in my inbox.

INNOVATION

It was a one-line message from the Bishop of London: "No surrender!" That was enough for me. I picked myself up, trusting in God, and reapplied. The second time around—to my horror—there were multiple applicants. Having been rejected once, I stood no chance. Yet miraculously, the people making the decision changed their minds, and I was appointed. Looking back, I realise how easy it would have been to quit. I could have let the first rejection define the story. Instead, I learned a life lesson that day—the final characteristic of courageous creativity: Don't give up. Keep going. Learn to develop resilience.

Yes and . . .

Creative resilience often involves learning to keep going and not break your flow. A great lesson on this comes from the world of improvisation theatre. The most basic principle in improv is simple: Don't stop. Improv actors are trained not to stop but to keep the process flowing when facing some impossible imaginary scenario. The natural inclination when facing a challenge or a roadblock is to say, "Yes, but. . . ." In doing so, we place limitations, find reasons something won't work, and shut down our creative flow before we've hit the magic. So, to get around this, improvisation teaches us a golden rule: Replace "Yes, but . . ." with "Yes, *and*. . . ." Rather than "Yes, but there are a thousand reasons this won't work." Try instead, "Yes, *and* let's build on that idea." "Yes, *and* what if we try this direction?" "Yes, *and* how could this idea feel more wonderful?"

"Yes, *and* . . ." is your secret weapon for growing resilience. It will give you the ability to keep going, especially when you feel stuck, when ideas run dry, and when you can't seem to bring things to a conclusion. Learn to turn your cul-de-sacs and dead ends into roundabouts and on-ramps.

Still Waters

You really do have an unfair advantage—the ability to hydrate your bruised creative soul with the Creator Spirit. Psalm 23:1–3 reminds us, "The LORD is my shepherd. . . . He leads me beside quiet waters, he refreshes my soul." In a world that drains and depletes, let the inner power of the Holy Spirit heal your disappointments and give you the strength to keep going. This is where true resilience ultimately comes from—not just grit or willpower, but the dynamic power of the Creator working in you. And this will require time. As Stephen Covey wisely said, we must never be too busy to take time to "sharpen the saw."[11]

CHALLENGE

Schedule one creative Sabbath each month. No output—just input.

+ Allow your soul to be recharged by beauty.
+ Visit something stunning—an art gallery, nature, an outstanding piece of design.
+ Let fresh ideas spark something new in you.

> *There is some magic I suppose, but mostly it's hard work . . . a constant review of the idea that you've had.*
> —John Pawson

We've explored these five key ingredients of innovation:

1. Execution: Make a Start
2. Dedication: Knead the Dough
3. Disruption: Add the Salt
4. Refining: Shape the Loaf
5. Resilience: Water the Dough

When you commit to working these five ingredients together, you'll begin to create something wonderful. It may take awhile, but you will see your ideas come to life. Plenty of attempts will go wrong. But know that in the end, you'll taste the fruit of your endeavours.

INNOVATION

Now it's time to put these ideas into action. Take a moment to go back through these last few chapters on innovation and reflect on the takeaways that you can apply to your creative practice. Do the hard work. Don't be afraid to revisit the ideas that stretched you. Talk them through with friends. Ask yourself honestly which of these characteristics you struggle with the most.

Because here's the truth: The spark that the Creator has placed in you isn't just flickering in your imagination; it's coming to life. You're moving beyond the lightbulb moments of inspiration; your idea is incubating, forming, taking shape. It's turning into realities that are going to make a difference. And if you commit to pursuing innovation—if you develop this muscle over time—you'll find that your courage begins to outweigh your fear. You'll be capable of far more than you ever dreamed possible.

> [God] . . . is able to do immeasurably more than all we ask or imagine, according to his power that is at work within us.
> —Ephesians 3:20

That "immeasurably more" is yours. And as we'll see next, there is extraordinary impact when you start to turn your ideas into action.

SPARK CIRCLE

Circle back through this chapter of Spark.

Notice
Which part of the baking metaphor connected most with how you start (or stall) new things?
Did anything help you see perseverance or preparation differently?

Name
What's one project, idea, or dream you've been feeding quietly in the background but haven't dared to start? Name it.
Go back through the chapter and review the Challenges. What will you try?

Next Step
This week, pick one creative idea you've been sitting on. Don't overthink it—just mix the ingredients. Start. Try setting a timer; give it thirty focused minutes.
Provide feedback to your Spark Circle on what happened when you finally started working through the dough.

MOVEMENT FOUR

Impact

CHAPTER 9

High Hopes

Art is the highest form of hope.
—Gerhard Richter

Hackney, *Shared Sky*.
Tears are streaming down her cheeks, down her tired face. Each drop glimmers in the shifting light before splashing down onto the screen below, magnifying and distorting the glowing pixels. The young woman is standing between two skies—her face turned upward; her eyes caught in the glow of the installation. Weeks earlier she had fled the relentless barrage of bombing and bloodshed that had engulfed her homeland, Ukraine, and she had found her way to the community at SAINT.

Wandering into the chapel by the front door, she stumbled upon Es Devlin's installation *Shared Sky*. Two skies. One beneath her feet. One high above. And in between, this young refugee stood, caught up in a cloud of haze and reflected light.

To her astonishment, the sky above was her sky: Kyiv, Ukraine. The space had become a focus for our prayers for peace, even as the world wrestled with the horrors of war. Standing there, looking up at the heavens above her country—the vivid azure sky of Ukraine stretched wide, streaked with soft clouds drifting past, the sound of birds winging gently overhead—she turned to me and whispered, "I can't go home. But here, I have hope."

IMPACT

Hope in Motion

Creativity takes us home. Creativity is hope in motion. Every idea, act, work, thought, and dream opens a window of opportunity for divine impact. Your God-given creativity has power to connect with that fierce longing in every soul—for a better day, for a place to belong, for homecoming—and in doing so, to restore that most powerful oxygen to the soul: hope. And in today's world, hope is often in short supply. Theologian Lesslie Newbigin hit the nail on the head, noting that one of the most alarming features of contemporary culture is the "disappearance of hope."[1]

At times we have every reason to feel hopeless. Life is hard. Creating is costly. We wonder if our work will ever matter. We ask ourselves, "What difference can my small contribution make against the great darkness around me?" And sometimes that question shakes our faith in the calling to remake the world. If we don't pay attention, we risk silencing the potential of our creativity. We bury the gifts God has placed within us. We shrink back from the very thing that could bring light until we become indifferent to the power of what we carry. Holocaust survivor and Nobel laureate Elie Wiesel put it like this:

> The opposite of love is not hate, it's indifference.
> The opposite of art is not ugliness, it's indifference.
> The opposite of faith is not heresy, it's indifference.
> And the opposite of life is not death, it's indifference.
> —*Elie Wiesel*[2]

Don't be indifferent to your creative potential. There's nothing more tragic than drifting through life, unaware of the hope that longs to express itself through your creative soul. But that's not going to be your story.

This is a chapter about high hopes. Together we're going to peer through the darkness and haze toward a better way of creating—and in doing so, we'll find ourselves coming home to a new kind of creative hope.

The Creative Minority

British historian Arnold Toynbee conducted one of the most comprehensive studies of human civilisation ever written—twelve volumes, three million words, seven thousand pages—through which he traced the stages that all civilisations go through: genesis, growth, trouble, and finally, disintegration.[3] His conclusion about how great cultures and civilisations rise to shape the world was striking. What changed the game? It wasn't geography. It wasn't biology. It wasn't philosophy or theology. It wasn't military might or political power.

Time and again throughout history, the world has been changed by creativity. When a tribe, people, or nation faces the threat of extinction—backs up against a wall—something extraordinary happens. Toynbee observed that every great breakthrough in history begins with a small group of individuals who come together, driven by a sense of urgency, and start to innovate. Inspiration sparks ideas. Ideas lead to solutions. Solutions create prosperity. And through this process of creative resistance, everything begins to change. Jonathan Sacks, summarising Toynbee's work, described these moments as "the birth of the creative minority."[4]

History has always been changed by creative minorities. People like you and your friends. The ones you love. The ones who inspire you. The ones who bring you hope. Small groups of creative thinkers unlocking imagination, daring to dream bold ideas, and innovating against the odds have rewired the world and rewritten the story. While creativity is the key, what is not as certain (the biggest variable historically) is what actually drives the creative minority. What is the motivation? What is the vision? Is it hope or despair? Love or hatred? Justice or tyranny? Light or darkness? And this leads us to a simple choice—whether our creative spark will bring hope and light or darkness and despair. What kind of impact will you choose? What sort of future will you choose to imagine? What kind of world will you dream into reality? And how do you get there? As wise old Dumbledore says to Harry Potter, "It is our choices, Harry, that show us who we truly are, far more than our abilities."[5]

The Fundamentals of Creativity

Five hundred years before Jesus, Plato wrestled with the big question of meaning and purpose—those hidden qualities of life that bridge being, beauty, and meaning—and those fundamentals have become one of the great threads of theology and philosophy to this day: *truth, beauty,* and *goodness*.[6] Augustine, writing in the fourth century, would develop these fundamentals, describing them as windows we see through to glimpse the nature of God himself, a beauty so ancient and so new.[7] Fast-forward to the thirteenth century, and Thomas Aquinas built these transcendental ideas into the heart of Christian theology, arguing that truth, beauty, and goodness are God's nature:

> God is the cause of being to all things.
> He is the cause of the truth of all things . . .
> He is the cause of goodness to all things.[8]

Truth, beauty, and goodness become windows into heaven: truth our gateway to holy reality; beauty an echo of God's creativity; and goodness the guide that shapes that which is right. Together they open up the windows of our shared sky and let us see a glimpse of home. And it was these principles of truth, beauty, and goodness that set the direction for the modern world. They became one of the common threads linking the classical world to the medieval world, and the interest in recovering them led to the theological, philosophical, and artistic rebirth that we now call the Renaissance.

Aquinas lit the fuse, and the church fanned the flames, acting as the greatest of artistic patrons.[9] The explosions of light, creativity, and innovation that followed—the wonders of Leonardo da Vinci's creative genius, the grace of Raphael's masterpieces, the works of Titian and Botticelli and Dürer—would illuminate a world emerging from the Dark Ages. The works of writers from Erasmus to Shakespeare, the science of Galileo and Copernicus, the architectural glory of Brunelleschi—suddenly the whole world was caught up in a wildfire of re-imagination and re-enchantment that swept everything along in its path.

We desperately need a new renaissance today: that people everywhere would once again capture a vision for a rebirth of truth, beauty, and goodness. That we all would see creativity as essential—not periphery—to the future. There has never been a more urgent moment for you and me to catch fire again with a vision of creative hope—one that can illuminate the cold darkness around us. Because when the creative minority pursues truth, beauty, and goodness, we witness the spark of divine inspiration spread until it becomes a furnace of hope, burning through the culture, lighting everything in the wildfire glow of creative revival.

Creative Direction

A story is told of Albert Einstein travelling by train. As the ticket collector moved down the carriage, checking each passenger's ticket, Einstein reached into his pockets—only to realise he couldn't find his. He stood up, rummaging through his belongings, searching under his seat, growing increasingly flustered. When the inspector finally reached him and saw his distress, he gently reassured him: "Don't worry, Professor. We all know who you are. It's okay—you don't need a ticket."

Einstein looked up and replied, "I too know who I am. The problem is—I don't know where I'm going."[10]

Truth, beauty, and goodness are our compass home. They give us direction. They open the windows of our experience, letting us glimpse that far-off country our souls are dreaming of. They are—as theologian Abraham Kuyper put it—a common grace: one of the ways God moves in and through the world to illuminate the darkness.[11]

1. Tell the Truth

It's everywhere. From unfiltered selfies (carefully curated) to my kombucha (an authentic blend of live cultures). Almost ubiquitous—every brand, lifestyle store, coffee shop, and social cause dripping with that most imitated quality: authenticity. It's become a buzz word. Our culture is obsessed with it. But I have bad news. Ultimately, authenticity is an illusion. It's a vapour. Authenticity is the logical outworking of a culture where everything is subjective. Authenticity is centred on the self; it's the ultimate expression of "my truth"—with a really small *t*.

Pursuing creative authenticity alone is a hollow goal that will leave your soul cold. It's a false hope built on the shifting sands of circumstance. What we've really been longing for all along is something far more real because hope demands something concrete, universal, and transcendent. That something, which is altogether more powerful, is Truth—with a capital *T*.

Truth is objective, not dependent on the whims of style or the fads of fashion. Truth can't be bought or sold, cancelled or commoditised. Why? Because Truth isn't a concept—he's a person. Jesus said, "I am the way and the truth and the life. No one comes to the Father except through me" (John 14:6). This same Creator Spirit is also called "the Spirit of truth" (John 16:13).

Creator's Cameo

There is a deep, almost spiritual connection between the artist and the artist's work. What we create doesn't just reflect us; it reveals us. Like a kid who scrawls "I was here" on a school desk, we leave our mark on the world. Theologian Jeremy Begbie says that when we create, we are "set in the midst of a God-given world vibrant with a dynamic beauty of its own . . . a gift for us to interact with vigorously, shape and reshape, form and transform."[12]

The creative act is not detached; it's incarnational. We pour ourselves into our work. And often we vanish into it, only to reappear on the other side of the canvas, the camera, or the composition.

I spent my twenties working in the film industry, immersed in the world of moviemaking magic. I read screenplays day and night, worked with directors, sat through endless screenings, and visited film sets. One of the quirks of living inside that world was noticing just how enmeshed we become in the creative process.

Time and time again, I saw how visionaries would submerge themselves in the world of their own vision. The willing suspension of disbelief that creative work invites is an act of faith—and so often the creators themselves can't resist stepping into the world they so deeply believe in.

Take the great directors of cinema. Many of them end up appearing in their own films in a cameo or a walk-on part. And once you start noticing this, you can't stop. It's everywhere: Alfred Hitchcock appears in thirty-nine of his films. Stan Lee—creator of the Marvel Universe—pops up in every one of the Marvel films. Martin Scorsese rides in the back of the taxi in *Taxi Driver*. Quentin Tarantino disposes of bodies in *Pulp Fiction*. Peter Jackson is in every installment of *Lord of the Rings*, throwing spears, fighting Legolas. Francis Ford Coppola even cast himself as a TV director shouting at the soldiers in *Apocalypse Now*.

The point is this: If you're the creator, you love to step into the picture. The creative soul has the urge to say, "Here is the created world—full of the truth we are telling—and I, too, have arrived in it with you." In Jesus, God walks into the picture. And this moment changes everything. The Creator—goodness, beauty, and truth—in human form, among us, enters the scene, inviting us into the world he has imagined. And in this, we understand—we see—and we believe. Jesus comes among us full of grace and truth (John 1:14). Isaiah said our eyes would see his beauty (Isaiah 33:17). And he described himself as the Good Shepherd (John 10:11).

To see Jesus—the image of the invisible God—is to come face-to-face with the source of all that is true, all that is beautiful, and all that is good. That changes everything. Hope now has a name and a face. And this isn't just a historical moment—it can be a lived reality for you and me. The spark of the Creator, the presence of God within us, means the qualities and character of Jesus are near.

In Jesus, God invites us to walk with him in our imaginations—his footsteps echoing in the cool of the garden of our souls. And standing beneath his sky, learning to see with his eyes—our focus realigned with his vision—we begin to understand that truth, beauty, and goodness are not only our ticket home but are the very architecture of the world God

IMPACT

is creating and the destination toward which he is leading us. What does this mean for us? The first frame of hope-filled creativity is to focus your vision on the world Jesus is imagining—because you'll find him here. Sometimes hiding in plain sight, a quiet cameo on the margins of your vision. At other times, front and centre in your story.

When the presence of Jesus takes centre stage in your creative world, his vision, his reality, and his truth begin to shape your mind, your ideas, and your impact. And no—God is not here to spoil your fun. This isn't about being moralistic. Great art is rarely tame, bossy, or boring. It's about being truthful in a world that's starving for integrity in the creative act. We've all seen creativity twisted toward the dark, the hopeless, and the godless. Art that controls. That demands. That dehumanises. And this kind of negative, shadow creativity never breathes hope, only despair. Deep in our bones, we know this can't be true creativity. It's a counterfeit.

Don't tell lies with your art. Don't paint fake sky with false hope. Don't let your mind be taken captive by hollow and deceptive philosophies, rooted in nothing but empty human tradition. Don't give the untruths of our generation starring roles in the stories you tell and the worlds you weave, because lies die quicker than truth. Darkness only absorbs light; it never creates it.

Instead, pull the focus of your soul's creativity upward—toward the God light. To the high and holy places where divine glory blazes. Where every pixel, pen stroke, and plotline is infused with God's marvellous light. Don't settle for the suburbs of the soul. Head for the high places of holy hope. Let your creativity flow toward the Way, the Truth, and the Life. Lead people through the fog of hopelessness until they glimpse that far-off country every human heart is longing for. Dorothy Sayers put it like this: "The recognition of the truth we get in the artist's work comes to us as a revelation of new truth. It is new, startling, and perhaps shattering, and yet it comes to us with a sense of familiarity. We did not know it before, but the moment the poet has shown it to us, we know that somehow or other, we had always really known it."[13]

Great creativity tells the truth—even when it's uncomfortable.

Guernica

During the Second World War, Picasso was living in Paris under occupation. One day a Nazi officer visited his apartment and noticed a photograph of *Guernica*. *Guernica* is one of Picasso's most famous works—a masterpiece. The painting pulls no punches, brutally depicting the horrors of the Nazi-supported bombing of a Spanish town during the Spanish Civil War. It is a raw, unflinching portrait of human suffering at the hands of tyranny.

The image caught the officer's eye, and he leaned in to examine it more closely. Staring at the chaos of destruction, broken bodies, and anguished faces, he turned to Picasso and, gesturing toward the painting, asked, "Did you do that?"

Picasso replied: "No. You did." [14]

Your creativity can show the world as it is—and, even more powerfully, as it could be. Your work holds up a mirror, reflecting injustice, failure, and pain. But just as mirrors reverse and reorder, your creativity can open a window into a different reality. You illuminate the landscape of the heart with true light—the truth of God's love that redeems, restores, and makes all things new.

Stereo Not Mono

Don't create in one dimension. To get to the fullness of truth, you need unity and relationship. Think of creativity as a multi-camera shoot—it's never in mono, always in stereo. And the best magic happens when you have all the angles covered. There's always a conversation happening: between the artist and the viewer, the storyteller and the audience, the architect and those who inhabit the space. You never create in a vacuum. Great creativity involves community. We need one another to truly grasp reality. Truth is something we're designed to discover together.

True creative interdependency is the sacred tension of collaboration that invites us into deeper truth through shared vision, vulnerability, and trust. Will you turn your creativity outward? Or will your hope, faith, and love turn in on themselves? If we want to change the world, we have to imagine together—and prefer the other. Don't go it alone. As Mumford & Sons put it, in their anthem "Delta":

> Does your love prefer the other,
> or does your love just make you feel good?[15]

Collaboration changes everything. If we want our creativity to impact people, we need to learn to work with others, especially those who are different from us.

The Gift of Difference

In Acts 13 we witness a moment of great innovation when the early church sends Paul on what would become his first missionary journey. For the first time, the good news of Jesus would spill beyond the Jewish believers, reaching the ends of the earth. Most of us are here today, reading this, because of that decision. But what's fascinating about this great innovation is how it happened.

> Now in the church at Antioch there were prophets and teachers: Barnabas, Simeon called Niger, Lucius of Cyrene, Manaen (who had been brought up with Herod the tetrarch) and Saul. While they were worshiping the Lord and fasting, the Holy Spirit said, "Set apart for me Barnabas and Saul for the work to which I have called them." So after they had fasted and prayed, they placed their hands on them and sent them off.
> —Acts 13:1–3

It's hard to picture a more diverse group of people—different backgrounds, different voices, different stories. Simeon was African. Lucius came from modern-day Libya. Barnabas was from the island of Cyprus. Manaen had grown up among the royal elite. And Saul, the former persecutor, was a rabbi turned revolutionary. Yet together they helped birth something world-changing. Think about that for a moment. This is a model of how imagination, ideas, and innovation lead to real impact. Not one genius with a calling, but a group of people, vastly different from one another, working together to bring truth to the world. If you want your creativity to lead people to truth and reality, you'll need to enlist those who are different from you. You'll have to step outside your comfort zone—collaborate with people from different backgrounds, disciplines, ethnicities, and skills. That will require humility. Preferring others. Listening well.

And the result? Far greater impact than you could ever achieve alone. As Helen Keller, who from an early age was deaf and blind, and went on to become a global voice for justice, said, "Alone we can do so little; together we can do so much."[16] She knew, perhaps more than most, that collaboration isn't weakness—it's power. That creative interdependence is how light breaks through. Collaboration around purpose sparks an explosion of creativity. If you want to make the best, most truthful, most powerful creative decisions, ones that will have the biggest impact, you need difference built in from the start. And this is not just a nice idea; there's hard data behind why this gives you a competitive advantage over those who choose to go it alone.

No Smoking

I once met Deborah Arnott, the woman who led the UK campaign to ban smoking in public spaces, a change described as "the single most important public health reform in generations."[17] The Prime Minister at the time, Tony Blair, had asked her to head up a body that would deliver the policy—a seemingly impossible task. Big Tobacco was against her. Powerful lobbyists were out to stop her. But in 2007, against the odds, her campaign succeeded, and the law was changed. In the year that followed, almost half a million people in the UK gave up smoking. A decade on, smoking related deaths from heart disease had fallen by 20 percent.

Intrigued, I asked Arnott, "How did you do it? It must have felt impossible." Her answer was simple but profound. "I had to build a team, a coalition of all the possible opinions. That way we saved a huge amount of time. I had everyone in the same room: Big Tobacco, scientists, politicians, policymakers. Sure, there were moments when it was bumpy, but in the end, together we achieved what none of us could have done alone."

Everywhere you look in the world of creative innovation, the message is clear: Variety really is the spice of life. Research from McKinsey & Company shows that diverse teams are 35 percent more likely to outperform industry norms in both profitability and innovation.[18] *Harvard Business Review* found that the more varied the makeup of your team, the greater the innovations you're likely to produce.[19] Columbia University points to plurality of perspective as a key ingredient in stronger decision-making.[20] And Google's innovation labs uncovered the same truth: The highest-impact ideas and breakthroughs came from radically diverse teams that had learned to collaborate and break new ground together.[21]

Embracing difference as a gift from God isn't just a nice idea—it's a massive creative advantage. And the truth is that your creativity—your work, your ideas, your imagination—has never been more needed than it is today. By embracing difference, we hold up a mirror to the brokenness of the world while painting a prophetic picture of the kingdom come. Our imaginations, innovations, the way we create all help reveal truth to a world that might otherwise be lost in the echo chamber of self-serving similarity. Working together, our creativity has the power to reflect truth to the world around us.

Nothing Can Separate Us

During the COVID lockdowns in London, one piece of art captured the moment—a single image that spoke to the pain of separation and the longing for connection we all felt. It was by the artist Lakwena Maciver, and it featured a bold, unmissable message: "Nothing Can Separate Us."

Inspired by a passage in Romans 8, this phrase appeared across multiple public installations in London, including a giant fourteen-hundred-square-metre mural on the roof of Temple Station.[22] With the city in lockdown—apart, afraid, and alone—this truth went viral, landing on magazine covers and reverberating across the city.[23] It connected with a deep human truth: our need for belonging, unity, and hope.

Your creativity has the power to connect. It can be a vehicle for truth—a way of meeting people in their deepest need. So let light shine through your imagination, your ideas, and your innovations. Let your creativity speak. Let it resonate. Let it impact the world around you.

How might you use the skills, capacity, and calling you've been given to point people toward the truth—that there is a God who is creative, that we are made in his image, that we are loved, chosen, and called? And how might you do this with others—collaborating, creating, imagining together—and in doing so, have a far greater impact than you ever could have on your own?

2. Build Beauty

Beauty will save the world.
—Fyodor Dostoevsky

Your creativity has the unique ability to reveal true beauty to a world longing for the mysterious, the other, the transcendent, the heavenly. True beauty points the heart to God. It's never neutral; it's powerful. Beauty connects with the soul in the most profound way.

And yet, we don't always know what to do with beauty. It's often misunderstood, dismissed as superficial. We tell ourselves that the Lord looks at the heart, not at the outward appearance. We're afraid that we'll get caught up in superficial notions of beauty, and we don't want to appear to be vain, materialistic, or objectifying. But beauty was never meant to be shallow. It is profound and fundamental to life. As philosopher Roger Scruton argues, "Beauty matters. It's not just a subjective thing, but a universal need of human beings. If we ignore this need, we find ourselves in a spiritual desert."[24]

So how do we approach this most transcendental creative quality?

IMPACT

Kalos

Jesus talked about beauty as being a powerful force for changing the world. He used the word καλός (*kalos*), meaning whatever is beautiful, noble, or good. In Matthew 5:16 he said, "Let your light shine before others, that they may see your good deeds (καλός)"—in other words, your actions that are good, beautiful, and true—"and glorify your Father in heaven."

The kind of creativity God calls us to deserves to be infused with beauty because beauty is one of the lenses through which the world encounters the mysterious grace of God. To reduce beauty to mere aesthetics is to miss the point. Beauty is not decoration; it's revelation. It sits at the heart of God's mission to remake the world. As C. S. Lewis wrote, "We do not merely want to see beauty... we want something else which can hardly be put into words—to be united with the beauty we see, to pass into it, to receive it into ourselves, to bathe in it, to become part of it."[25]

We live in a generation longing for wonder. As G. K. Chesterton said, the world is starving "for want of wonder."[26] Wonder helps us come alive. The human soul is a sponge for beauty. Think of that view that takes your breath away. That piece of art or music or poetry that articulates your deepest longings. In such moments, your soul is experiencing the transformational power of beauty.

When the first astronauts went to space and looked back at Earth, they were overwhelmed by a sense of beauty and awe. Psychologists call this the overview effect—a mind shift brought about by the sheer scale and wonder of seeing the planet from outer space. Studies have found that sensations of wonder and awe, sparked by experiencing something truly beautiful, increase positive emotions, sharpen the mind, and deepen our emotional capacity. Beauty awakens something in us—it restores, refocuses, and expands our perspective.

Being exposed to beauty is, it turns out, literally mind-blowing. It improves your mental health, firing up parts of your brain that dream, release dopamine, and help reduce stress. Exposure to beauty changes how you see the world, making you more aware of its fragility, wonder, and interconnectedness.

The Holiness of Beauty

Beauty is a vitamin for the creative soul—it changes you from the inside out. The answer to a cynical, burnt-out, distracted, and distraught world is not more content or more bandwidth; it's more beauty.

> *Art is capable of making visible our need to go beyond what we see, and it reveals our thirst for infinite beauty—for God.*
> —Pope Benedict XVI

Beauty is essential to human spiritual flourishing. It awakens the soul, stirring a longing for something beyond itself—something deeper, truer, and more real than what we can see. There's a kind of indescribable holiness to beauty—something that we can't quite grasp but that we instinctively know draws us upward toward heaven. Theologian Hans Urs von Balthasar put it like this: "Every experience of beauty points to eternity."[27]

And this is where your creativity comes in. You have a role to play in helping others recover true beauty and wonder in a world saturated with synthetic stimulation, sinking in cynicism, and starving for meaning. When your creativity unlocks beauty in the eyes of the beholder, you are drawing that person closer to the holiness of God. There is a spiritual, almost sacramental nature to beauty. So don't settle for the flatlands of your faith. Go "further up, come further in!" to the mountaintops of glorious encounter.[28]

Here, the presence of God transfigures the world around us. Just as creativity leads us to truth, it also unlocks the power of beauty, revealing it in ways that make the world come alive. N. T. Wright explains it like this: "The arts are not the pretty but irrelevant bits around the border of reality. They are the highways into the centre of a reality which cannot be glimpsed, let alone grasped, any other way. The present world . . . is like a violin waiting to be played—beautiful to look at, graceful to hold—but if you've never heard it in the hands of a musician, you wouldn't believe the new dimensions of beauty yet to be revealed."[29]

IMPACT

So, here's a challenge for you: How can you make room for a bounty of beauty in your life? How can you make space for more wonder? Learn to see beauty and mystery as sacramental gateways into the glory of God. You must keep fuelling the fire of your creative soul with beauty. But let me warn you—choosing to prioritise this will be hard. As Fyodor Dostoevsky wrote in *The Brothers Karamazov*, "Beauty is mysterious . . . God and the devil are fighting there, and the battlefield is the human heart."[30] There's a battle around what beauty grows into: between a turning inward, until it becomes poisoned with the toxins of narcissism, fuelling selfishness, comparison, and vanity; and a redeeming beauty that turns outward and upward to God. You and I are called to impact the world with the latter— with beauty that heals, uplifts, and reveals the divine.

Here are some practices you may find helpful:

Start to notice beauty.

Identify the things you consider beautiful—the sights, sounds, and smells that lift your soul higher. Really do stop to smell the roses. Watch the sun go down. Make room in your life for all the small, sacred moments of wonder.

> *Drawing makes you see things clearer,*
> *and clearer and clearer still, until your eyes ache.*
> —David Hockney

Keep a beauty journal.

Capture what moves you. Snap a photo, jot a note, fill your sketchbook or notes app with moments of awe. Then, each month, return to them. Let them re-inspire you—a dose of soul vitamin distilled into fuel for your imagination. The artist is, above all, one who notices, who pays attention—just as the Creator is described as "the God who sees" (Genesis 16:13).[31]

Date your creativity.

Regularly set time aside to expose your soul to beauty and

wonder. Get out of your house. Visit a gallery. Walk through nature. Climb a hill. Sit and watch the sunset. Listen to the sound of water. Try new tastes. Watch live music. Just as you can build your physical strength through training, build your creative capacity for awe and wonder by spending time with beauty. In *The Artist's Way*, Julia Cameron calls this practice the "Artist Date," a weekly ritual of creative nourishment, where you step away from the noise and reconnect with wonder.[32]

Detox from artificial beauty.

Break the spell of digital hypnosis. Go offline. Go off-grid. Fast from the never-ending cycle of stimulation, and let what is true, real, and good soak into your soul.

Find what works for you. But don't skip this part of the process. Beauty is not optional. It's oxygen for your creativity. So, a creativity that brings hope is true, it's beautiful, and thirdly, it's good.

3. Grow Goodness

Imaginary evil is romantic and varied; real evil is gloomy, monotonous, barren, boring. Imaginary good is boring; real good is always new, marvellous, intoxicating.
Simone Weil

In the beginning, God created, and he said it was good. Six times he made this point, and then, after his creation of humanity, he said that all he had made was "very good" (Genesis 1:31).

Your creativity was always intended to redeem, to renew, and to make the world good. Now, don't misunderstand me—I'm not talking about some goodie-two-shoes version of goodness. We're not called to a saccharine version of Christian creativity that settles for the vanilla, drowning in its own blandness. What we're talking about is a radical, disruptive, revolutionary kind of good—a redemptive kind of goodness. One that takes the broken pieces of the world and remakes them. One that thinks outside the box. That imagines differently. That is ablaze with holiness and heavy with glory. This is the kind of good we're called to.

Think of it this way: The cross of Jesus Christ is the singularity of the creative soul. Because of the cross—the central, overcoming, human event horizon—all things can truly be made new. The code is written for the future of the human race. And our joy as creatives is to take that code and use it to reprogramme the world.

As a result, your imagination has more than purpose—it has urgency. You're part of the solution, the antidote, the remedy. Your mission and purpose as someone who creates—whether in the arts, business, science, or education—is to live out the creativity that began in Genesis, passed through the cross, and continues into the new kind of future God is making. The ongoing work of God's creativity expressed through your life is not an ending but a beginning.

Now, let's take a little detour and have a conversation about something we really need to talk about.

On Christian Creativity

At a recent Renaissance gathering, I was set to interview a young artist who has been gaining critical acclaim and serious momentum in the music industry. Just before our conversation—set to take place in front of hundreds of creative leaders—she seemed unusually nervous. I pointed out that only the night before, she'd performed in front of an arena crowd of thousands. So why, I asked, did this setting feel so intimidating?

She hesitated, then admitted she was worried that people were expecting her to explain how her art was somehow "Christian." She said, "Look, I'm not sure if people expect my music to be Christian. It's not—I'm just trying to make the best music I can."

I gently pushed back. "That's exactly why your art is Christian," I suggested to her. "Because it's done with excellence, to the glory of God. You're called to make the best music you can—to the glory of God." She looked relieved.

Here's the thing: There's no such thing as Christian art and non-Christian art. There's only good art and bad art. Made by people who are Christians. Or not (yet). The subject of the art, well, that's a different matter. My point is that all creativity can glorify God. And all creativity can lie to us. Sticking the label "Christian" on it won't save it or make it good. And calling it "Christian" won't make bad art acceptable. The acid test is simple: Is it true? Is it beautiful? Is it good?

> *What a Christian portrays in his art is the totality of life. Art is not to be solely a vehicle for some sort of self-conscious evangelism.*
> —Francis A. Schaeffer

So, here's the charge: Let your Spirit-fired creativity aim to be insanely good. Tell stories that move the soul. Plumb the depths of emotion. Take people to the mountaintops of wonder. Make the most profound impact you can with what you've been given. Do everything to the glory of God. And don't settle for playing it safe. You carry the spark of the Creator within you, so your work should be extraordinary. Don't shortchange your calling. Instead—invest in your gifts. Practice. Keep going. Get better. Dream big. Aim high. Set the sights of your soul on glory. Dorothy Sayers put it simply: "The only Christian work is good work well done."[33]

The world needs your best ideas and your boldest creativity. They are water to a thirsty generation. And when you create—when you make art, protest, innovate, invent, dream, build, tell stories that shape reality, and bring hope to others—what you're doing is making good. Your creativity matters: It's not just about truth and beauty. God has placed creativity in you so that your life might bring goodness into the world. There is an inescapably moral quality to creativity. The creativity of your soul reflects the goodness of God and contributes to the flourishing of society. As Trevor Hart argues, the world is a "project divinely begun and established, yet one that is handed over to us with 'more to be made of it yet' and inviting our responsible participation in the making."[34]

And God wants you to be part of making the world better—it's your calling, your mandate, your purpose. Just as Jesus takes bread and wine—the fruit of human culture and creativity—and transforms them, he also wants to take your ideas, your output, and your imagination, and work through you and in you to gather the broken bits of the world into the redeeming power of his death and resurrection. True creativity renews and resurrects—it's an act of love. It's the outward, not inward, motion of the soul.

Creativity Unlocks Heaven

Your creativity has the power to remake the world—justly. The renaissance of culture isn't about perpetuating cycles of brokenness but about unlocking the image of God in one another and seeing the healing power of his kingdom come. That means restoring what's right, repairing what's wrong, and making good. To act justly, to love mercy, to walk humbly (Micah 6:8)—these are not passive ideals. Creativity and justice go hand in hand. Holy creativity and holy justice always walk together, because righting the wrongs of yesterday will always demand creative thinking. Reconciliation is relational innovation.

Over the past few years in the US, one of the ways communities have begun to address the injustice of racial division is through a process called the "witness circle"—a space where Black and white leaders—often pastors and elders—gather to apologise, repent, and reconcile. These are powerful moments where historical documents related to slave ownership are read aloud and leaders today step forward to acknowledge the failings of the past.

One such gathering took place on February 7, 2023, on the campus of Asbury University in Kentucky. A witness circle brought together the college president and both Black and white leaders from the local community for a moment of historic repentance and renewed commitment to unity. Slave owners' deeds were read publicly. There was deep, heartfelt confession. Tears. Forgiveness. Reconciliation.

A student gospel choir led worship during the gathering. They later described something shifting in the room—a change in the spiritual atmosphere. When the circle concluded, they didn't want to stop. So they moved to a nearby chapel on campus, where students would gather the following morning for a regular, mandatory chapel service.

The next day that same choir led worship again. My friend Zach Meerkreebs was preaching. And at the end of the service, something extraordinary began to unfold. The presence of God filled the room. The Holy Spirit began to move—in quiet, unmistakable power. It was sovereign and supernatural: Day and night the presence of God filled that place. Students dragged mattresses into the space, not wanting to leave. And for sixteen days and nights, the outpouring continued. Tens of thousands of people queued all night to experience this movement of God, leading to the local authorities closing down the town to all incoming traffic. The flashing hazard traffic signs read: "Revival over Capacity." *The New York Times* would later describe what became known as the Asbury Outpouring as the first revival of the twenty-first century in the West.[35]

But what many don't realise is that behind the scenes of this historic move of God was a creative convergence—forgiveness, reconciliation, and worship—that opened the doors for heaven to move. And it was as the choir sang of the goodness of God that the heavens began to open.

When you use your creativity to heal, restore, and reconcile, all of heaven draws close because you're doing the very thing the image of God in you was designed to do. Ask yourself not "Will this be successful?" but "Will it light up the darkness?" Decide what your red lines are and stick to them. Choose not to create what dehumanises others. Let the ethics of heaven flow through your creative work so that it points unmistakably to the goodness of God. Watch for the signs of the creative Spirit at work around you and follow him with everything you have. Discover where the Creator Spirit is moving and invest your life there.

I have high hopes for your creativity. Your life is going to be an inbreaking of what is to come—a down payment of a future kingdom. Your creativity has the potential to help save the world, to make all things new. Think about this: What truth will you tell? What beauty will you show the world? What will you build that is good?

Christians Create Futures

You are someone who is involved in creating a future that will look radically different from the chaos of the past. As Erwin McManus says, "Christians create futures."[36] Not just because we're dreamers but because we follow a God who makes all things new (Revelation 21:5). To be made in the image of God is to carry his creative essence—and the future belongs to those bold enough to imagine and build what doesn't yet exist. McManus concludes, "The past will be the future unless you create a different one."[37]

This is the Christian calling: not just to resist darkness but to shine light. Not just to critique what is but to imagine what could be. The church at her best has always been future building—raising up ancient cathedrals, founding schools that shaped generations, launching movements that reformed society, defending the vulnerable, and singing the new songs that point to the world that is to come. It's no accident that, as Robert Darden points out, "Gospel music was the soundtrack of the civil rights movement."[38]

We don't just inherit the past; we build the future. What you will create doesn't just matter now; it echoes into eternity. Creativity is not escapism; it's eschatology. It's the future breaking in. Whether you're designing software, writing music, raising children, or leading a church, you are shaping what tomorrow will look like. In a world overwhelmed by entropy and despair, the Spirit invites us to join in the divine act of creation—to push forward, not backward.

Now, I'm not saying this will be easy. You'll need extraordinary persistence, but your life will have an impact. Your creativity will not be wasted. The great pioneer of missions, Hudson Taylor, put it like this: "There are three stages to every great work of God: first, it is impossible; then, it is difficult; then, it is done."[39] Your creativity has the power to change the world. Create. Heal. Illuminate. Lift your eyes to the horizon of hope.

> *Whatever is true, whatever is noble, whatever is right, whatever is pure, whatever is lovely, whatever is admirable—if anything is excellent or praiseworthy—think about such things.*
> —Philippians 4:8

SPARK CIRCLE

Circle back through this chapter of Spark.

Notice
What did this chapter stir in you?
Was there a line, image, or story that made you believe creativity really could change things?

Name
How might beauty, truth, and goodness shape your creativity?
How can you shine light with your work?

Next Step
This week, create something rooted in one of the three foundations: beauty, truth, or goodness. It could be a word of encouragement, a piece of work, a conversation—whatever flows from your creativity.
Don't wait for perfect conditions. Just start, and then share with your Spark Circle what happened when you created with hope in mind.

CHAPTER 10

Overwhelmed with Wonder

But lo! men have become the tools of their tools. The man who independently plucked the fruits when he was hungry is become a farmer; and he who stood under a tree for shelter, a housekeeper. We now no longer camp as for a night, but have settled down on earth and forgotten heaven.
—Henry David Thoreau

As soon as all the people saw Jesus, they were overwhelmed with wonder and ran to greet him.
—Mark 9:15

Congratulations! You're living in extraordinary times. But navigating this insane world? Bewildering. As I write this, I'm sitting in a coffee shop in San Francisco, where we're gearing up to launch the first Renaissance event on the West Coast. But my journey here this morning was unlike any other I've ever taken. I opened my phone, ordered a taxi, and a minute later the car pulled up. My friend and I jumped in the back. So far, so good. The traffic was normal, the car comfortable, a typical taxi ride—except for one unusual detail: The car had no driver. We were being driven by a robot.

My first trip in a driverless car felt like something from childhood sci-fi dreams. I sat in awe as the steering wheel spun by itself, guided by some invisible force. By the time you read this, it might feel like old news, and the early adopters among you are probably zipping around in a drone taxi. But as I sit in this café watching daylight unfold over San Francisco, my mind is racing as I consider the new technological era that is dawning. In the moment, it feels both bewildering and exhilarating in equal measure.

One thing is clear: Whether we like it or not, technology is transforming the world around us. It's not a bad feeling; it's just new. And new is, well, a lot. On one hand, we have more information and greater processing power at our fingertips than ever before. On the other, this high-change world leaves us dizzy, irritated, even travel sick, as we speed through our existence, fingernails clinging to the upholstery in the back seat. And, to stretch this metaphor a little further, it can feel like life's steering wheel is spinning out of control and we have no say in where we're headed. So, here's my question: How do we navigate this?

This chapter is about how your divine creativity will help you navigate this rapidly changing world. We're going to need to look out the window—pay attention to the landscape, notice the patterns, and read the signs along the way. Because they're trying to tell us something. So, fasten your seat belt, because this journey is about to become far more exciting than we could imagine. We're about to explore some ideas that can change the very direction of this cultural moment.

Motion Sickness

If you've ever felt confused, disoriented, or like you don't quite fit—if you've struggled to understand your place in the world—take heart: You're not alone. This feeling is the standard human reaction in times of rapid change. When history accelerates, it can feel like being swept away by a tide of change. What once took decades now happens in minutes. And the compound effects of rapid change make us feel a little travel sick.

So much of our world—both individually and collectively—seems like it's in a constant state of flux. The solid ground we once built our lives upon now feels like it's liquifying beneath our feet. We're living through a sea change. The tide of technology is rising so fast that the very nature

217

of what it means to be human—our spirituality, our creativity, our place in the world—is facing a full-blown identity crisis. Sociologist Zygmunt Bauman describes this as liquid modernity, where "change is the only permanence, and uncertainty the only certainty"; and as a consequence, "individuals face a continuous process of renegotiation and adaptation."[1]

Times like these send shockwaves through the cultural, spiritual, and technological frameworks we rely on, shaping the future in ways we can't yet fully see. So, it's no surprise that the revolutionary environment you're existing in feels deeply unsettling. Alvin Toffler, in his book *Future Shock*, warned that in times of rapid change, "people suffer from shattering stress and disorientation" due to an "inability to cope with the pace of change." The result? They are left "dizzy, disoriented, and disconnected."[2] That's certainly how I feel on days like today, as I watch my driverless car speed off into the distance without a care in the world.

And yet, while moments of high change can feel overwhelming, if we can find a way to navigate them, they are also moments of extraordinary opportunity. The future is a blank canvas, waiting for the new. Who gets to fill that blank canvas? The picture of the future that will emerge will be painted by those who have learned to harness the power of their creativity. The thoughts, dreams, ideas, and longings that exist deep in your soul are the sketchbook of the future God is longing to create through you. Because it's in these moments of extraordinary flux that something new is born. We are entering a time of transformation—the age of a new renaissance.

The Age of Renaissance

Time and again, when history speeds up, a familiar pattern emerges: Revolution leads to renewal, which births renaissance.

Understanding that this pattern always surfaces in seasons of disruption helps us frame what comes next, because at every breakthrough moment in history, these three are always present. Let's dig a little deeper into this, as the pattern here is uncanny:

1. First, there's a *technological revolution*—a radical advancement that fundamentally changes the way humans interact with the world. Unsettling, bewildering, disorienting.
2. Next, there is an accompanying *spiritual renewal*—a revival of faith, the return of a generation to God, that is often both amplified by and in response to this new technological landscape. The two go hand in hand through history.
3. Finally, the impact is a significant *cultural renaissance*—the rebirth and flourishing of human creativity, community, and intellect. From the swirling maelstrom of change, a fresh reality begins to emerge, one that shapes the world, coalesces, and solidifies into the new normal.

And here's what is so fascinating: When we map these three patterns across the arc of human history, we begin to see a golden thread that links together the great moments of transformation:

Revolution rearranges the foundations.
Renewal restores the soul.
Renaissance reshapes the future.

Let's do a little experiment. Imagine for a moment that you can order a taxi from an app on your phone, and what arrives is a little bit more DeLorean time machine from *Back to the Future* than self-driving car. Instead of taking us from A to B, we can travel from AD to BC at the click of a button, complete with complimentary water bottles, soothing music, and pre-selected interior temperature.

Campfires

Our first stop is the farthest back in time: 40,000 BC. It's a time of wild things, beasts, pre-history. The human race is in the middle of our first great revolution: what's known as *pyrotechnology*—the fancy word for the domestication of fire. Our ancestors are beginning to use fire as a tool, not just to keep warm and scare off big hairy things with long teeth. Around those campfires, the first communities have been formed, drawn together for warmth and safety. Fire starts to be used to create tools for hunting, hardening stones, and baking primitive ceramics.

Alongside this pyrotechnological breakthrough, something else begins to emerge: spiritual renewal. People seem to start believing that their lives are more than just the span of their days, that there must be a soul that travels on beyond death. For the first time, around this period in history, people start burying their loved ones in elaborate ways with possessions, empathy, and ritual. And at the same time—around 40,000 BC—the first figurative, recognisable works of art begin to emerge in the form of cave paintings or simple carved sculptures like the *Lion Man* of Hohlenstein-Stadel.

Our first revolution was fire, and this sparked the original spiritual activity of the human race alongside the first cultural expression of creativity. Professor Randall White, a leading authority on Paleolithic art, observes that the earliest hearths served not only as sources of warmth and sustenance but also as the birthplaces of artistic expression and ritual activity.[3] The same sparks that lit the campfires of prehistory also ignited the spiritual imagination of the human race. What followed was more than just survival—it was the birth of culture. The first myths were told. The first stories passed from one generation to the next. This was the first renaissance—a moment when the technological, the spiritual, and the creative fused together, shaping the trajectory of humanity in a radical way—not just survival, but a "relationship with the things unseen."[4]

Easy as ABC

Jump back in that time machine and punch in the year 3000 BC, where on the dusty plains of what is modern-day Iraq, another revolution is taking place: The people are developing writing. The shapes carved into those first clay tablets mean that their ideas, stories, and laws are no longer bound to memory—they can now be preserved and passed down through each generation. Up to this point, communication has all been word of mouth. Now someone is taking notes.

Our pattern is also here. The breakthrough in technology is matched with a spiritual awakening—the genesis of the Abrahamic faiths—and a cultural renaissance. We still have their creative output from the centuries that followed: Literature, poetry, sacred songs, great epics, the first drama and theatre, written histories, and the birth of ideas as philosophy were all beginning to flourish. Writing didn't just record knowledge—it expanded imagination and reshaped civilisation. Societies became structured and organised as laws were codified for the first time. This was the world of the Bible: the stories of the Old Testament, of Egypt, Babylon, and other kingdoms of the Middle East. The human race had turned a new page.

All Roads

As my driverless car disappears into the distance, it is still relying on one of the most (literally) groundbreaking technologies ever invented by the human race: the road. The road was the technology that allowed a small collection of tribes from central Italy to conquer the known world, stretching their influence from Scotland to the Persian Gulf.

The year we jump to next is 300 BC, and the technological revolution of the Roman Road is reshaping the world. Rome's success was built on this simple innovation: More than just a network of stone and mortar, it transformed connectivity, trade, and movement, laying the foundation for what would become the Roman Empire. The ability to move armies, goods, money, and ideas rapidly across vast distances was a game changer. The Roman Road didn't just connect cities; it held the empire together, making expansion and control possible on an unprecedented scale. Rome's achievement was not just an empire of conquest, but as historian Tom Holland puts it, an empire of infrastructure that spread along roads that would outlast Rome itself.[5] The road was Rome's greatest legacy, one that still shapes the whole world today.[6]

What about the spiritual renewal? Well, this one may be a little more familiar: At the height of Roman power, a lone figure from a small, forgotten backwater of the empire entered the story. His life, death, and resurrection ignited a movement that spread along those roads like the flame on a fuse. Without the Roman road, the good news about Jesus would have crawled along—slow, fragmented, confined. But speeding down those highways, its impact became explosive, a revolution that reshaped the world. The good news about Jesus moved at the pace of the Roman road.[7] Two millennia later, the spiritual legacy of that creative breakthrough grows by the day.

Press Print

Jump back into your time machine for one last stop: Fast-forward to the middle of Europe in the fifteenth century. It was a time of plague and darkness, tyranny and servitude. Knowledge moved at a painstaking pace. Every book, every manuscript, every idea had to be copied by hand—a slow, laborious process. Books were rare, expensive, and accessible only to an elite few. But in the 1440s, everything changed.

When Johannes Gutenberg created a way of arranging movable type into the printing press, he enabled information to flow into your hands. And as we know, information is power. Overnight the printing press illuminated a universe of knowledge. The invention democratised learning. For the first time in history, the written word could be mass produced. Whether you're reading this on a screen or holding a physical book, you have Gutenberg to thank. The printing press was arguably the most transformative leap in human communication since the invention of language itself.

OVERWHELMED WITH WONDER

And as with every major technological revolution, this one helped spark a spiritual renewal: the Reformation. The printing press placed the Bible into the hands of ordinary people, allowing them to read it in their own language. This new accessibility ignited the flames of reformation, spreading the radical ideas of Martin Luther and the early Reformers, and unleashing a great spiritual awakening. If you're reading this on a Kindle (other devices are available) or listening to the *Spark* audiobook (subtle plug), you're still riding the Gutenberg wave.

As always, a cultural renaissance followed. The intellectual and artistic energy already bubbling across Europe was suddenly accelerated by this technology. A seismic shift unfolded—giving rise to the European renaissances that swept the continent in the generations that followed. It was a time of creativity, exploration, and intellectual flourishing that reshaped Western civilisation. Much of today's art and culture trace their roots back to this explosive moment. The towering giants of the Renaissance—Michelangelo, Leonardo da Vinci, and Donatello—laid the foundations for the great European masters, shaping the trajectory of art all the way through to the radical movement of the twentieth-century's modernists and beyond. It's hard to overstate just how profound this eruption of beauty and imagination was.

The Reformation and Renaissance laid the groundwork for what came next: the Enlightenment, the rise of modern science, and ultimately, the digital age. From the printing press to the internet, each leap in communication has sparked a new cycle of revolution, renewal, and renaissance, reshaping how we think, create, and believe. We shape our technologies, and then our technologies shape us.[8]

Finally, our time machine lands back on the road outside the coffee shop in San Franscisco, and we step out into the fresh air of today's fast-paced, high-change world. Let's map this pattern of revolution, renewal, and renaissance onto the world you and I exist in. What kind of renaissance will emerge from this revolution? Will this change even be positive? The jury is still out on whether this will be an age in which we recover what it truly means to be human. One in which our imaginations spark a new world of light, freedom, and life. Or alternatively, will the human ability to dream, to make good, to renew, to imagine be snuffed out, leaving us in darkness and despair? Perhaps, like the ex-driver of my now driverless car, we will be left thumbing a lift on the sidewalk of history.

The Big One

This is not a drill. One thing is certain: We're living through the early stages of The Big One, a technological revolution like none the planet has ever experienced. The brilliant physicist Stephen Hawking recognised the scale of this shift, describing the rise of AI as "the biggest event in human history."[9] I would take a slightly different view—the incarnation seems a little bit more, well, physically and eternally significant, but it is certainly true that the scale and implications of the revolution we're living through make every other human technological shift look like a warm-up lap. The reality is that we've already crossed the Rubicon.

Everywhere we look, the world is being rewired. Machine learning is not just automating tasks—or ordering your online shopping—it is reshaping how we think, our ethics, and challenging our understanding of human creativity, intelligence, and uniqueness. What it means to be human is being challenged, even at the most fundamental level of the human imagination, leading Yuval Noah Harari to conclude that when machines begin to take control of human imagination, then the future of humanity itself will be truly at stake.[10] So, to put it bluntly, this current technological revolution is the most profound and impactful shift yet to have happened to the human race.

Will we so have anaesthetised our creativity that we will simply have ceased to dream? Will we, under a blanket of technological fog, forget what the stars in the heavens look like? That, ultimately, will depend on whether this revolution is accompanied by a deeper renewal of the creative soul, a spiritual awakening that reclaims what it means to be truly human.

Babel 2.0

> *We have allowed our technology to*
> *outdistance our theology.*
> —Martin Luther King Jr.

The book of Genesis relates a cautionary tale about the people of Babel, who built a tower to make a name for themselves. Starting in Eden, the desire for God-like intelligence has always led us into trouble. Babel, a bold act of self-reliance that ended in disaster, was no exception. The result? Division, confusion, and a technological tower that crumbled into dust.

Today Babel is back. The revolution we've unleashed is threatening everything from creativity and ethics to agency and autonomy. The question is: Where will it lead? We can't just keep building higher, faster, bigger. Because if we do, we'll miss the music of the soul in the process. Imagination will be bypassed, and meaning will become secondary to function. As Andrzej Turkanik describes in *The Robot Will See You Now*, "Left to its own devices, however, I am afraid that AI will provide us with technically smooth and sleek material, which is, at the same time, lacking in intention, imagination, and the thought-world of meaning and purpose. And those are uniquely human—or, should I say, God-like—traits."[11]

For the first time in history, we've entered what's known as the Anthropocene Age, an era where humankind is the dominant force shaping the very fabric of the planet. Our technology, production, and consumption are taking more than they give. And the consequences are stacking up: sociological, economic, environmental. Eden is still burning.

Now, I don't say this to alarm you or to fuel that most post-modern malaise of technological anxiety. You can of course sit back, fasten your seat belt, and let the self-driving car of change speed off into the sunset, but to bury your head in the sand at this moment in history would be a mistake. This is a time for a move of God, for a recovery of spiritual fire and the awakening of a generation. Otherwise, the future will be pretty bleak.

Start Paddling

So, revolution? Tick. But what kind of renaissance happens next will be directed by one crucial factor: the spiritual renewal that will bridge the two. Will there be a move of God in this generation? What will it look like? And how can we position our creative souls to experience the full force of the wave that is coming?

I once went surfing with a world champion. Fresh off a global title win, my host encouraged me out into a serious surf break off the eastern coast of Australia. The swell was massive, the sky stormy. As we paddled out, he tried to reassure me with a fast and loose interpretation of Philippians 1:21, "To live is Christ and to die is gain." It didn't help. I found myself panicking. It took ages to get to the back of the break. When I finally made it—exhausted—I paused to catch my breath. Then my friend pointed to the horizon.

"That one's yours," he said.

I watched as a towering wall of water glided toward us. I started paddling, but it was too late. Before I knew it, my feet were flying over my head, and I was being rolled down toward the reef. My wetsuit scraped along the rock, my board dinged, I crawled up the beach coughing salt water, dazed and winded.

An hour later, having regrouped and caught my breath, I was back in the water. This time, sitting at the back of the break, my friend explained what I was doing wrong. "You're not getting ready for the wave soon enough," he said. "The moment you spot the wave, you have to start paddling—lining up your board, building momentum. If you wait till the wave's already on top of you, it's too late. You'll never catch it." I put his advice into practice, and to my astonishment, I found it worked. I was standing and gliding down the face of the biggest wave I've ever seen. In the distance, I could hear my friend cheering as I walked on water.

We face a choice in this moment in history: to start paddling or to sink to the bottom of this sea change moment. The water is changing fast: a technological revolution is sweeping all around us. Watch out for the spiritual renewal that will surely come rolling in from the horizon, and prepare for the renaissance that must follow. If we want to catch this wave, we have to start paddling now. If we sit back as spectators or leave it too late, we'll find ourselves rolled in the surf.

So, what do we make of this moment? Are there any waves of hope on the horizon? Is faith a distant memory, or is something new rolling in?

The Wave Is Here

Well, as I write, there's undoubtedly a ripple on the horizon. The first waves of the set are already starting to break around us. Change is in the water. We are in the early stages of a spiritual awakening, especially in the most secular parts of the world and, most strikingly, among younger generations. The post-pandemic years have unearthed a deep spiritual hunger. Those born after the turn of the century are abandoning the casual secularism of their parents. They are half as likely to identify as atheists. Everywhere you look, there's talk of revival.

The early data backs this up. Belief in God in London has jumped significantly: Just five years ago, only a quarter of Londoners claimed to believe in God; now it's well over half.[12] Any way you look at it, that's a huge shift. Leading atheists and cultural figures have come to faith.[13] Churches are seeing unexpected spikes in young men attending services.[14] Bible sales among Gen Z are surging.[15] People have a hunger, a longing, a desperation for something more. We're beginning to see outpourings of the Holy Spirit on university campuses, in local churches, in unexpected corners of the globe.[16] The revival fire that has been burning across Asia, Africa, and Latin America is starting to spread to the most secular places on the planet.

No question: We are entering an age of spiritual renewal. So now is the time to start paddling. In that sense, everything we've explored in this book has been building to this moment. How do we allow the spark of divine creativity—the Holy Spirit—to set our whole lives on fire with renewing power so that we might see a new renaissance?

Mountaintop Movements

To unpack this, let's rewind to a mountaintop moment with God—a spiritual encounter that changed everything. Mark's gospel tells the story of how Jesus led his closest friends—Peter, James, and John—up a high mountain. And there, before their eyes, Jesus was transfigured. His clothes dazzled, radiant with glory. In that moment, the cloud of creative glory—the presence of the Creator Spirit—descended on them all. It was a life-changing encounter. Peter never wanted to leave. He wanted to capture it, bottle it, stay in it forever. But instead of staying in that place of spiritual ecstasy, Jesus led them back down the mountain into the heart of the culture. Your creativity—the spark in you, the cloud of God's presence, the glory resting on your life—is not there just for your own benefit. God draws close to your soul so you can go down the mountain to a generation longing for spiritual renewal.

When Jesus and his friends came down the mountain, the scene they encountered was similar to what we would experience today. Mark 9:14 records, "When they came to the other disciples, they saw a large crowd around them and the teachers of the law arguing with them." In other words, coming down from an encounter with God often leads us straight into the fight, the chaos at the heart of the culture. A world of conflict, confusion, arguments, division, and fragmentation.

It's normal for your soul to experience creative tension, for your ideas to be misunderstood, for what God has birthed in you to stir jealousy, judgment, even resistance. Whenever you carry something new into the world, a crowd will always be ready to shoot it down. Just as gravity pulls everything down, the human race has a way of dragging down innovation and suffocating the new. Then we see something extraordinary happen—a template for how true revolution flows into renaissance: "As soon as all the people saw Jesus, they were overwhelmed with wonder and ran to greet him" (Mark 9:15).

How can you become a vehicle for glory if you're not experiencing that glory for yourself? How can you see renewal if you're not being renewed inwardly? Sure, you can go a long way on your own gifting.

You're made in the image of God, after all. You can perform, persuade, and pull something off. But the truth is, your mission flows from your mountaintop. You might be gifted, brilliant, and talented, but unless you're experiencing deep spiritual renewal and encounter with the creative Spirit for yourself, you will eventually burn out. This has been the story of so many creatives and innovators over the years. They were called by God. They started out in his presence, on the mountaintop. But somewhere along the way, they tried to do things in their own strength. And if what they were building was founded on their own glory, not God's, it could not last.

As the disciples walked down the mountain with Jesus, something extraordinary began to happen—people flocked to Jesus. Perhaps it was the look on his face—maybe he was still radiating glory from the transfiguration—but something about him was utterly irresistible. The same is true today: The answer to this cultural moment is not technology or sociology or theology or philosophy—it's an encounter with the presence of the risen Christ, the one who holds space and time in the span of his hands.

See Jesus

The first thing that happened is that "all the people saw Jesus." Spiritual renewal ignites at the heart of culture when people carrying the fire walk into the chaos of revolution. Others begin to see the *imago Dei* ablaze in you. The fire in your creative soul wasn't meant for the mountaintop alone—it was meant for the marketplace. For the start-up incubator. The casting studio. The boardroom. The school. The science lab. The library.

As soon as all the people saw Jesus, something shifted. And take note of this—it wasn't just *some* of the people. The ones with their Bibles under their arms, just waiting for God to show up. It was not the super keen and the squeaky clean. It was everyone. All of them. There's no sacred-secular divide here. The glory of God cannot be contained. True renaissance begins when the saturation of God's divine presence flows beyond the church and into the culture. He is, after all, not a tame lion.¹⁷ God is not restricting himself to the boundary you draw around him. Instead, as Gerard Manley Hopkins put it, "Christ plays in ten thousand places."¹⁸ Jesus will walk down the mountain into whatever corner of the creation he wishes to.

So today—open the eyes of your heart.
Fix your gaze on Jesus.
Let something extraordinary happen.
See him in all his beauty.

Be Overwhelmed with Wonder

Mark recorded next that when Jesus and his friends came down the mountain, as soon as the crowd saw Jesus, "they were overwhelmed with wonder" (Mark 9:15). We're living through a wonder drought. The world is starved of awe, but Jesus is the answer to that longing. He is the key to wonder. Spending time in his presence immerses our hearts in the headwaters of awe.

This is the pattern: The more we see Jesus, the more we experience the Creator's love and fire, the more we are overwhelmed with wonder. A virtuous circle of glory is set in motion: The more we see, the more we love. And from that place dreams are born, imaginations come alive, ideas catch fire, and impact flows from inspiration. Everything changes. Your best ideas won't come from pressure or striving; they will flow from presence. From awe. From encounter. So make room to allow yourself to be overwhelmed with wonder, and keep returning to that place over and over again.

Run to Greet Him

And then, Mark wrote, the people "ran to greet [Jesus]." Before spiritual revival comes, there must be relational revival. The crowd that greeted Jesus after his transfiguration didn't hesitate. They ran. They raced. They rushed. And not just a few of them—all of them. This wasn't an individual moment. It was a shared experience. The whole crowd moved: the "entire multitude," according to the Greek. The whole culture was swept up in running to Jesus, to meet him, to welcome him, to draw close to him.

You harbour this same divine radiance in your soul. And through your creativity, your life, your work, your love, people are going to experience Jesus. The gift of your creative faculties is a highway of holiness through which God will meet with people. The spark of divine creativity in you isn't there to make you look good. It's there to bring the world running to the fire of God's glory.

The creative life is a bridge between the chaos of revolution and the beauty of the renaissance to come. What the world needs right now isn't more technologists full of revolutionary zeal. It's a creative minority full of the Holy Spirit. There is a generation around you aching to glimpse just one flicker of glory. As the old saying goes, you may be the only Bible they ever read. Your spark may be their only connection to heaven. The call on your life is to feed the fire of the Holy Spirit in your soul and let it burn through your work—your creativity, your character, your calling, your imagination—so that extraordinary things start to catch fire. So that people see Jesus and run to him, overwhelmed with wonder. That's the shape of the coming renaissance.

God will stir a revolution in your life if you'll make space to be overwhelmed with wonder again. So make space for the mountaintop moments. Let your creative soul be unveiled before the majesty of heaven. Invite the Holy Spirit to saturate you. And then—and only then—let God's presence lead you down the mountain, into the heart of the revolution. Let your life burn with holy fire, and let God's reflected glory light up the world around you.

And when you do, you'll realise something powerful: A true renaissance isn't just possible. It has already begun.

SPARK CIRCLE

Circle back through this chapter of Spark.

Notice
How is this moment of revolution impacting your creativity? What might a new renaissance look like in your life?

Name
Describe a mountaintop moment when you've encountered the Creator.
How might creativity help people experience the wonder of God?

Next Step
If you've never encountered God in a personal way, why not try praying to Jesus?
Where might God be sending you? Share with your Spark Circle.

EPILOGUE

Cathedrals of Creativity

> *Creativity is God's gift to us. Using our creativity is our gift back to God.*
> —Julia Cameron

Boxing Day, December 26, 2004.

It was a perfect day on the beach: the tropical sun shone gently as heat ripples danced across the golden sand. Palm trees swayed in the soft Indian Ocean breeze. Olivia and I were lying on a delicate golden sandbar in the middle of a picture-postcard river estuary. A picnic, two towels, a beach bag, and a parasol. It was paradise.

Little did we know that within minutes our lives would change forever, and that from that day on, we'd mark our lives as *before* and *after*. We were in our mid-twenties, newly married, and trying to figure out what to do with our lives. Olivia had just completed the latest stage of the gruelling training that would eventually allow her to practise as an architect. I was hustling hard trying to make it as a young film producer. Exhausted, we'd hit a wall. The remedy, of course, was that classic carefree twentysomething solution: We'd blown what little savings we had and taken a month off work to travel across Asia. By the time we reached the coast of India, it was Christmas, and we found ourselves sitting on this immaculate beach, talking about life, our dreams, and what we would like to do with our futures.

EPILOGUE

However, all of that was about to change. Just hours earlier, the most powerful earthquake ever recorded had struck the Indian Ocean: A 9.1 magnitude earthquake deep under the ocean off the coast of Indonesia triggered a devastating tsunami, with waves over thirty metres high. The Boxing Day Tsunami became the worst natural disaster of the century, claiming a quarter of a million lives—destroying communities all around the Indian Ocean—leaving millions homeless, bereaved, and changed forever. But now here we sat, toes in the water, oblivious to the danger of the deadly tsunami that was racing across the ocean straight toward the coastline of India.

The first sign something was wrong came when the sea began to recede—fast. One minute the water was lapping around our feet, the next minute the tide had pulled back so far that it looked as if the ocean had disappeared. We sat there on our towels, puzzled, discussing this phenomenon. I remember every word of the conversation: We talked about how strange it was since there were no tides where we were. *"It's so weird; where did the sea just go?"* Thinking about it still makes me shudder all these years later.

Then, without warning, the water came rushing back in. A surge tore up the beach, drenching us, soaking everything in sight. Suddenly we were on our feet, trying to make sense of what was happening. The sandbar we were standing on was abruptly cut off, and we were stranded in the middle of the sea. The flood of water was now swirling all around us, the whole sea level rising in and out, like the cycle of the tides repeating every few minutes. With no phone signal—no advance warning—we were oblivious to the full magnitude of what was happening. All we could do was watch, spectators in a tectonic drama playing out of our control.

Mercifully for us, by an accident of geography, the shape of the coastline where we were located meant that we had been sheltered from the full destructive force of the tsunami and escaped to tell the story. It was not until later that day that the full gravity of what we'd been a part of began to emerge. Our families back home in London had awakened to the devastating headlines of what had happened: Entire coastal regions washed away. First came the frantic text messages: *"Are you alive?"* And

CATHEDRALS OF CREATIVITY

then came the phone calls. *"We're okay. Unharmed. Safe."* And then the spine-chilling realisation: We had escaped the deadliest natural disaster of the twenty-first century by a whisker. A different beach, a different day, and I would not be writing these words.

That Boxing Day changed everything for me. For a while I tried not to think too hard about the *what ifs*—but the reality is that near misses put everything into perspective. That day we experienced something profound: the truth that all our lives are short. Fragile. Fleeting. "But a breath," as the psalmist wrote (Psalm 39:5). There's nothing like a near-death experience to focus your mind on the beautiful urgency of every day. Ever since that moment on the beach, I've felt like I've been living on borrowed time. It's funny what a sense of mortality does for the bravado of youth. Perspective changes. Some ambitions are recognised as idols. And in their place, a different kind of hope begins to burn.

The greatest tragedy of all is not dying but never really learning to live your life in the first place. Through the journey of these pages, I've tried to encourage you to live for a different flame: to follow the heavenly vision for your life. The message has been simple: You are made in the image of your Creator, and he longs to fill you with his holy fire. The Holy Spirit wants to keep on fanning into flame the divine spark of your creative potential so that your life burns with heaven's creativity.

Over this journey together, we've unpacked this calling. We've looked at the power of your imagination, the deep places your inspiration flows from. We've explored how change happens miraculously, and how by nurturing the innovation of heaven in our lives we can see everyday miracles break out. We've traced the highs and lows of fears and failures. We've learned how to dig deep and find that creative courage that will sustain us. And then, finally, we talked about impact—the holy legacy your life can have when you begin to live out the fullness of this creative calling. All the way through this journey, you've done the hard work: wrestling with these ideas, sketching and mapping your own journey, making space for God to speak to you.

Now, as we come to the closing pages, I want us to visit one final place together.

EPILOGUE

London Calling

If you and I were to trace the winding streets of the city of London back to its oldest point, we'd cross the medieval grid of alleyways and lanes, ancient buildings and Roman foundations, until we'd come to a hill that rises from beside the Thames. Here, on a hilltop in the middle of the city a place of worship has stood for two millennia. First, a pagan shrine, then from AD 60 a Roman temple. In 604 St Mellitus, the first Bishop of London, founded a Saxon church here, which was replaced in 1087 by a Norman cathedral dedicated to St Paul. London was built up around this great place of worship. Then in 1666 the great fire of London tore through, destroying two-thirds of the city. As the smoke cleared, all that remained of great St Paul's was a charred skeleton of broken beams. Today's building is what rose from the ashes. And we come to it now on our walk up that hill, a towering giant of a cathedral dominating the skyline of the city to this day.

When you first approach St Paul's Cathedral, the scale of the place is breathtaking. Completed in 1711, the great dome is still one of the largest in the world, second only to St Peter's in Rome. A golden cross stands on top of the cathedral at a height of 365 feet—one for each day of the year. It was, until the mid-1960s, the second tallest building in London. Designed by Sir Christopher Wren, construction took thirty-five years, resulting in one of the most magnificent buildings ever built. The structure is entirely built from one hundred fifty thousand tonnes of Portland stone, which was carefully carved by hand into a million stone blocks by a team of over a thousand stonecutters and craftsmen working around the clock.

Wren was meticulous about the quality of the work, insisting that it must be executed to the highest standard. He would religiously visit the building site each week. The story is told of one occasion when he saw three stonecutters at work. He asked them one by one what they were doing. The first replied that they were cutting the Portland stone into blocks to be used for building a wall. The second replied that he was earning a week's wage by working hard. The third stonecutter set down his tools and turned to face the great architect. "Sir," he replied, "I am building this great cathedral to the glory of God!"[1]

Your Life's Work

What are you building with your life? What is the purpose you see in your day-to-day, your creativity, your imagination?

Is it just getting by brick by brick or to make money? While those are necessary, they're not the real prize here: God has placed his spark in you so that you might lift people's eyes to heaven and point people to an eternity of hope. Over the course of your life, you will spend over eighty thousand hours working and four million minutes creating, dreaming, solving, building, and loving.[2] Each hour you'll think hundreds of unique thoughts.[3] Each day you'll make thirty-five thousand decisions.[4] Each of us will make millions of choices about how we will spend this one life we have been given. Will we simply do the task in front of us, or will we build cathedrals of creativity with our lives that will leave a lasting legacy on the skyline of people's hopes?

Your creativity is the most powerful thing about you. People miss this all the time: It's not your intellect or your ambition. It's your ability to think creatively, to imagine a different world. The great solutions and breakthroughs of the next generation won't come from people with the biggest brains, but from those who dare to dream the most audacious dreams. And when you combine that creative spark with purpose, when you live a life turned outward, extraordinary things will begin to happen. Your creativity, what God ignites in you, can transform the lives of everyone around you in the most remarkable ways.

How do we make the most of the time we have? Well, consider the great cathedral: On the top of the highest point, the cross stands tall, casting its long shadow of redemption over the city skyline. The key to building a truly divine creative legacy—just like the great cathedral—is understanding that at the end of the day, everything that you create with your life must happen under the cross. Three hundred sixty-five days a year, your creativity must sit under the death, surrender, and sacrifice of Jesus—here, only, can all things truly be made new. Surrendered, there is no limit to the power and potency of what God will create through your life. You will be free to write a radically different kind of creative story.

EPILOGUE

The Thankyou Story

Daniel and Justine Flynn, cofounders of the social enterprise Thankyou, were just nineteen and twenty-one years old when they were deeply moved by the global water crisis. In 2008, fresh out of high school, these young Australians decided to do something with their lives to impact the hundreds of millions of people who didn't have access to clean water. Rather than play it safe, they had a wild idea: What if they used their gifts and talents as budding entrepreneurs to build a business that would pump profits into life-changing water projects, helping those most in need? It felt like a call from God to use their creative gifts to turn the entrepreneurial model upside down.

The public rallied behind them, and Thankyou became one of Australia's great success stories. Daniel and Justine have become well known for their groundbreaking marketing campaigns. They first started with bottled water, then expanded into personal care. By 2013 their products were gaining momentum—with a notable exception—no national supermarket chain would stock them. They pitched. They emailed. They tried every angle. But every retail giant just kept turning them down.

It's moments like this when the spark in you really counts. Instead of going quietly into the night, admitting defeat, they allowed their imaginations to dream. They had a final shot: They booked meetings with all the biggest supermarkets for the same day to try one last time to persuade the executives to stock their products. Instead of playing it safe, they decided to try something brave.

They hired two helicopters, which they flew in circles around the two biggest supermarkets', Coles and Woolworths, headquarters. Suspended from the helicopters were massive twenty-thousand-square-foot banners that read: "Hey Coles/Woolworths, thanks for changing the world (if you say yes)." The bold stunt made national news. And finally, the humour, the creativity, the intrigue, and the sheer audacity of it worked. Daniel and Justine didn't just get one yes; all the major supermarkets in the country said yes, and not long after, Thankyou products landed on those last remaining supermarkets' shelves.

CATHEDRALS OF CREATIVITY

Now if all of that sounds inspiring, wait till you hear the craziest part of their story. Before the business had earned a penny, Justine and Daniel made a bold decision. I interviewed them at a recent Renaissance gathering, and they shared the story of how they decided on day one to assign a portion of the profits from the company into a charitable trust that would help lift people out of poverty. They described how they started discussing the percentage they wanted to give: Should they give 10 percent? It's a good biblical number, a tithe. Should they split the profits of their hard work 50/50? They kept going and landed on the idea of keeping only 10 percent while giving the rest away. But as they prayed, they felt that was not the answer.

In the end, they said, "What if we just gave it *all* away—100 percent? Every penny of profit. That would be crazy. No one does that." So that's what they decided to do. Right at the start, before things kicked off, they made the decision to live for impact, to use their creativity to make a difference. And what happened next? Well, today Thankyou has gone on to become one of the most successful consumer goods brands in the southern hemisphere, turning over tens of millions of dollars in sales each year. And this has enabled them to give millions and millions of dollars away through Thankyou's charitable foundation.

You have boldness built into your soul. Your best ideas are just waiting for your creative courage to spark them into life. And you will never do this with greater impact than when you do it to make the world a better place. Because the truth is you can't take anything you create with you. Your legacy will be measured not by what you got but by what you gave. The creativity God has placed in you isn't for building a brand, reputation, or personal empire. It's not for lining your pockets in this world. Instead, you're called to move through the world pouring yourself out and leaving behind you a trail of goodness.

The great Baroque composer Johann Sebastian Bach would begin his composition manuscripts with the initials *J. J.*—*Jesus Juva*—Latin for "Jesus, help," and would end them with—*S. D. G.*—an abbreviation for *soli Deo gloria*, meaning "To God alone be the glory." Bach understood that the aim of the work he created was not vanity: to make himself look good. He believed that everything we create should direct the praise and the glory away from ourselves and up toward God alone. Drawing no distinction between his church compositions and his mainstream works, Bach understood that all human creativity was to be crafted from a place of dependence, as co-creators, and all glory was to be credited back to God.[5]

What would this look like in your life? As you journey onward into your creative future, perhaps let this be your motto: "Jesus, help, and to you alone be the glory." Choosing to offer our creativity at the cross, in surrender and dedication to God, frees us from the prisons of egotistical ambition and worldly pride. Instead, our souls are set free to soar, to think radically, to be braver than we thought possible.

To the entrepreneurial mind: Dare to dream the impossible.
To the storyteller: Paint the most powerful canvas possible.
To the filmmaker: Tell stories that move the human heart.
To the musician: Lift the human spirit toward the horizon of hope.
To the designer: Trace the architecture of that new Jerusalem.

Whatever you do, whatever field you're in, however creative or "uncreative" you think you are, know this: Your life can have extraordinary impact. Because you are a part of the creativity of all believers and the priesthood of the creative. You were made to make, called to create, to spark something lasting—a cathedral of creativity with your life.

Build a Cathedral of Creativity

Extravagant beauty, whether in creation or in artistic acts, is not the problem. Selfish excess is. So if it seems good to you and to the Holy Spirit (and to the city council), then build a cathedral and let it give glory to God.
—W. David O. Taylor

You're not just crafting a career or fuelling passion; you're building a spiritual cathedral with your creativity. This is not something you do on your own, you're doing it collaboratively with God and others.

Imagine what could happen if in every community around the world there was a collective of people championing the creativity of all believers. What if every local church became an incubator for truth, beauty, and goodness—cathedrals of creativity in every corner, crackling with divine possibility?

In the European Renaissance, the church was the great patron of the arts, supported by the generosity of people with vision. The churches were the incubators, places that became the backdrops for the masterpieces of Michelangelo, Donatello, and Leonardo da Vinci. In the same way today, every church community across the globe should be that kind of place, an incubator, alive with God's great creativity.

Keep the Flame

You carry this holy fire. And the community that gathers around you will help fan it into flame. It's always been local churches—humble, ordinary, beautiful—that become the great altars on which God kindles his fire. We are to be keepers of the flame. God commands his people in Leviticus 6:9–13, "The fire must be kept burning on the altar." In this short passage, he repeats that command three times, as if to make sure they don't miss it. In the same way, God is calling us to keep the fire of his Spirit alive on the altar of our creativity. So, here's the challenge: Keep fanning into flames the gifts he's placed within you. Continue to fuel the goodness in one another. Tend to one another's fires. Just as a coal removed from the hearth won't stay lit for long but needs the other coals to burn strong, so we are to keep the flame on the altar of our souls hot. Surround yourself with others who carry the spark, and you'll burn hotter, longer, brighter.

With every increasing day, the world needs the light of your fire more and more. As we enter this new era, the human race is realising that the power of creativity isn't just something nice to have. It is vital to human flourishing. Studies are uncovering more and more benefits to creative thinking. For instance, for health—how artistic activities reduce symptoms of dementia and help fight depression and anxiety.[6] A recent Yale University study revealed that "moments of awe in everyday life can improve depressive symptoms and overall well-being."[7] Creativity helps people to flourish in life—from education where imagination fuels deeper learning, to innovation, where companies that prioritise creativity are more than three times as likely to outperform their competitors.[8]

Here's the life we're called to live: one that finds the spark in one another, fans it into flame, and fuels that fire until the imagination of a generation is ignited. Just imagine what might happen if you spent a lifetime fanning your spark into flame. Imagine the impact of your best ideas bringing hope over decades. Imagine if your life and that of your friends, your community, and your church became a furnace of divine hope. The code of the future won't be written in the echo chambers of the algorithm. It will be written in God-sparked imaginations of ordinary people who choose to see cathedrals of creativity rise from the ashes.

This is where our journey ends and your great adventure begins.

Your life will be a map. People will follow you. They'll trace the patterns and the footsteps of your soul. They'll dance to the soundtrack of your songs and navigate by the light of your creativity. It's always been that way. Your spark means that you are a cartographer of hope.

Mappa Mundi

In one of the giant stairwells at St John-at-Hackney hangs a work of art by East London–based contemporary artist Ewan David Eason. His work depicts the geography of the city with the viewer's location—the spot where the work hangs—at the centre point of a golden map. The piece is based on an old sacred art tradition, the *Mappa Mundi*, or Chart of the World. These were medieval visualizations of the world, usually showing Jerusalem at the centre—pinning the life, death, and resurrection of Jesus as the centre of the whole of the universe. From this spiritual reference point, every journey, distance, and adventure was understood as a coming and going—to and from—the epicentre of God's remaking of the world. Then, with reference

CATHEDRALS OF CREATIVITY

to Charles Booth's famous *Descriptive Maps of London Poverty* from 1889, the streets around the city are gilded—paved with gold—a foretaste of that new Jerusalem that one day will be our home.[9]

I often stop to gaze at Ewan's work. I trace the streets of the city. The hospital where I go to pray for the sick and sit with the dying. I see the outlines of the urban estates where some of the highest poverty levels in the country are recorded. I'm reminded of that thin red line, haemoglobin-red, tracing the staggering steps of the man bleeding out on the street. I see the places that have become home—each street tells a story—paved with potential. And here, I remember how the miraculous power of God's creativity has worked through our little community to spark hope.

That promise from God—that the place would throng with people—has come true.

Now we're not just opening the doors for funerals. Each week hundreds gather. The place is packed. Multiple services full to the brim. The church is vibrant—alive, like the neighbourhood it serves. And the room is young, bursting with energy and expectation. Teenagers falling over themselves to find a seat. Families—young and old. Generations side by side.

Every week thousands are impacted by hope. The homeless fed. The hopeless embraced. The lonely welcomed home. And none of this has happened because of human brilliance or strategy or talent. It's the result of thousands of small, unseen choices made by a community of people determined to let the spark of God's creativity light the way.

What we've learned is this: God is more eager to answer our prayers than we are to pray them. It was only ever the ceiling we placed on our faith that held back the flood of his mercy—ready to sweep through these city streets and pave them with gold.

This is not just our story. It's the story of church communities all over the world. Everywhere we look, the old structures of empty religion are collapsing like the charred beams of some forgotten cathedral, and something alive is rising amid the ancient ashes. Communities of hope. Movements of renewal. Waves of creativity and healing.

There's a sea change coming. Not a flood of destruction but a tide of hope. So, wherever you're reading this, even if you feel alone, know this:

EPILOGUE

You are not. You are part of a great swell of creative hope sweeping the world. You were born for such a time as this.

The New Renaissance

This is the new renaissance. Everywhere I look, everywhere I go, I find the same song of hope being sung. The long shadow of the secular myth is fleeing away in a glorious sunrise of wonder. I've told you stories from one neighbourhood, but I can't wait to hear the stories you will tell of what happens when you fan the spark into flame in your life, your church, your neighbourhood. This really can be an age of wonder, a time when our souls recover the truth, beauty, and goodness of what it means to be human, made in the image of our Creator. Your courage, imagination, and creativity will be the map by which a generation will navigate their homecoming.

This is your moment—a time for creative courage. A time not to hide away or shrink back but to follow the call God has placed deep in your soul. This is your renaissance. Your life will make a difference. You're here not by accident, not by chance. You are a carrier of the flame. What world will you imagine? What beauty will you create? What courage will you bring on behalf of others? What truth will you reveal, and what goodness will you leave behind? Just as Moses stood in wonder before the burning bush, let your life burn with holy purpose so that when you arrive on the shores of eternity, you'll look back and see that not a moment was wasted.

You have not been put here to build a monument to yourself, but cathedrals of hope with your creativity. When you create, you lift people's eyes beyond the gutter, beyond the horizon, toward the stars. You stretch their vision from the immediate to the far-off. From the urgent to the eternal. From what is to what could be. And all around you, the world is longing, groaning, straining to see what you will build.

When Sir Christopher Wren had finally completed his great work, he died and was buried by his family in a quiet corner of St Paul's

CATHEDRALS OF CREATIVITY

Cathedral. Compared to some of the great tombs, his is a very modest one. But if you find it today, you'll see written on the stone these words:

Si monumentum requiris, circumspice.
—Translation: If you seek his monument, look around you.[10]

The legacy of your life will be the spiritual cathedrals of creativity you build. Your monument will be the love, hope, and joy you bring: that creative explosion of life that inspires and encourages others through the power of the divine spark God has put in you. And here's what will happen: Your creativity won't just serve you—it will have turned outward. The spark will have brought renewal to your friends, family, community, and industry. You'll help write the spiritual code for a generation that is fighting to recover what it truly means to be human. How do I know? Because this has been the dream of God since the beginning: that you would catch fire with his divine creativity and set fire to the world around you.

So, we end where all great stories begin—with a spark.

This is the start. The world is your Eden—waiting to be remade.

Go with the sunrise of wonder on your face and the wind of the Spirit at your back.

Know this: God isn't just beside you—he's already running ahead, calling you on.

Carry childlike joy.

Trust the holy "That's funny."

What animals will you name?

What worlds will you imagine?

Create boldly.

Love wildly.

Now, go build something eternal.

> *May the God of hope fill you with all joy and peace*
> *as you trust in him, so that you may overflow*
> *with hope by the power of the Holy Spirit.*
> —Romans 15:13

SPARK CIRCLE

Circle back through the epilogue.

Notice
What moment in the epilogue moved you most emotionally or spiritually?
How has your view of creativity changed while reading *Spark*?

Name
What kind of "cathedral" are you being invited to build with your life?
What lasting beauty—small or great—could your creativity offer to the world?

Next Step
This week write a commissioning prayer. Name the people you feel called to serve, the beauty you long to build, the injustice you hope to challenge.
Bring your prayer to your Spark Circle, and pray together for the commissioning of the Creator Spirit.

Embers

Share these lines from Spark with your friends, and see what catches fire in them.

Your imagination is your forgotten superpower.
History belongs to the dreamers.
You were created to create and made to make.
Creativity isn't lost—it's unlearned.
Creativity makes the invisible visible.
Creativity is your birthright, the rich spiritual inheritance of your soul.
Creativity is the birthplace of the new.
To create is to partake in the divine.
Creativity isn't a solo act—it's a symphony.
Every human act of creativity is a participation in God's divine work.
Your creativity has the potential to help save the world, to make all things new.
Your creativity was always intended to redeem, to renew, and to make the world good.
To be human is to create.
Creativity is not escapism; it's eschatology. It's the future breaking in.
Your creativity is sacred ground. It has a sacramental quality.
The creative act is, at its core, a spiritual one. Creativity is prayer, and prayer is creativity.
You carry heaven's blueprint within you. You hold the raw materials of redemption.
Your soul is the beating heart of your creativity. As a result, your spiritual life—the place of interface and interaction with God—is the key to unlocking your richest and most profound creative work.
Failure isn't fatal. It's formational.
Necessity may be the mother of invention, but boredom is the mother of imagination. You carry heaven's blueprint within you. You hold the raw materials of redemption.

Thank You

To my darling Olivia—thank you for being the inspiration behind *Spark*. Your fingerprints are all over this book. Years of conversations, adventures, and pursuing beauty and wonder together have shaped this story more than words can express. Everything good here reflects the great gift you are to me. Thank you for your relentless encouragement, patience, kindness, and, above all, your love.

To my precious children—Kester, you have stunning insights, wisdom beyond your years, and natural sense of beauty, truth, and goodness. Thank you for inspiring me, and I pray this book will be helpful for you in the years to come as you continue to be fascinated by the world. Talia, thank you for your inspiring energy, contagious joy, and love. You are a force of nature, lighting up every room with the creative spark in you. Please keep fanning it into flame in the years to come. Grayson, thank you for seeing the world through wonder-filled eyes. You continue to teach me so much. And, yes, thank you for letting me steal your excellent Lego story, which you tell much better than me.

To Tom Dean at A Drop of Ink Literary Agency—you are an amazing agent and an even better friend. Thank you for taking crazy risks; jumping on planes; your tireless diligence, patience, and kindness; and above all your deep love and care. You're extraordinary and I so appreciate you.

To everyone at Zondervan Reflective and HarperCollins, especially my editor Ryan Pazdur for choosing to believe in this project and helping to nurture it along every stage of the way. You've been amazing to work with. Thank you. And to the whole Zondervan Reflective & Harper

THANK YOU

Collins team who have worked so hard on Spark, including the brilliant Matt Estel, Laura Weller (thank you for the linguistic gymnastics with the British English), Daniel Saxton, Emily Voss, Tammy Johnson, and, of course, Ian O'Reilly and the Harper Collins UK team. I'm so grateful for you all and for your hard work.

To those many friends who have helped behind the scenes—James Jackson for your advice, James Mumford for your wisdom, and to all those who foolishly agreed to patiently read early drafts of *Spark*—you know who you are—especially Jo Soda, Temi Taiwo, Isaiah Morris. Thank you to Mark Batterson for the wise advice. Thanks to Lucy Thorne for the stunning artwork that accompanies this book online. Thanks to Marcus Mumford for kindly agreeing to lending me your lyrics. To the category-defying talent of Deborah Pritchard for composing the original soundscape that accompanies this book.

Thank you to the extraordinary community at SAINT for keeping the fire of creativity and love burning. It is an honour to tell your story here. The best is yet to come. Thank you to the talented team I have the privilege of getting to work with, including all the staff at SAINT. You are the kindling for so much of this story. Thank you to Zac Lloyd for your faithfulness, friendship, and fun, and for always being up for an adventure, especially culinary ones. To Naomi Maxwell-Babtunde, thank you for carrying the fire and loving our community so well. You are an extraordinary gift. And Geneva Peters, thank you for creating the space for me to write, and your kindness, encouragement, and prayers.

Thank you to the whole Renaissance family around the world who are part of this adventure, including Ale and Ben Seikmeier, Zac and Clare Gageler, Dave Lochhead, Daniel and Justine Flynn, Ben and Shauna Pilgreen, Annie Phillips, Michael Hands, Ruth and Ayo Afolabi, Sam and Katrina Lawson Johnston—special thanks to Katrina for not just reading drafts but also taking photos. Your friendship and constant encouragement mean so much. Thank you to all those who have shaped this story with their faith, tears, and laughter: John and Jackie Parmiter, Jen Jamie, Mark Nelson, Tosin Oladipo, Jacquie Driver, Anntoinette Bramble, and Joanne Grenfell. Thank you to Nicky and Pippa Gumbel

THANK YOU

and everyone at HTB and Alpha for the years of formational faith that taught us to step out and dream big.

Thank you to all those whose creativity I have witnessed first-hand, and whose vision, talent, spark, and passion I've tried to capture in this book. To John Pawson and your extraordinary team, including Stefan Dold and Chris Masson, thank you for your gentle generosity, and to Clive England at Thomas Ford & Partners for turning this vision into reality. To Es Devlin, thank you for challenging us to dream big and open the windows. To Sam and Sam Clark for letting your gift of hospitality overflow. To Tom Herbert for being such an inspiring friend, and for making bread fly. To Reggie (we miss you) and Holly, Markus, and the team behind Hackney Church Brew Co. for your courage and faith in those early days. To Louise Lateur and everyone at E5 Bakehouse for feeding the hungry with us. To the genius that is James Kape at OMSE for helping spark our imaginations over and over. And to all those many others whose stories are reflected in this book: You know who you are, and I am forever grateful to you.

And finally, to God my Creator—Jesus, you have rescued me from darkness and brought me into your light, and ever since then my soul has been ablaze. I'm captivated and fascinated. Thank you. All of this is yours. I give it back to you, and to you alone be the glory.

Soli Deo Gloria!

Notes

Prologue: The Creativity of All Believers

1. Brené Brown, *The Gifts of Imperfection* (Hazelden, 2010), 108.
2. Eric Haseltine, "How Many Thoughts Do We Have Per Day?" Big Think, March 25, 2021. https://bigthink.com/neuropsych/how-many-thoughts-per-day/.
3. Jennifer Guttman, "Decision-Making: Facing the Challenge of Making 35,000 a Day," *Psychology Today*, July 16, 2019, https://www.psychologytoday.com/us/blog/sustainable-life-satisfaction/201907/decision-making-facing-the-challenge-making-35000-day; see also "How to Elevate Your Decision-Making Skills," *Psychology Today*, July 18, 2025, https://www.psychologytoday.com/za/blog/emotions-in-our-lives/202507/how-to-elevate-your-decision-making-skills.
4. Maya Angelou, interview by Lynn Neary, "At 80, Maya Angelou Reflects on a 'Glorious' Life," *Weekend Edition Sunday*, NPR, April 6, 2008.
5. Plato, *Symposium*, trans. Alexander Nehamas and Paul Woodruff (Hackett, 1989), 206e–209e.
6. NIV 1984.
7. Pete Greig, endorsement quoted at RenaissanceMovement.org.
8. IBM Corporation, *Capitalizing on Complexity: Insights from the Global Chief Executive Officer Study* (IBM Institute for Business Value, 2010), 24, https://www.hrbartender.com/images/Capitalizing_on_Complexity.pdf.
9. Wendell Berry, *Life Is a Miracle: An Essay Against Modern Superstition* (Counterpoint, 2000), 54.
10. Yuval Noah Harari, *Homo Deus: A Brief History of Tomorrow* (Random House, 2016), 462; Yuval Noah Harari, interview by *Today*, BBC

NOTES

Radio 4, June 2018, "We are probably one of the last generations of Homo sapiens." Transcript audio: https://www.bbc.co.uk/programmes/p045qlkd.

11. Globally, 35 percent of food production is dependent on pollinators, and their disappearance would severely undermine global food security and biodiversity. Food and Agriculture Organization of the United Nations, "Declining Bee Populations Pose Threat to Global Food Security and Nutrition," 2019, https://www.fao.org/newsroom/detail/Declining-bee-populations-pose-threat-to-global-food-security-and-nutrition.

Chapter 1: Your Secret Superpower

1. In the previous recorded year, 2015, London had experienced a notable increase in homicides, with a total of 118 cases, marking a 25.5 percent rise compared to 2014. Metropolitan Police, "Crime in London," Wikipedia, https://en.wikipedia.org/wiki/Crime_in_London. "Homicides rose from 94 in 2014 to 118 in 2015 (a 25.5 percent increase)."
2. Dylan Thomas, *Do Not Go Gentle into That Good Night* (1951; repr., Penguin, 2025).
3. "Let the little children come to me, and do not hinder them, for the kingdom of heaven belongs to such as these" (Matthew 19:14).
4. Karen C. Barrett, Patpong Jiradejvong, Lauren Jacobs, and Charles J. Limb, "Children Engage Neural Reward Structures for Creative Musical Improvisation," *Scientific Reports* 15, no. 11346 (2025), https://doi.org/10.1038/s41598-025-95619-1.
5. George Land and Beth Jarman, *Breakpoint and Beyond: Mastering the Future Today* (HarperBusiness, 1993), 21.
6. L. S. Vygotsky, "The Role of Play in Development," in *Mind in Society: The Development of Higher Psychological Processes*, ed. Michael Cole, Vera John-Steiner, Sylvia Scribner, and Ellen Souberman (Harvard University Press, 1978), 102.
7. Madeleine L'Engle, *Walking on Water: Reflections on Faith and Art* (Convergent, 2016), 58.
8. Leland Ryken, "I Have Used Similitudes: The Poetry of the Bible," *Bibliotheca Sacra* 147, no. 587 (1990): 259–73. Ryken said, "One-third

of the Bible is not too high an estimate" for the amount of Scripture that can be classified as poetry (260).
9. C. S. Lewis, *Selected Literary Essays* (Cambridge University Press, 1969), 265.
10. See Psalm 90:2.
11. Trevor Hart, *Making Good: Creation, Creativity, and Artistry* (Baylor University Press, 2014), Kindle loc. 157.
12. James Joyce, *Ulysses*, ed. Hans Walter Gabler (Vintage, 1986), 733.
13. George Steiner, *Grammars of Creation* (Yale University Press, 2001), 20.
14. "So God created mankind in his own image, in the image of God he created them; male and female he created them" (Genesis 1:27); my use of *bara'ed* in text.
15. *Chariots of Fire*, written by Colin Welland, directed by Hugh Hudson, performances by Ian Charleson and Ben Cross (Warner Bros., 1981).
16. Carola Baumgardt, and Jamie Callan, eds., *Johannes Kepler: Life and Letters* (Philosophical Library, 1953). Also, Johannes Kepler, *The Harmonies of the World* (1619).

Chapter 2: Ignite Your Imagination

1. Karl Barth, *Die kirchliche Dogmatik* (Evangelischer, 1945), 3:1.
2. Wolfgang Amadeus Mozart, letter quoted in Friedrich Rochlitz, *Allgemeine musikalische Zeitung* (published c. 1798–1818).
3. Jake Fairnie, author interview, 2024. Used by permission.
4. Pablo Picasso, quoted in "Through the Eyes of Picasso," *Antiques and the Arts Weekly*, February 20, 2018, https://www.antiquesandthearts.com/through-the-eyes-of-picasso/.
5. C. S. Lewis, *Surprised by Joy: The Shape of My Early Life* (Bles, 1955), 228.
6. George MacDonald, *Phantastes: A Faerie Romance for Men and Women* (Smith, Elder, 1858).
7. Lewis, *Surprised by Joy*, 135.
8. Andrew Newberg and Mark Robert Waldman, *How God Changes Your Brain: Breakthrough Findings from a Leading Neuroscientist* (Ballantine, 2009), 90.
9. "Younger People More Likely to Pray Than Older Generations, Survey

NOTES

Finds," Church of England press release, based on a Savanta ComRes survey of 2,073 UK adults (July 2022).

10. Simone Weil, *Waiting for God*, trans. Emma Craufurd (Harper Perennial Modern Classics, 2009).
11. John Donne, Sermon LXXX, preached at the funeral of Sir William Cokayne, KNT., Alderman of London, December 12, 1626.
12. D. Kapogiannis, A. K. Barbey, M. Su, G. Zamboni, F. Krueger, and J. Grafman, "Cognitive and Neural Foundations of Religious Belief," *Proceedings of the National Academy of Sciences of the United States of America* 106, no. 12 (2009): 4876–81.
13. Walter Brueggemann, *The Prophetic Imagination* (Fortress, 1978), 8.
14. Quoted in Giorgio Vasari, *The Lives of the Most Excellent Painters, Sculptors, and Architects*, trans. Julia Conaway Bondanella and Peter Bondanella (Oxford University Press, 1991), 474. Vasari also notes how central Michelangelo's faith was to his art: "As the admirable Christian he was, Michelangelo took great pleasure from the Holy Scriptures, and he held in great veneration the works written by Girolamo Savonarola, whom he had heard preaching in the pulpit. He dearly loved human beauty, which could be imitated in art, where the essence of the beautiful could be separated from beautiful things, since without this kind of imitation nothing perfect can be created" (474–75).
15. Rick Rubin, "Pharrell Williams," *Tetragrammaton with Rick Rubin*, podcast, December 4, 2024, https://www.tetragrammaton.com/content/pharrell-williams.
16. Pablo Picasso, epigraph to "Modern Living: Ozmosis in Central Park," *Time*, October 4, 1976, https://time.com/archive/6852180/modern-living-ozmosis-in-central-park/.
17. Quoted in Darragh Johnson, "Betting on a Bass That Belts Them Out; Singing Fish Becomes Season's Unlikely Hit," *Washington Post*, July 30, 2000, C1.
18. Traditional African proverb. Commonly cited in leadership and cultural discourse; original source unverified. See "It Takes a Village to Determine the Origins of an African Proverb," Goats and Soda, NPR, July 30, 2016, npr.org/sections/goatsandsoda/2016/07/30/487925796/it-takes-a-village-to-determine-the-origins-of-an-african-proverb.
19. Walter Isaacson, *Steve Jobs* (Simon & Schuster, 2011), 148.
20. Steve Jobs, "You've Got to Find What You Love," commencement

NOTES

address at Stanford University, Palo Alto, CA, June 12, 2005; excerpted in *Stanford Report*, June 14, 2005, https://news.stanford.edu/stories/2005/06/steve-jobs-2005-graduates-stay-hungry-stay-foolish/.

21. Elizabeth L. Eisenstein, *The Printing Press as an Agent of Change: Communications and Cultural Transformations in Early-Modern Europe* (Cambridge University Press, 1979).
22. James A. Dewar, *The Information Age and the Printing Press: Looking Backward to See Ahead* (RAND Corporation, 1998), 3, https://www.rand.org/pubs/papers/P8014.html.
23. Alphonse de Lamartine, *Memoirs of Celebrated Characters* (Richard Bentley, 1854).
24. David Bentley Hart, *The Doors of the Sea: Where Was God in the Tsunami?* (Eerdmans, 2005), 72.

Chapter 3: The Spark That Lights the Fire

1. Leonard Cohen, "Prince of Asturias Award for Literature 2011: Acceptance Speech," Prince of Asturias Foundation, Oviedo, Spain, October 21, 2011, online transcript: https://www.fpa.es/en/princess-of-asturias-awards/laureates/2011-leonard-cohen/?texto=discurso. "In other words, if I knew where the good songs came from I'd go there more often."
2. *Abstract: The Art of Design*, season 1, episode 3, "Es Devlin: Stage Design," directed by Brian Oakes, produced by RadicalMedia and Godfrey Dadich Partners, Netflix.
3. "*Shared Sky*: Es Devlin in Conversation with Al Gordon," filmed interview for Renaissance, a ministry of SAINT. Used by permission of the Parochial Church Council (PCC) of the Parish of Hackney (2021).
4. "*Shared Sky*."
5. Giorgio Vasari, *The Lives of the Most Excellent Painters, Sculptors, and Architects*, trans. Gaston du C. de Vere (Modern Library, 2006), cited in Evan Nicole Brown "A Detail You May Not Have Noticed in Michelangelo's Sistine Chapel," Atlas Obscura, October 29, 2017, https://www.atlasobscura.com/articles/michelangelos-sistine-chapel-figs.
6. Vasari, *The Lives of the Most Excellent Painters*, 406.
7. "When the Lord saw that he had gone over to look, God called to him from within the bush, 'Moses! Moses!' And Moses said, 'Here I am'"

NOTES

(Exodus 3:4). In the Hebrew, the phrase is *Hineni* (הנני), which suggests a state of readiness, attentiveness, and availability to God.
8. Edwin Hatch, "Breathe on Me, Breath of God," *Anglican Hymns Old and New*, revised and enlarged (London: Kingsway Music, 2008), hymn no. 87a.
9. Romain Rolland, "George Frideric Handel," *Romain Rolland's Essays on Music*, ed. David Ewen (Dover, 1959), 215.
10. Blaise Pascal, "Mémorial," in *Pensées and Other Writings*, ed. Honor Levi (Oxford University Press, 1999), 178.

Chapter 4: Lightbulb Moments

1. See John 2:1–11.
2. W. David O. Taylor, ed., *For the Beauty of the Church: Casting a Vision for the Arts* (Baker, 2010), 36.
3. Anne Craig, "Discovery of 'Thought Worms' Opens Window to the Mind," *Queen's Gazette*, July 13, 2020.
4. For full list of awards, visit https://hackneychurchbrew.co/pages/our-awards.
5. James C. Kaufman, "The Sylvia Plath Effect: Mental Illness in Eminent Creative Writers," *The Journal of Creative Behavior* 35, no. 1 (2001): 37–50; see also "Sylvia Plath Effect," Wikipedia, https://en.wikipedia.org/wiki/Sylvia_Plath_effect.
6. Simon Kyaga et al., "Mental Illness, Suicide and Creativity: 40-Year Prospective Total Population Study," *The Lancet Psychiatry* 379, no. 9814 (2012): 2102–10, https://www.thelancet.com/journals/lanpsy/article/PIIS2215-0366(12)70217-3/fulltext.
7. "Mentally-Healthy Survey 2024—70% of Industry Reports Burnout," UnLtd, August 20, 2024, https://lbbonline.com/news/mentally-healthy-survey-2024-70-of-industry-reports-burnout.
8. Marc Hogan, "Musicians Way More Likely to Be Depressed and Anxious, Study Shows," Pitchfork, November 2, 2016, https://pitchfork.com/news/69507-musicians-way-more-likely-to-be-depressed-and-anxious-study-shows/.
9. Roberta Comunian and Dave O'Brien, "Freelancers in the Creative Economy," Creative Industries Policy and Evidence Centre, Arts

NOTES

Council England, 2021, https://pec.ac.uk/policy_briefing_entr/freelancers-in-the-creative-industries/.

10. Gillian W. Shorter, Siobhan M. O'Neill, and Lisa McElherron, *Changing Arts and Minds: A Survey of Health and Wellbeing in the Creative Sector* (Belfast: Inspire/Ulster University, 2018), 6.
11. If you are struggling with mental health or emotional distress, free, confidential support is available globally through Befrienders Worldwide at https://www.befrienders.org.
12. Jun'ichirō Tanizaki, *In Praise of Shadows*, trans. Thomas J. Harper and Edard G. Seidensticker (Vintage Classics, 2019), 14.
13. Gerard Manley Hopkins, "God's Grandeur," in *Poems and Prose*, ed. W. H. Gardner (Penguin, 1953), 105–6.

Chapter 5: The Priesthood of the Creative

1. Andy Hargreaves, "100 Quotes to Teach and Lead By," accessed May 22, 2025, https://andyhargreaves.weebly.com/100-quotes-to-teach-and-lead-by-26-50.html.
2. Batya Friedman and Steve Lyons, "The Progressive Interview: Frank Zappa: Revolt Against Mediocrity," *The Progressive*, November 1986, vol. 50, no. 11, p. 36.
3. Susana Pérez Posada, "In the Age of On-Demand Streaming, Have Solo Stars Killed Off UK Bands for Good?" *Skoove Blog*, accessed May 22, 2025, https://www.skoove.com/blog/decline-of-bands-uk/.
4. Ben H. Bagdikian, *The Media Monopoly* (Beacon, 1983).
5. Michael Copps and Bernie Sanders, "Rule Change Would Favor Big Media," *Politico*, December 18, 2012, https://www.politico.com/story/2012/12/fcc-rule-change-would-help-big-media-085262.
6. Amanda Petrusich, "Nick Cave on the Fragility of Life," *The New Yorker*, March 23, 2023.
7. "The Lance of Pallas," in John Ruskin, *Modern Painters*, vol. 5 (Smith, Elder, 1860).
8. Matthew 5:14–16 (MSG).
9. J. R. R. Tolkien, *Tree and Leaf; Mythopoeia; The Homecoming of Beorhtnoth Beorhthelm's Son* (HarperCollins, 2001), 97.

NOTES

10. Trevor Hart, *Making Good: Creation, Creativity, and Artistry* (Baylor University Press, 2014), Kindle edition, loc. 155.
11. Hart, *Making Good*, loc. 155.
12. *The Blues Brothers*, directed by John Landis, Universal Pictures, 1980.
13. Iris Murdoch, *Metaphysics as a Guide to Morals* (Chatto & Windus, 1992), 215.
14. N. T. Wright, *Surprised by Hope: Rethinking Heaven, the Resurrection, and the Mission of the Church* (HarperOne, 2008), 155.
15. T. S. Eliot, "East Coker" in *Four Quartets* (Harcourt, 1943), pt. 5.
16. Hart, *Making Good*, loc. 205.
17. Brian Eno, interview by Sissi Makropoulou, "Brian Eno—Stories," *Apartamento* 22 (2018), https://www.apartamentomagazine.com/stories/brian-eno/.
18. Teresa M. Amabile, *The Social Psychology of Creativity* (Springer, 1983).
19. "The Ethics of Elfland," in G. K. Chesterton, *Orthodoxy* (John Lane, 1908).
20. Widely attributed to Francis Bacon; original source unverified.
21. John Micklethwait and Adrian Wooldridge, *God Is Back: How the Global Revival of Faith Is Changing the World* (Penguin, 2009).
22. Sandy Millar, personal correspondence. See also *All I Want Is You* (Hodder & Stoughton, 2019).

Chapter 6: Courageous Creativity

1. Bryan Stevenson, *Just Mercy: A Story of Justice and Redemption* (Spiegel & Grau, 2014), chap. 15.
2. Martin Palethorpe, "Paradigms: Are You a Flea in a Jar?" *Unbounded*, September 19, 2017, https://www.be-unbounded.com/blog-list/paradigms-are-you-a-flea-in-a-jar.
3. Penelope Green, "Q&A: John Pawson," *The New York Times*, September 8, 2010.
4. Deyan Sudjic, *John Pawson Works* (Phaidon, 2000).
5. "John Pawson in Conversation with Al Gordon," filmed interview for Renaissance, a ministry of SAINT, December 16, 2022. Used by permission of the Parochial Church Council (PCC) of the Parish of Hackney.

6. Steve Jobs, interview by the Silicon Valley Historical Association, 1994, included in *Steve Jobs: 1994 Uncut Interview (Visionary Entrepreneur)*, accessed via YouTube, https://www.youtube.com/watch?v=RyzJx68TJa8.
7. "John Pawson in Conversation with Al Gordon."
8. "John Pawson in Conversation with Al Gordon."
9. David Bayles and Ted Orland, *Art & Fear: Observations on the Perils (and Rewards) of Artmaking* (Image Continuum, 2001), 29.
10. Malcolm Gladwell, *Outliers: The Story of Success* (Little, Brown, 2008), 38–42.
11. "The Wholehearted Life: Oprah Talks to Brené Brown," Oprah.com, https://www.oprah.com/spirit/brene-brown-interviewed-by-oprah-daring-greatly.

Chapter 7: Make Friends with Failure

1. Thomas A. Edison, quoted in *Forbes Epigrams*, ed. B. C. Forbes (Funk & Wagnalls, 1922), 90.
2. Tom Kelley and David Kelley, *Creative Confidence: Unleashing the Creative Potential Within Us All* (Crown Business, 2013), 41.
3. Kelley and Kelley, *Creative Confidence*.
4. Ken Robinson, *The Element: How Finding Your Passion Changes Everything* (Viking, 2009), 6.
5. Robbie Williams remains, at time of publishing, the best-selling solo artist in UK chart history. Alex Green, "Robbie Williams Becomes Solo Artist with Most Uk Number One Albums," *Evening Standard* (culture section), 16 September 2022: "Robbie Williams has overtaken Elvis Presley to become the solo artist with the most UK number one albums."
6. Cees W. De Jong, ed., *Dieter Rams: Ten Principles for Good Design* (Prestel, 2021), 122.
7. Plato, *Apology*, trans. Benjamin Jowett, in *The Dialogues of Plato*, vol. 2 (Clarendon, 1871).
8. Plato, *Apology*.
9. Daniel R. Ames and Markus Baer, "From the Head and the Heart: Locating Cognition- and Affect-Based Trust in Managers' Professional Networks," *Academy of Management Journal* 55, no. 6:1224–42, https://doi.org/10.5465/amj.2010.0126.

NOTES

10. Yeun Joon Kim and Chen-Bo Zhong, "Ideas Rise from Chaos: Information Structure and Creativity," *Organizational Behavior and Human Decision Processes* 138 (January 2017): 15–27, https://doi.org/10.1016/j.obhdp.2016.10.001.
11. Paul Batura, "The Christian Origins of LEGO—and the Company's Missed Opportunity Today," *Daily Citizen*, November 4, 2022, https://dailycitizen.focusonthefamily.com/the-christian-origins-of-lego-and-the-companys-missed-opportunity-today/.
12. Ian Sample, "Isaac Newton's Apple Tree Cuttings Headed for Space," *The Guardian*, May 9, 2010.
13. Igor Stravinsky, *Poetics of Music in the Form of Six Lessons*, trans. Arthur Knodel and Ingolf Dahl (Harvard University Press, 1947), 65.
14. Giorgio Vasari, *The Lives of the Most Excellent Painters, Sculptors, and Architects*, trans. Julia Conaway Bondanella and Peter Bondanella (Oxford University Press, 1991), 427.

Chapter 8: Start the Work

1. G. Cacciotti, J. C. Hayton, J. R. Mitchell, and A. Giazitzoglu, "A Reconceptualization of Fear of Failure in Entrepreneurship," *Creativity and Innovation Management* 30, no. 2 (2021): 439–57.
2. Tom Eisenmann, "Why Start-Ups Fail," *Harvard Business Review*, May–June 2021, https://hbr.org/2021/05/why-start-ups-fail.
3. "Rick Owens Inspiration & Execution," Hommeschool, November 2, 2014, https://hommeschool.com/rick-owens-inspiration-execution/.
4. "E5 Bakehouse Sourdough Classes," Time Out, May 10, 2023, https://www.timeout.com/london/things-to-do/e5-bakehouse-sourdough-classes.
5. Philip Roth, "Works in Progress," *The New York Times Book Review*, July 15, 1979.
6. "John Pawson in Conversation with Al Gordon."
7. Matt Carlson, "The Joke," Carnegie Hall, April 10, 2020, https://www.carnegiehall.org/Explore/Articles/2020/04/10/The-Joke.
8. Ralph Keyes, *The Quote Verifier: Who Said What, Where, and When* (St. Martin's Griffin, 2006), 292.
9. Sir Arthur Quiller-Couch, *On the Art of Writing: Lectures Delivered in*

the *University of Cambridge, 1913–1914* (Cambridge University Press, 1916), 203.
10. *Showrunners: The Art of Running a TV Show*, directed by Des Doyle (United States and Ireland: Black Sheep Film Productions, 2014).
11. Stephen R. Covey, *The 7 Habits of Highly Effective People: Restoring the Character Ethic* (Free Press, 1989), 147.

Chapter 9: High Hopes

1. Lesslie Newbigin, *The Other Side of 1984: Questions for the Churches* (World Council of Churches, 1983), 1.
2. Elie Wiesel, "The Opposite of Love Is Not Hate, but Indifference," *The Arizona Republic*, October 26, 1986, C6.
3. Arnold J. Toynbee, *A Study of History*, 12 vols. (Oxford University Press, 1934–61).
4. Rabbi Jonathan Sacks, "On Creative Minorities," First Things Erasmus Lecture, October 21, 2013, video, posted by The Rabbi Sacks Legacy, https://rabbisacks.org/videos/erasmus-lecture-creative-minorities/.
5. J. K. Rowling, *Harry Potter and the Chamber of Secrets* (Bloomsbury, 1998), 333.
6. Plato, *Symposium*, trans. Alexander Nehamas and Paul Woodruff (Hackett, 1989).
7. Augustine, *Confessions*, trans. Henry Chadwick (Oxford University Press, 1991).
8. Thomas Aquinas, *Summa Theologica*, pt. 1, Q. 6, trans. Fathers of the English Dominican Province (Benziger, 1947).
9. Paul Johnson, *The Renaissance: A Short History* (Weidenfeld & Nicolson, 2000).
10. Probably apocryphal, widely told, but see Vibhuti Verma, "Einstein's Lost Ticket: A Journey of Humility and Purpose," September 20, 2024, https://medium.com/%40thisisvibhuti/einsteins-lost-ticket-57e5e626801b.
11. Abraham Kuyper, *Common Grace: God's Gifts for a Fallen World*, trans. Nelson D. Kloosterman and Ed M. van der Maas, ed. Jordan J. Ballor and Melvin Flikkema, vol. 2 (Lexham, 2019), 153.
12. Jeremy S. Begbie, "Created Beauty: The Witness of J. S. Bach,"

NOTES

in *The Beauty of God: Theology and the Arts*, ed. Daniel J. Treier, Mark Husbands, and Roger Lundin (InterVarsity Press, 2007), 19–44.
13. Dorothy L. Sayers, "Towards a Christian Æsthetic," in *The Whimsical Christian: 18 Essays*, ed. V. A. Demant (SPCK, 1944), 60–61.
14. Gijs van Hensbergen, *Guernica: The Biography of a Twentieth-Century Icon* (London: Bloomsbury, 2005), quoted in Colin Marshall, "The Gestapo Points to Guernica and Asks Picasso, 'Did You Do This?'... Picasso Replies 'No, You Did!,'" Open Culture, May 31, 2017, https://www.openculture.com/2017/05/the-gestapo-points-to-guernica-and-asks-picasso-did-you-do-this.html.
15. Mumford & Sons, "Delta," *Delta*, released through Gentlemen of the Road, Island Records, and Glassnote, 2018.
16. Joseph P. Lash, *Helen and Teacher: The Story of Helen Keller and Anne Sullivan Macy* (Delacorte, 1980), 489.
17. Haroon Siddique Campbell, "Smoking Ban Tops List of 21st Century Uk Public Health Achievements," *The Guardian*, December 23, 2019, https://www.theguardian.com/society/2019/dec/23/smoking-ban-tops-list-of-21st-century-uk-public-health-achievements.
18. "Why Diversity Matters," McKinsey & Company, December 5, 2003, https://www.mckinsey.com/featured-insights/diversity-and-inclusion/diversity-matters-even-more-the-case-for-holistic-impact: "Companies in the top quartile for racial and ethnic diversity are 35 percent more likely to have financial returns above their respective national industry medians."
19. Henrik Bresman and Amy C. Edmondson, "To Excel, Diverse Teams Need Psychological Safety," *Harvard Business Review*, March 2022, https://hbr.org/2022/03/research-to-excel-diverse-teams-need-psychological-safety. "The vast majority... believe more diverse teams will outperform... particularly when the project involves innovation."
20. Katherine Phillips and Adam Galinsky, "Diversity in the Workplace Can Be a Reality, Says New Study," Columbia Business School, February 26, 2016, https://business.columbia.edu/press-releases/cbs-press-releases/diversity-workplace-can-be-reality-says-new-study. "Demographically diverse groups make better decisions and produce more innovations, because they bring in different perspectives."
21. Bresman and Edmondson, "To Excel, Diverse Teams Need Psychological Safety."

22. "For I am convinced that neither death nor life, neither angels nor demons, neither the present nor the future, nor any powers, neither height nor depth, nor anything else in all creation, will be able to separate us from the love of God that is in Christ Jesus our Lord" (Romans 8:38–39).
23. theCoLAB, "Lakwena Maciver: Back in the Air–A Meditation on Higher Ground," https://www.thecolab.art/lakwena.
24. Roger Scruton, *Why Beauty Matters*, directed by Louise Lockwood (BBC Two, 2009).
25. C. S. Lewis, *The Weight of Glory and Other Addresses* (HarperCollins, 2001), 12.
26. G. K. Chesterton, *Tremendous Trifles* (Methuen, 1909), 39.
27. Hans Urs von Balthasar, *The Glory of the Lord: A Theological Aesthetics*, vol. 1: *Seeing the Form*, trans. Erasmo Leiva-Merikakis, ed. Joseph Fessio and John Riches (Ignatius, 1982), 18.
28. C. S. Lewis, *The Last Battle* (Geoffrey Bles, 1956), 151.
29. N. T. Wright, *Simply Christian: Why Christianity Makes Sense* (SPCK, 2006), 235–36.
30. Fyodor Dostoevsky, *The Brothers Karamazov*, trans. Constance Garnett (Bantam Classics, 1990), 316.
31. "[Hagar] gave this name to the LORD who spoke to her: 'You are the God who sees me,' for she said, 'I have now seen the One who sees me'" (Genesis 16:13).
32. Julia Cameron, *The Artist's Way: A Spiritual Path to Higher Creativity* (TarcherPerigee, 1992), 9.
33. Dorothy L. Sayers, "Why Work?," in *The Mind of the Maker* (Religious Book Club, 1942), 57.
34. Trevor Hart, *Making Good: Creation, Creativity, and Artistry* (Baylor University Press, 2014), Kindle loc. 229.
35. *The New York Times*, cited in Al Gordon, "How the Asbury Outpouring Changed Our Church for Good," January 31, 2024, Premier Christianity, https://www.premierchristianity.com/features/how-the-asbury-outpouring-changed-our-church-for-good/17109.article.
36. Erwin Raphael McManus, "The Soul as Art," *Outreach Magazine*, July 3, 2014, quoting from *The Artisan Soul*: "Bees create hives, ants create colonies, but humans create futures."
37. Erwin Raphael McManus, "The Secret to Living Without Fear,"

NOTES

Relevant Magazine, April 11, 2024, https://relevantmagazine.com/life5/erwin-mcmanus-secret-living-without-fear/.
38. Robert Darden, quoted in Melvin L. Butler, "Commentary: Why Black Gospel Music Still Matters Despite the Rise of Contemporary Christian Music," *Chicago Tribune*, March 2, 2020, https://www.chicagotribune.com/2020/03/02/commentary-why-black-gospel-music-still-matters-despite-the-rise-of-contemporary-christian-music/.
39. James Hudson Taylor, *A Passion for the Impossible: The Continuing Story of the Mission Hudson Taylor Began*, ed. Leslie T. Lyall (OMF, 1965), 5.

Chapter 10: Overwhelmed with Wonder

1. Zygmunt Bauman, *Liquid Modernity* (Polity, 2000), Kindle loc. 82.
2. Alvin Toffler, *Future Shock* (Random House, 1970), 21.
3. Randall White, *Prehistoric Art: The Symbolic Journey of Humankind* (Abrams, 2003).
4. Neil MacGregor, presenter, Paul Kobrak, producer, "The Beginnings of Belief: Living with the Gods" (BBC Radio 4, October 23, 2017), 06:08 minutes in, https://www.bbc.co.uk/programmes/b09c1mhy.
5. Tom Holland, *Rubicon: The Last Years of the Roman Republic* (Little, Brown, 2003).
6. Mary Beard, *SPQR: A History of Ancient Rome* (Liveright, 2015), 415.
7. Rodney Stark, *The Rise of Christianity: A Sociologist Reconsiders History* (Princeton University Press, 1996), 29.
8. Marshall McLuhan, *Understanding Media: The Extensions of Man* (McGraw-Hill, 1964): "We become what we behold. We shape our tools and thereafter our tools shape us."
9. Stephen Hawking, Stuart Russell, Max Tegmark, and Frank Wilczek, "Transcendence Looks at the Implications of Artificial Intelligence—but Are We Taking AI Seriously Enough?," *The Independent*, May 1, 2014, https://www.independent.co.uk/news/science/stephen-hawking-transcendence-looks-at-the-implications-of-artificial-intelligence-but-are-we-taking-ai-seriously-enough-9313474.html.
10. Yuval Noah Harari, *Homo Deus: A Brief History of Tomorrow* (Harvill Secker, 2016).

NOTES

11. Andrzej Turkanik, "Art, Music and AI," in *The Robot Will See You Now: Artificial Intelligence and the Christian Faith*, ed. John Wyatt and Stephen Williams (London: SPCK, 2021), Kindle loc. 230
12. "The Quiet Revival: Gen Z Leads Rise in Church Attendance," Bible Society, April 2025, https://www.biblesociety.org.uk/research/quiet-revival.
13. "'A Revival Is Happening': Church Hails Resurgence Among Young in UK," *The Guardian*, April 2025, https://www.theguardian.com/world/2025/apr/26/a-revival-is-happening-church-hails-resurgence-among-young-in-uk.
14. Justin Brierley, "A 5-Fold Increase . . . The Phenomenal Rise in Young Men Attending Church. Dr. Rhiannon McAleer on the UK's 'Quiet Revival,'" Think Faith, April 8, 2025, https://justinbrierley.beehiiv.com/p/a-5-fold-increase-the-phenomenal-rise-in-young-men-attending-church-dr-rhiannon-mcaleer-on-the-uk-s.
15. "Bible Sales Surge Among Gen Z: SPCK's Role in the Growing Demand," SPCK, March 2025, https://spckpublishing.co.uk/blog/bible-sales-surge-among-gen-z-spck-s-role-in-the-growing-demand.
16. Josh Green, "Asbury Revival: An Incredible Move of the Spirit—and It's Touching the UK Too," Premier Christianity, February 15, 2023, https://www.premierchristianity.com/opinion/asbury-revival-an-incredible-move-of-the-spirit-and-its-touching-the-uk-too/14912.article.
17. C. S. Lewis, *The Last Battle* (Geoffrey Bles, 1956), 155.
18. Gerard Manley Hopkins, "As Kingfishers Catch Fire," in *Poems and Prose*, ed. W. H. Gardner (Penguin, 1953), 105–6.

Epilogue: Cathedrals of Creativity

1. Bruce Barton, *What Can a Man Believe?* (Bobbs-Merrill, 1927), 150.
2. Benjamin Todd, "Introduction: Why Should I Read This Guide?," 80,000 Hours, April 2016, updated May 2023, https://80000hours.org/career-guide/introduction/; OECD, "Time Use Across the World," 2021, https://www.oecd.org/gender/data/time-use.htm. Adults in the UK spend an average of two to three hours daily on creative, social, and leisure activity.

NOTES

3. Crystal Raypole, "How Many Thoughts Do You Have Per Day?," Healthline, February 28, 2022, https://www.healthline.com/health/how-many-thoughts-per-day.
4. Jennifer Guttman, "Decision-Making: Facing the Challenge of Making 35,000 a Day," *Psychology Today*, July 16, 2019, https://www.psychologytoday.com/us/blog/sustainable-life-satisfaction/201907/decision-making-facing-the-challenge-making-35000-day. See also Anna Rostomyan, "How to Elevate Your Decision-Making Skills," *Psychology Today*, July 18, 2025, https://www.psychologytoday.com/za/blog/emotions-in-our-lives/202507/how-to-elevate-your-decision-making-skills.
5. Stephen Nichols, "Johann Sebastian Bach: J.J.," 5 Minutes in Church History, Ligonier Ministries, March 6, 2013, https://www.5minutesinchurchhistory.com/johann-sebastian-bach-jj/.
6. Junyu Zhao, Hong Li, Rong Lin, Yuan Wei, and Aiping Yang, "Effects of Creative Expression Therapy for Older Adults with Mild Cognitive Impairment at Risk of Alzheimer's Disease: A Randomized Controlled Clinical Trial," *Clinical Interventions in Aging* 13 (July 24, 2018): 1013–20, https://www.ncbi.nlm.nih.gov/pmc/articles/PMC6063252/.
7. Maria Monroy, Michael Amster, Jake Eagle, Felicia K. Zerwas, Dacher Keltner, and Javier E. López, "Awe Reduces Depressive Symptoms and Improves Well-Being in a Randomized-Controlled Clinical Trial," *Scientific Reports* 15, no. 16453 (May 12, 2025), https://doi.org/10.1038/s41598-025-96555-w.
8. Forrester Consulting, commissioned by Adobe, "The Creative Dividend: How Creativity Impacts Business Results," August 2014, 2–3, https://landing.adobe.com/dam/downloads/whitepapers/55563.en.creative-dividends.pdf. Adobe's analysis found that "companies that foster creativity outnumber their less creative counterparts by a factor of more than 3.5 to 1 on key business measures such as revenue growth."
9. See https://saint.church/ewan-eason/.
10. "Christopher Wren," *Britannica*, last modified April 2025, https://www.britannica.com/biography/Christopher-Wren.

Renaissance

Join the Movement

Want more?

Download free discussion guides and bonus content here:
renaissancemovement.org/spark

Scan the QR Code to Access Bonus Content

- Group leader guides
- Spark Circle video series
- Creative resources for your church or team